TEACHING SCIENCE 3–11

Also available from Continuum:

Mark O'Hara: Teaching 3–8
Lucy O'Hara and Mark O'Hara: Teaching History 3–11
David Owen and Alison Ryan: Teaching Geography 3–11
Len Newton and Laurence Rogers: Teaching Science with ICT

Reaching the Standard
Series editor: Mark O'Hara

Teaching Science 3–11

THE ESSENTIAL GUIDE

Christine Farmery

continuum
LONDON • NEW YORK

For my father
Cyril Eades

Continuum

The Tower Building   370 Lexington Avenue
11 York Road   New York
London SE1 7NX   NY 10017–6503

www.continuumbooks.com

First published 2002

British Library Cataloguing-in-Publication Data
A catalogue record for this book is available from the British Library.

ISBN   0–8264–5585–9 (paperback)

Designed and typeset by Ben Cracknell Studios
Printed and bound in Great Britain by Biddles Ltd, Guildford and King's Lynn

Contents

SECTION 1: Knowledge and understanding

SECTION 2: Planning, teaching and class management

SECTION 3: **Accountability, special educational needs, equal opportunities and whole school issues**

Acknowledgements

I would like to thank friends, colleagues and pupils at East Dene J and I School for their help in the writing of this book and for providing some of the exemplar materials, which illustrate the book. I would also like to thank the Head, Howard White, for allowing me to reproduce material in the book from East Dene. I am particularly grateful to Mark O'Hara for his comments and valuable criticisms concerning the material in this book. Finally, thanks to my family for the ongoing support they give me in my passion for primary science.

Preface

This book covers various aspects of the process of the teaching and learning of science, one of the core subject areas in the National Curriculum (DFEE, 1999a). Within the National Curriculum specific content and skills to be delivered to children aged 5 to 11 is detailed. The Early Learning Goals, which form the curriculum for the Foundation Stage of learning, does not have science listed as a subject in its own right. Although the Foundation Stage does have its curriculum, it is not structured specifically along subject boundaries, as in the National Curriculum, but is organized under six general areas. Science coverage is to be found mainly under the heading of 'knowledge and understanding of the world'. The difference in the curricula is based upon current understandings of how our younger pupils learn, in that they do not necessarily make the same subject distinctions that adults use to organize teaching and learning. The under-5s curriculum is consequently organized into Areas of Learning, which reflect rather than mirror the subjects within the National Curriculum. In nursery and reception classes planned activities often offer starting points for learning which encompass a number of the areas of learning and, accordingly, a number of the recognized National Curriculum subjects. Our youngest pupils are thus successfully introduced to science through a variety of beginnings; almost all of which will involve the children's natural curiosity regarding their immediate surroundings. Within this Foundation Stage the children will begin to develop the knowledge, skills and understanding which not only help them make sense of the world now, but will form an excellent foundation for their later work in science.

Children in the Foundation Stage will be introduced to the skills and attitudes of:

- Exploration
- Observation
- Problem solving
- Prediction
- Critical thinking
- Decision making
- Discussion
- Communication

- Interest
- Curiosity
- Care for others
- Care for the environment

The terms *science*, *curriculum*, *primary* and *school* will be used throughout the book where the material is applicable to the full age range of 3 to 11 years. The terms *knowledge and understanding of the world*, *Foundation Stage*, *nursery* or *reception* will only be used when referring specifically to science in the Foundation Stage, i.e., to where 3–5 age group settings are exclusively being discussed.

It must also be noted here that, as many of the early years settings are actually outside the mainstream education system, the contents of the Early Learning Goals are not compulsory in the same way that National Curriculum Order for science is compulsory. However, readers who are about to embark on school experience with children in the Foundation Stage, need to be aware of the skills and attitudes contained in the list above, and to consider first and foremost how these are to be developed. The skills and attitudes are vital for the child's understanding of science, indeed throughout the book it will be emphasized that science is not purely a body of knowledge but that the development of skills, attitudes and understanding is important at all stages of learning. The early-years practitioner must also be aware that the Early Learning Goals set out a range of desired learning outcomes for all children upon completion of their reception year. Therefore, those nurseries that are part of mainstream education, as well as reception classes, are consequently expected to be using the Early Learning Goals to structure their work with pupils aged 3–5 years. Therefore, whilst noting the slightly different status of the Early Learning Goals to the National Curriculum Order, the provision of science for all pupils aged between 3 and 11 years of age will be covered in this book.

Standards Information

This book is aimed at both newly qualified teachers and students in teacher training, who are working in the 3–11 age range. It is intended to be of use to all teachers and students, whether they have non-specialist science knowledge or a subject specialism in this area of the curriculum. The Standards and requirements for the subject knowledge and understanding in science are set out in the DfEE Circular 4/98 *Teaching: High Status, High Standards* (DfEE, 1998). The requirements for primary science are found in Annexe E of this circular, where the specific content for science is prescribed. (Please note that at the time of writing the Standards are being reviewed and updated.)

The Annexe contains three sections:

- Pedagogical knowledge and understanding to secure pupils' progress in science (Section A);
- Effective teaching and assessment methods (Section B);
- Personal knowledge and understanding of science (Section C).

The three sections are summarized below.

Section A

All students and newly qualified teachers need to be able to demonstrate that they:

- Know some of the reasons why it is important for all pupils to learn science (Annexe E, Section A, 1);
- Are aware of the requirements of Early Years science (Annexe E, Section A, 2);
- Know the importance of ensuring pupils' progress in science (Annexe E, Section A, 3);
- Have an understanding of the key aspects of science and how these underpin the pupils' progress in acquiring scientific knowledge, understanding and skills (Annexe E, Section A, 4a);
- Are able to structure practical science activities (Annexe E, Section A, 4b);
- Are familiar with the specific language of science (Annexe E, Section A, 4c);
- Understand the value of engaging all pupils' interest in science (Annexe E, Section A, 5).

Section B

All students and newly qualified teachers have to demonstrate the ability to:

- Recognize and address common pupil errors and misconceptions in science (Annexe E, Section B, 6a);
- Know how and when to use skilfully framed questions (Annexe E, Section B, 6b);
- Provide effective exposition to promote pupils' scientific understanding (Annexe E, Section B, 6c);
- Know how and when to use practical science activities (Annexe E, Section B, 6d);
- Make effective links between science teaching and other areas of the curriculum (Annexe E, Section B, 6e);
- How to teach pupils to communicate their scientific understanding (Annexe E, Section B, 6f);
- Give due attention to ethical and environmental issues (Annexe E, Section B, 6g);
- Manage science in the classroom (Annexe E, Section B, 7);
- Assess and evaluate teaching and learning in science (Annexe E, Section B, 8).

Section C

For personal knowledge and understanding of science, the students and teachers are required to demonstrate:

- Knowledge and understanding of the nature of science (Annexe E, Section C, 13a);
- Knowledge and understanding of the processes of planning, carrying out and evaluating scientific investigations (Annexe E, Section C, 13b);
- Knowledge and understanding of the methods employed in scientific investigation (Annexe E, Section C, 13c);
- The use of clear and precise forms of communication in science (Annexe E, Section C, 13d);
- Knowledge of health and safety issues (Annexe E, Section C, 13e);
- That they know and understand life processes (Annexe E, Section C, 13f);
- That they know and understand materials and their structure (Annexe E, Section C, 13g);
- That they know and understand physical processes (Annexe E, Section C, 13h).

The structure of the book does not follow the order of the Standards or address every Standard contained within the Annexe. However, the grid below provides the reader with a guide to where requirements within each section of the Standards may be located within the book.

Standards	Chapters
• Section A – Pedagogical knowledge and understanding to secure pupils' progress in science.	1, 2, 3, 4, 5, 7, 8.
• Section B – Effective teaching and assessment methods.	3, 4, 5, 6, 8, 9.
• Section C – Personal knowledge and understanding of science.	1, 2, 4, 8, 9.

Introduction

The content of this book is to be of use to both teacher-training students on 3–11 courses and for newly qualified teachers. The student will find the book to be useful as an introduction to science in the primary setting whilst the newly qualified teacher will find it a source of reference. The aim of the book is to provide the reader with insights into the nature of the subject in the primary and foundation settings, with effective ways of planning and teaching science and then how to assess the outcomes of the teaching. Within these three strands the book will also consider various issues that lead to effective teaching and learning in science. Cross-curricular considerations that affect teaching and learning in all subjects such as equality of opportunity and special educational needs (SEN) will also be addressed. The final part of the book is concerned with the role of a science specialist in school with responsibility for coordinating science across a whole school, together with the issues surrounding the wider community.

Chapter 1 begins the section of the book that deals with knowledge and understanding in science. It aims to define the term *science,* both in terms of the nature of science as a subject and science within the primary setting. It raises questions about what constitutes *science* and argues that although science involves a body of knowledge, it is the skills, understandings and attitudes that it both develops and uses, that make the subject complete. The chapter concludes by discussing the reasons for including science in the curriculum for children prior to their secondary education.

Chapter 2 examines the current science curriculum in England and Wales. It deals with the requirements of the National Curriculum at Key Stages 1 and 2 and the content of the Early Learning Goals. The chapter also begins to consider the use of ICT in the primary setting, and how it can lead to developing knowledge and understanding in the science curriculum. The chapter concludes by focusing on how science is linked to the whole curriculum.

Chapter 3 begins the second section of the book. It focuses on the three strands of planning used in schools: long-term, medium-term and short-term planning. It explores how the three strands fit together, by considering the development of planning from whole school long-term plans, through to year group and class medium term planning, and then on to short term planning – involving individual science lessons and/or sessions. Through this, the chapter demonstrates how the three strands ensure continuity and progression in the subject across the 3–11 age range.

Chapter 4 deals with issues surrounding teaching methods used in science. It begins by briefly considering the theories of how children learn and then goes on to explore the use and development of effective teaching methods in science. The relative merits of whole class teaching, group work, paired work and individual work in science are noted. The chapter then considers the structure of science lessons and details a range of strategies and approaches that are appropriate to teaching in science. The role of play in science learning is given particular attention in this chapter. The term *differentiation* is then given due regard, by defining the term and outlining a number of different approaches to differentiation in science, in order to cater for individual needs. It therefore considers the use of differentiation by outcome, by task and by support. Case studies from across the age range are used to illustrate how differentiation is used in practical settings. This leads on to a consideration of children's misconceptions in science, the ideas that pupils may hold which are different to the accepted ideas in science, and how these may be dealt with. Finally, the chapter concludes with guidance on improving the quality of teaching and learning in science through self-evaluation and the use of further sources of information and research.

Chapter 5 focuses on the provision of an effective learning environment. The chapter begins with an overview of the health and safety issues surrounding establishing a learning environment for science. The consideration then takes note of how the available space is used to create a learning environment, the role of display and reviews some of the resources needed for teaching and learning in science. It considers the range of resources required to deliver the primary curriculum and how these can be organized within an effective learning environment. The use of ICT as a resource is explored, together with the use of audio-visual materials and written documentation. The chapter concludes with an exploration of the use of environments and resources beyond the nursery or school, using case studies to illustrate how a visit may be used to enhance science learning in the classroom, and the use of adults to support learning in science.

Chapter 6 begins the section of the book dealing with monitoring, assessment, recording, reporting and accountability. The chapter considers first the require-ment of teachers to be accountable for their work and its effect on the learning of their children. The chapter suggests how children's learning in science can be monitored and assessed, and how assessments are used to develop learning. The use of assessment in providing feedback on pupil progress and to inform future planning is considered. The chapter ends with a review of the statutory requirement to record and report children's attainment and the introduction of target setting as a tool to improve standards of attainment.

Chapter 7 is concerned with the area of special needs in education. It considers the entitlement of all children to a science curriculum and how this can be ensured for the 20 per cent of pupils with special educational needs in science. The needs of these children vary widely and include physical disabilities, learning difficulties, emotional and behavioural difficulties and children who may be identified as very able, gifted or talented. The chapter outlines some of the special needs that teachers may encounter and offers suggestions on how the science curriculum can be adapted and delivered to support the scientific learning of children with special educational needs. The chapter looks specifically at physical difficulties, learning difficulties, emotional and behavioural difficulties and the needs of gifted and talented pupils.

Chapter 8 considers the potential for teaching and learning in science to make a positive contribution to the provision of equal opportunities within the classroom. The chapter begins with a consideration of the term and examines strategies that teachers can employ in their science teaching to foster fairness, equity and social justice in their classrooms. Within the consideration of equality of opportunity, specific reference is made to gender issues and to the promotion of multi-cultural, anti-racist science teaching.

Chapter 9 begins to investigate the wider relationship of science teaching to whole school issues. It begins by exploring the need to keep parents and governors informed regarding the science curriculum, using case studies of science curriculum evenings and other science initiatives. The chapter then goes on to liaison between key stages within and beyond the 3–11 age range, using case studies to illustrate how effective liaison may be achieved. The role of a curriculum coordinator, a role that most teachers now often take on early in their careers, is then considered. The responsibilities of a science coordinator are examined, and some of the challenges facing coordinators are discussed. The chapter specifically considers the role of the science coordinator in managing and initiating change in the science curriculum across a school. The chapter concludes by exploring some of the key skills that a science coordinator needs to employ in order to be effective in the role. The key skills are identified through a consideration of an inspection report from the Office for Standards in Education (Ofsted) into the teaching and learning of science in a hypothetical school, and includes the school's response to the report.

SECTION 1

Knowledge and understanding

Science

The term *science* is given various interpretations. To many adults it conjures up smelly chemicals, housed in a strange room, used for a variety of inexplicable experiments. To others it brings back a fear of the unknown. Garson (1988) considered the meaning of science to pupils, teachers, parents and administrators, and subsequently worked on the provision of a list of words that they might have used to express the feelings evoked by their classroom experiences of science. The list included such words as boring, repetitive, confusing, incomprehensible, frustrating. Fortunately, to many of us, the term *science* invokes the idea of an exciting and interesting discovery. It is important that all teachers share this view as it is reported (Nott and Wellington, 1993) that how we as teachers respond to science is critical to our teaching of the subject, that teachers teach science in ways that may be linked to their own perception and understanding of the subject. It is therefore important that the student or newly qualified teacher is taken through an exploration of what is meant by the term at the outset, in order to set the rest of the book in context. The chapter will therefore enable the reader to consider their own experiences of science, and their reaction to it, and lead on to promoting valuable experiences in science for our primary aged children.

The chapter begins with a consideration of what is science, using various definitions and interpretations. It identifies four aspects of science – a body of scientific knowledge, a collection of scientific skills, scientific attitudes and a unique scientific language. It concludes that the subject is a complex one involving interplay of these four aspects and goes on to relate the findings to the primary curriculum. It begins by exploring the arguments for teaching science to children prior to their secondary education. Science was a feature of the primary curriculum for many children prior to the introduction of the National Curriculum in 1989, but the coverage was patchy, and often very different to the science on offer to children today. The National Curriculum established the right for every child to be offered a relevant science curriculum, with a set of prescribed areas of study. The chapter considers how the present science curriculum was arrived at.

Finally, the chapter considers the potential educational and economic benefits to be gained from teaching and learning in science. Longair (DfEE/QCA, 1999a) describes science as '. . . an integral part of modern culture', and states that it '. . . stretches the imagination and creativity of young people.' Its challenges are 'quite enormous.' The chapter discusses this view, in order to investigate the potential effects of the primary science curriculum, and argues that science is not only to be studied for its own worth, but for what it can contribute to children's development towards being an adult in a world increasingly affected by scientific endeavour.

What Is Science?

Sykes (1982, p. 939) defines science as '. . . systematic and formulated knowledge . . .' that is '. . . based mainly on observation, experiment and induction . . .' This basic definition leads on to the identification of science as a dual subject, consisting of the two inter-related disciplines – *knowledge* and *skills*. The science curriculum for the primary age range, as set out in the National Curriculum Order for science, is based upon this classification, and yet the term *science* encompasses so much more than the designation indicates. In reality science is a multi-disciplinary subject, including study from a range of related subjects: this is what makes science unique. A list of the disciplines under the umbrella of science would begin with physics, chemistry and biology and may then widen to include such subjects as biochemistry, astronomy, genetics and so on.

Activity

List all the scientific or science related subjects you know of.

_____

_____

_____

_____

_____

_____

_____

_____

If the definition of science as a collective term for various disciplines that are scientific or science related, then its study immediately begins to become unmanageable. The definition would indicate that the scientific knowledge to be acquired would need to be taken from all the known disciplines, thus making its study virtually impossible. Therefore, in order to make the subject manageable, particularly for the primary age range, the definition of science must be developed from this basic definition, and be more specific than the reference to all that is science-related. In order to arrive at such a definition, it is important to look at the two identified strands of science – knowledge and skills – and to consider their contribution to science as a whole.

Francis Crick, together with James Watson, is best known for his work on DNA (genetic material). Crick completed his physics degree in 1937 and then carried out graduate studies on the measurement of viscosity of water at high temperatures. Later he worked with Arthur Hughes on the physical properties of cytoplasm (the material within cells where all chemical reactions vital to life take place). He thus carried out research using a range of investigative skills – measurement, observation, etc. When Crick began working with Watson they used their respective knowledge of x-ray diffraction of proteins and bacterial genetics to begin to uncover the structure of DNA. Their specific knowledge of two areas of science therefore led to their use of investigative skills to generate further scientific knowledge.

(Adapted from 'Francis Crick', Devitt, 2001)

Scientific knowledge

Scientific knowledge, also known as the content of science, does not on the surface rely on scientific understanding. For example, it is a commonly known scientific fact that 'plants take in carbon dioxide and give out oxygen', and yet to know this does not require a detailed understanding of the process of photosynthesis. Scientific knowledge has therefore traditionally been accepted to be merely the acquisition of a body of known facts. However, Selley (in Wellington, 1989) writes that scientific knowledge is now regarded not as that which is objectively true, but as that which scientists have accepted as true. In other words, the facts are what generations of scientists have given as the conventions of science. Peacock (1998) stresses that science is not to be defined by the ideas it encompasses and that to be a scientist involves much more than learning, and remembering, science facts. He reports that what is important, what constitutes science, is not the individual pieces of knowledge it provides but how we make sense of the knowledge. Therefore, although the knowledge is important to science as a whole, teaching and learning in science is not simply a matter of the transfer of knowledge, it is an active process involving teacher and learner. Consequently, to approach this aspect of science as simply a collection of facts ignores the original interpretation of the facts at source, the secondary interpretation by later scientists and the interpretation by the learner. This strand of science is thus a body of knowledge, formulated through dialogue between the scientific community.

In November 2000 it was reported (CNN.com) that scientists had discovered a *possible microbe from space*. An international team of scientists had made the discovery following the collection of bacteria by a scientific balloon. Chandra Wickramasinghe, a scientist at Cardiff University, described how the collection of bacteria was carried out and explained that the observations made from the collection, together with the findings of another related study, suggested the presence of living bacteria too high in the atmosphere to have originated from the surface of the planet. The bacteria sample study was led by Javant Narlikar of India; Wickramasinghe and Sir Fred Hoyle jointly published the report about the evidence found on the Web.

(Adapted from 'Scientists Discover Possible Microbe from Space', Stenger CNN.com)

Scientific skills

Scientific skills are also referred to as the process of science or the methodology of science. They are the skills needed for exploration in science and include observation, measurement, recording, drawing conclusions and communicating results. The skills need to be acquired in a systematic way, i.e., they are to be taught (and learned) explicitly. However, Selley (in Wellington 1989) warns against the assumption that the transfer of context-free processes or skills inevitably leads to knowledge about the methodology of science, and so scientific skills need to be taught within a relevant context. Scientific skills are needed to underpin science activity both in the school curriculum and in the wider world. For scientists, the skills are necessary to determine the establishment of new theories in science, through investigation into ideas and phenomena and the interpretation of observations and results. It is most unlikely that new theories of science will arise from a school-based exploration; the process of science is thus used to enable children to confirm what the scientific community already knows. Feasey (1993) describes the use of scientific skills, through investigation, as providing opportunities for children to use their scientific knowledge of a concept in a practical and relevant context. The uses of scientific skills in the classroom therefore serve to:

- reinforce scientific knowledge being taught;
- interpret the scientific knowledge being taught;
- lead to the development of scientific attitudes;
- contribute widely to the study of science as a whole.

The process of science is thus a way of working which is inextricably linked with the development of scientific knowledge, understanding and attitude.

The process of science is all that goes into scientific ways of working. It incorporates the actions of people wishing to *find out* about something. It involves questions such as:

- Why did they investigate that area?
- What ideas led them to investigate it?
- What evidence did they have for and against these ideas?

Scientists are therefore not simple fact finders; they have new ideas that they investigate and build up evidence about rather than just *find out*.

(Adapted from 'Planning for the Future but Learning from the Past' Sutton, 2001)

Scientific Attitudes

It can now be appreciated that to define science as merely a collection of facts is to provide an incomplete definition, as it rests on the assumption that there can be certainty about the facts and that they are independent of interpretation. This has been shown not to be true. Sutton (2001, p. 7) suggests that to pass on scientific knowledge as merely information is too simplistic a view, that it needs to be discussed as a '. . . set of ideas with evidence'. Similarly, the definition of science as a way of working, the methodology, is also incomplete. The definition must therefore encompass both these aspects. A third aspect has also now been introduced, that of scientific attitudes (see above). Scientific attitudes suggest the notion of science as a way of thinking, i.e., through the demonstration of curiosity, through the use of questioning and the ability to think through problems. Further attitudes that science teaching and learning build up include care for the environment, care for plants and animals and care for the pupils themselves. Equally as important as these scientific attitudes are the attitudes towards science itself. Many writers in the field of school science, and in particular primary science, refer to the development of such attitudes. Nott (1992) considers that education about scientists, as now included in the primary curriculum, aids in both the acceptance of scientific ideas and gives pupils an understanding of the nature of science. He suggests that through this type of study, children develop more positive attitudes towards science.

 *Case study*

Reverend Richard Dawes weighed up the needs of the children in the neighbourhood. He taught science to the children to lift them with a sense of understanding of the world around them and to nurture in them feelings of competence, integrity and self-respect. He believed that a knowledge of local things would make the children better informed and help them with their sense of identity. They would become people who could reason about the world around them.

(Adapted from 'Planning for the Future but Learning from the Past' (Sutton, 2001)

What is of interest to the student and newly qualified teacher regarding scientific attitudes is the reported evidence (Hodgson & Scanlon, 1985) that such attitudes towards science are formed very early in a child's life, and that the most significant aspects in determining the type of attitudes formed are the teaching styles used by the teacher *and* the teacher's own image of science. It is for this reason that this exploration of what constitutes science is imperative for the student and newly qualified teacher. They therefore need to both investigate the rationale behind the inclusion of science in the primary curriculum *and* fully consider their own attitude towards science. This is essential if the teacher is to be confident and enthusiastic about primary science, in order to develop positive attitudes in their pupils (Harlen, 1992). However, this may require the reader to explore their own responses and the attitudes of others close to them *and* to overcome their own negative experiences of science. The main requirement for successful teaching in primary science is thus for the teacher to have a certain *feel* for what it is.

CS *Case study*

Miss R teaches a lively and inquisitive Year 6 class. Part of the science curriculum for the Year involves revision for the end of Key Stage 2 SATs. The children had investigated forces earlier in Key Stage 2 and so Miss R needed to recap on their knowledge. The lesson to be taught centred on the definitions of gravity, weight and air resistance. As a short revision session Miss R could have merely asked the children questions and instructed them to write a brief explanation of the three terms. In contrast, Miss R wanted to make the session fun yet at the same time explore the children's knowledge *and* understanding of the terms.

Miss R began the lesson by showing the children a 'Happy Birthday' balloon filled with helium. The children were invited to comment on the balloon and why it was floating. The children began to answer the question. Through skilful questioning and direction the children were able to use the three terms correctly to describe the floating balloon.

Miss R then introduced changing the weight of the balloon using paper clips and the children observed the effects. This led to the more able children discussing the effect of filling the balloon with helium and to wanting to investigate further the relationship of gravity, weight and air resistance. The children suggested investigating the relationship using parachutes. The children worked together in small groups to plan their own investigations.

Miss R's teaching thus involved the children in discussing together, considering evidence and providing more evidence to substantiate their ideas. They used present knowledge to suggest the investigation to be carried out and had the skills needed to plan their investigations (which were carried out during the next teaching session.) The children were also developing their attitudes towards science and to the world around them by considering the part science had to play in the development of everyday (fun) objects.

Science as a social construct

Throughout the preceding consideration of what is defined as science, the need for oracy skills was repeatedly noted. These skills – of communication through speaking and listening – are necessary for the student of science to be able discuss scientific facts, to articulate one's own interpretations of the facts, and to be able to share the results of investigations. The social aspect of science is therefore a further vital part of the subject.

I have stressed the view that science is a social activity and that the creation of scientific theories and the acceptance of procedures and results is also a matter of social negotiation. Scientists operate to social norms and those norms can be prescriptions, as well as justifications, for behaviour. It may be that science education should concentrate as much on the explicit development of a range of attitudes and norms as well as on knowledge and skills.

Nott, 1992, p. 13

Communication is therefore one of the most important skills to be acquired through science education. It is through communication that the scientific community is able to discuss together findings in science, and so develop the body of scientific knowledge. Prior to such discussions, the individual scientist must be able to make sense of the findings for him or herself. This indicates a need for the development of a knowledge and understanding of the specific language for ideas and phenomena in science. Science is thus a social activity by nature of the inherent need to communicate between scientists. It is the language of science, together with the common way of working within science, which allows scientists from all backgrounds, cultures, countries and language bases to communicate. Feasey (1999) defines science as a language, an international language, which all can have access to, and that the access is provided by scientific study. Yet another aspect to the definition of science is thus now added. Selley (in Wellington, 1989, p. 91) adds to this aspect of the definition by stating that an understanding of science is both '. . . culturally and temporally determined'. In other words, we make sense of science both through our own thoughts and through those of our cultural environment. Booth, McDuell & Sears (1999) report that our *cultural environment* is becoming a scientific world with new discoveries, inventions and technologies being made, and that everybody needs to know the words scientists use. The ability to communicate using the language of science is thus important both to understand and to question the direction the environment is taking.

A definition for science

Having considered various interpretations and explanations of what constitutes science study, we can now return to the statement made at the beginning of the chapter; that science is that which involves both a body of knowledge, and that the skills, understandings and attitudes it both develops and uses are what make the subject complete. If this statement is now used as the basis for a definition of science, then science not only encompasses both the identified strands of knowledge and skills, but also regards the content and procedural aspects of science as complementary and not as separate or sequential. The two strands can therefore be described as dependent on each other, i.e., science is a subject that involves the symbiotic relationship between evidence, interpretation and the establishing of accepted knowledge. This can further be refined and stated as the interplay between an investigation carried out by a scientist, past or present, and the analysis of its findings. The definition thus involves scientific skills, knowledge, language and attitudes.

A model of the interplay of the aspects of science

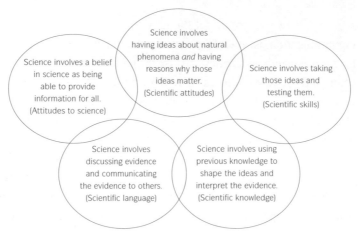

The model shows how each aspect of science helps to extend and enhance the understanding of the idea in question

The first part of the chapter has hence focused on defining science, and has concluded that it is a complex subject, which encompasses scientific knowledge, skills, interpretations, attitudes and language.

It is interesting to note here the relationship between the disciplines of science and technology. Traditionally, within schools, science is the study of how things work whilst technology is the application of science (DES, 1985). However the two disciplines are now considered to be complementary and inextricably linked (ASE, 1992). Rather than technology being an application of science, following scientific discovery and understanding, it is now regarded as a vehicle for the understanding of science. (Farmery, 1997).

Science for the 3–11 Age Group

The National Curriculum and the Early Learning Goals set out the academic requirements of teaching and learning for this age group. The National Curriculum is a statutory document that details the knowledge, skills and understandings that children should be taught within different Key Stages. It also determines how the performance of children will be assessed and reported. The Early Learning Goals do not provide a statutory curriculum. They establish a range of expectations for most children to reach by the end of the foundation stage and thus provide the basis for planning within the Foundation Stage of learning.

The National Curriculum lies at the heart of our policies to raise standards. It sets out a clear, full and statutory entitlement to learning for all pupils.

An effective National Curriculum therefore gives teachers, pupils, parents, employers and their wider community a clear and shared understanding of the skills and knowledge that young people will gain at school.

DfEE/QCA 1999a, p. 3

The National Curriculum and the Early Learning Goals include an entitlement of our youngest pupils to a relevant science curriculum. The main argument for this entitlement is that children will develop their ideas of the world regardless of whether they are taught formally or not, and that by guiding our pupils through a planned, relevant and organized science curriculum, they will be both better prepared and better informed to embark on the secondary phase of their education. Using the definition of science established in the first part of the chapter, for study in the primary curriculum to be classed as *science* it must reflect the aspects noted, i.e., it must include a balance of scientific knowledge, scientific skills, interpretations, attitudes and language. It is also important that the study is of significance to all the pupils, both those pupils who will study science at an advanced level and those pupils who will not. The National Curriculum Order for science prescribes such a curriculum, it includes:

- Scientific enquiry,
- Scientific content
- Knowledge of scientists and their work,
- Relevance of science to everyday life.

A science curriculum for the 3–11 age group would hence enable our youngest children to learn science, to learn about science, to develop scientific attitudes and to prepare for their further learning in the subject. This curriculum provision will be discussed in detail in Chapter 2; what is to be discussed further here is *why* this science curriculum is to be taught in the primary school.

Establishing a science curriculum for the 3–11 age group

The rationale for the National Curriculum is thus quite clearly stated. It was introduced to ensure a common entitlement to learning, with a set agenda of skills, knowledge and understanding to be developed. It must, however, be remembered that science was not brought into the primary curriculum for the first time through the introduction of the National Curriculum, but was in fact included in the curriculum for many children prior to this. Nevertheless, the provision of science varied widely and was not an entitlement for all. Hodgson & Scanlon (1985) reported that in the 1978 HMI survey of primary education, it was indicated that only around 10 per cent of schools incorporated science into their curricula, and that this was following approximately fifteen years of support in the area of primary science. They concluded that this showed how little progress was being made in this area that further stimulus and support was needed. This ultimately resulted in the introduction of a National Curriculum Order for science in 1989. The section below looks at the history of primary science prior to 1989 and some of the major developments between 1989 and the present day.

A brief history of science in the primary curriculum

Jenkins (1996) reports that students interested in the history of school science education will be faced with a substantial amount of literature. He cites many references, from Layton (1973) who writes about science education in the nineteenth century to Jenkins (1979) who writes about the form and content of school science curricula. He also notes curriculum projects (Waring, 1979; Fuller, 1992), the work of organizations and individuals who have been influential to science curricula, e.g., the Association for Science Education, William Tyndall (Brock et al., 1981) and J. H. Gladstone (Coleman, 1991). Jenkins notes that an understanding of the history of science education is needed in order to understand the current curricula.

Layton (1973) stated that the nineteenth century saw the beginnings of science education in schools. The Victorian classroom saw children participating in object lessons to '. . . develop in the children's minds an interest in the things around . . .' and to '. . . teach the use of all the senses and form habits of observation . . .' (Harlen, 2001 p. 10). There followed the construction of a general science curriculum in the early part of the twentieth century (Jenkins, 1979), although by the 1960s most primary school science involved 20 to 30 minutes of nature study per week, often in the form of reading and copying text and/or pictures from textbooks (Wastnedge, 2001).

The idea of a National Curriculum was first formally proposed in a consultation document in 1987 (DES/WO). Prior to this, teachers taught the '3Rs' with other areas taught 'as and when' (Alexander, 1992). In 1989 it became statutory that science was studied, through the introduction of the National Curriculum. Initially there were 17 Attainment targets but these were reduced to 14 Attainment targets for primary aged children – Attainment target 1, Exploration of science, covered scientific enquiry skills; others covered animals and plants, materials and their uses, energy and forces, light and colour and earth and space (Davies, 1989).

Russell et al. (1992) detail the process of evaluation and review, in 1991, of the 1989 National Curriculum Order for science. The University of Liverpool was awarded the contract to carry out the evaluation. Three issues were to be considered:

- Coverage – as not all Attainment targets were being studied effectively;
- Progression – the identification of areas of inappropriate progression;
- Differentiation – the appropriateness of the Order for the less able, the more able and the talented.

The research project was to last two years and involve LEAs, schools and individual teachers. Richards (1994) reported that it was an overload in the primary curriculum that resulted in proposals to modify the statutory regulations of the National Curriculum. The draft proposals were therefore issued in May 1994, the results of what was known as the Dearing Review, with the document being published by the DES in 1995. There were now four programmes of study – Experimental and investigative science, Life processes and living things, Materials and their properties and Physical processes – and a section setting out the introductory requirements of the programmes of study. The Dearing Review also promised schools a five-year moratorium, which meant no further changes to the National Curriculum would be made until the year 2000. In preparation for this, in 1998, the QCA advised the government on the need for, and nature of, changes to the National Curriculum. These changes resulted in Curriculum 2000, which is the document used in schools at the time of writing (DfEE/QCA,1999a). The main change to the science Order was the renaming of Experimental and investigative science, which now became Scientific enquiry, and the removal of the section setting out the introductory requirements of the programmes of study. The requirements became integrated into Scientific enquiry and other areas of the Order. There were other minor changes to the Order, e.g., the removal of the study of balanced and unbalanced forces from Key Stage 2 to Key Stage 3.

The National Curriculum clearly defines science in terms of its importance and content. It was included as a *core* subject, thus giving the subject the same status as maths and English. Whilst the fundamental importance of English and mathematics in enabling children to function in the modern world and to get the most out of their education is indisputable, it is perhaps less understandable why science was attributed the same degree of importance. However, Robinson (in Harlen, 1992) suggested that the science curriculum was academically desirable in terms of the potential educational and economic benefits to be gained from teaching and learning in science. The importance of science and its study is therefore the same as that of English and maths, in that it fulfils the same function. It is accordingly a core requirement for children to comprehend the world in which they live and to take an active part in it.

Educational benefits of studying science

Science, as a subject, is intrinsically fascinating to children and involves them in exploration and 'finding out' for themselves. Even the term *science* itself interests children. They expect the activity to be exciting and also expect to experience success. However, it has been noted within the preceding section of this chapter that what may be considered to be science is not always clear-cut, which could indicate that success cannot always be guaranteed. Far from this making science inappropriate as an area of study for children, it makes it extremely valuable and relevant. The opportunities science presents for encouraging children to think as well as remember are extremely important, indeed science offers the option for pupils to be critical about the world around them, encouraging the use of observation, evidence, logic and reasoning. Such opportunities necessitate the use of firsthand experience, which in turn offers children the chance to ask questions, reflect and predict as well as experimenting and playing with ideas. Introducing young children to knowledge and understanding of the world presents teachers with the chance to challenge pupil assumptions. Children have opportunities to find information for themselves, while their teachers provide experiences that allow them to explore important scientific ideas such as cause and effect. Although the promotion of thinking is not unique to one subject, science is an interesting arena within which to encourage children to review their actions and thoughts, to develop both their knowledge and understanding of science and scientific ideas. Within science, teachers are able to model the scientific process, by demonstrating strategies and explaining the processes involved. Stereotypical ideas of science that many adults hold can be challenged within science in the primary school.

Children hence come to science in the 3–11 setting with their own ideas of science and their own scientific theories; these may or may not reflect the ideas that scientists themselves hold. Harlen (1993) reports that there exists a substantial amount of research regarding pupils' ideas and their misconceptions, i.e., the ideas that children have which need developing (see Chapter 4). The research indicates that children develop their scientific ideas throughout their primary years and unless there is intervention in their learning, to develop the children's' misconceptions, then the ideas the children do develop may be non-scientific and may obstruct or impede learning at the secondary level. This is perhaps one of the more powerful reasons for including science in the primary curriculum, the view that it lays the foundation for learning at the secondary level and was one of the main reasons for introducing a National Curriculum for pupils aged 5–16 years, that of the continuity and progression in the pupil's learning.

The primary science curriculum:

Prepares children for the next stage of learning in science
Teaches scientific skills
Teaches scientific knowledge
Develops attitudes to self and environment
Develops attitudes to science

Teachers must provide opportunities for children to:

Explore scientific ideas
Research scientific facts
Share ways of working with others
Discuss their learning with others
Develop a sound, scientifically literate base

The lists above sum up the educational benefits of studying science with respect to scientific skills and knowledge; they also refer to the attitudes that a relevant primary science curriculum develops. These are manifold. DfEE (1999a) states that studying science enables children to:

- Develop an understanding of themselves and the world in which they live,
- Develop a caring attitude to themselves, to others and to the environment,
- Begin to appreciate quality of life, what affects quality of life, and how it may be improved,
- Distinguish the importance of science to their everyday life and ultimately the cultural significance of science worldwide,
- Challenge established ideas and explanations.

The impact of these attitudes is summed up by Feasey (1999, p. v) who quotes from the 'ASE Science Education for the Year 2000 and Beyond', that science enables learners to '. . . participate in a technological society as informed citizens, who understand the nature of scientific ideas and activity'. The benefits to a child's development through science in foundation and primary settings is not only to be justified in terms of its intrinsic usefulness, but also in terms of its usefulness to other subjects and areas of learning. These include:

- the development of key skills across the curriculum;
- unifying the primary curriculum;
- contributing to a child's intellectual development.

Development of key skills across the curriculum

The Education Reform Act of 1988 (ERA) placed a statutory responsibility upon schools to provide a curriculum that would, amongst other things, prepare pupils for the opportunities, responsibilities and experiences of adult life (NCC, 1990). For most pupils these will include employment opportunities, and the key skills developed through the science curriculum may be highly transferable in a working economy. Identified key skills, which may be developed through science, include:

- selection
- discrimination
- handling of data
- critical and creative thinking
- reasoning and evaluation skills

CS Case study

James, a Year 2 child, was studying 'Light' at school. For homework he was to list sources of light and sort them into groups. He enlisted the help of his father and older sister in preparing a list of sources. All ideas were written on a large sheet of paper. James looked at the list and began to sort the words into groups. He first tried natural and man-made as headings, but decided that sunlight was the only natural source, which made making two equal lists impossible. He started again and divided the list into sources that were powered by electricity and those which were not. This time he had two fairly equal lists.

Unifying the primary curriculum

Science can take the role of the unifying subject of the 3–11 curriculum by providing a topic context offering numerous opportunities for related work across the curriculum. It is able to offer an interesting vehicle for the development of literacy and numeracy, together with offering opportunities in many other areas of the curriculum such as art, geography or ICT (see Chapters 2 and 3).

 **Case study**

The study of the body in science provides a context for:

English	Descriptive writing, poetry, research skills
Maths	Data handling of measurements, e.g., heart rate, height, eye colour, etc.
Design Technology	Designing and making a team logo badge
ICT	Researching relevant information, data handling, presenting ideas
History	History of the Olympic games
Geography	Locating Olympic participants on a world map
Art	Body pictures, montages of athletes, etc.
P.E.	The effect of exercise on the body
Music	Appreciation of sporting themes from TV and film
R.E.	Religious choices made by athletes, e.g., Eric Liddell did not run in his preferred event at the 1924 Paris Olympics because the qualifying heats were held on a Sunday.

Intellectual development

One of the stated purposes for education as set out in the Education Reform Act of 1988 was to promote the *spiritual, moral, cultural, mental and physical development* of pupils and of society. DfEE (1999a, p. 8) indicates some of the specific ways in which the teaching and learning of science can contribute to these developments:

- Spiritual development, e.g., through the exploration of life – where it starts, where it comes from;
- Moral development, e.g., through discussion and recognition of both beneficial and harmful effects of scientific knowledge;
- Social development, e.g., through the development of the ability to form opinions and justify decisions;
- Cultural development, e.g., through the understanding that how scientific discoveries and ideas affect how people think, feel, behave and live, and that the extent to which scientific ideas are accepted and valued is dependent on cultural differences.

 **Case study**

A Year 5 class were considering 'changes' using the theme of food. The science work was being carried out within a cross-curricular topic and the children had visited a local fast-food restaurant as a starting point for the term's work. During the topic the problems with

BSE became known to the public. Within one science session the conversation turned to the scientific information being given out on the news, and the children's responses to the information. The children were able to discuss the issue, stating their opinions and justifying their views. The children were able to relate the issues to cultures where diet is of religious importance, i.e., to Muslims and Jews. They were also able to discuss the variety of information being given out by different experts.

Finally, perhaps the best way to appreciate the value of science in the 3–11 curriculum is to consider a curriculum that does not include science. The absence of science from the school curriculum would result in an impoverishment of children's educational experiences by denying them access to a body of knowledge, a set of practices and attitudes not to be found in any other area of the curriculum. Feasey (1999, p. vi) questions that if we accept children are involved in *art for art's sake* then we should also accept *science for science's sake*, thereby arguing the case for children to be involved in science purely because they enjoy it.

Economic benefits of studying science

The economic benefits of teaching science, and thus one of the arguments for including science in the primary curriculum, is ultimately embedded in its relevance to the modern world and its direct link to future employment. DfEE (1999a) reports that the study of science contributes to:

- Technical change
- Industry
- Business
- Medicine

This contribution in practice takes three forms:

- An understanding by the general public of scientific information;
- The confidence to challenge information and/or decisions made by both governments and industries;
- A willingness to work in a scientific industry.

A science curriculum that encourages children to develop scientific attitudes and to consider evidence, as proposed throughout the chapter, will aid in the understanding of scientific information by the adult population. It will also give support to the information required to challenge beliefs and decisions. The role of the science curriculum is therefore twofold – it is intended to meet the future needs of society, whilst also meeting the needs of individual children. Sutton (2001) suggests that science is wrapped up in ethics, politics and economics and the understanding of these issues is thus a part of science today and in the future. Science can therefore make a unique contribution to the needs of society and can have great personal relevance for children, developing, for some at least, into a lifelong hobby and interest. (Booth et al., 1999) meanwhile write that many people today work in science or subjects that rely on science, and so the curriculum must prepare children for their future as a member of the workforce.

Conclusion

This chapter has sought to provide the reader with a definition of science and to outline the argument for science to be included in the 3–11 curriculum. However, the chapter can only be considered to be an introduction to the issues raised; the student or newly qualified teacher may therefore need to research this area in greater detail. It is important for the reader to have an overview of the issues and to be able to answer certain questions about science for himself, in order to establish an informed view of the 3–11 science curriculum. Some questions to be considered, questions that this book seeks to give the reader clear answers to, are in the list below.

Questions about science in the primary curriculum

- What is science?
- What is the purpose of primary science?
- What is a scientist?
- In what ways does science contribute to the development of the child?
- In what ways can science help our pupils to become better readers and writers?
- In what ways can science help our pupils to become better citizens?
- In what ways can science help our pupils to gain insights into the workings of the modern world?
- In what ways can science be made enjoyable?
- In what ways can science meet the needs of society?
- In what ways can science meet the needs of individual children?
- What is the link between science and future employment?
- How can science motivate children?
- What is the personal relevance of science for children?
- What are the potential benefits of studying science?
- What opportunities does studying science bring?
- Are children natural scientists or naturally curious?
- In what way is science developmental?

REFERENCES

Alexander, R. (1992) *Policy and Practice in Primary Education*, London: Routledge.

Association for Science Education (1992) 'Technology' in *Policy Present and Future*, Hatfield: ASE.

Booth, G., McDuell, B. & Sears, J. (1999) *World of Science*, Oxford: Oxford University Press.

Brock, W. H., McMillan, N. D. & Mollan, R. C. (eds) (1981) *John Tyndall: Essays on a Natural Philosopher*, Dublin: Royal Dublin Society.

Coleman, D. (1991) 'The Life and Work of John Hall Gladstone (1827–1902) with Particular Reference to his Contribution to Elementary Science Education at the London School Board', unpublished PhD thesis, University of London.

Davies, S. (1989) 'Implementing the National Curriculum', *PSR* 11, pp. 19–21, ASE.

Department of Education and Science (1985) *Science 5–16: A Statement of Policy*, London: HMSO.

Department of Education and Science (1995) *Key Stages 1 and 2 of the National Curriculum*, London: HMSO.

DES/WO (1987) 'The National Curriculum 5–16: A Consultation Document', London: DES/WO.

Devitt, S. (2001) 'Francis Crick', http://emuseum.mankato.msus.edu/information/biography/abcde/crick_francis.html.

Farmery, C. (1997) 'The Relationship of Science and Technology in the Curriculum', *PSR* 50, pp. 19–21, ASE.

Feasey, R. (1993) 'Scientific Investigation' in *ASE Primary Science Teachers' Handbook*, Hatfield: Simon and Schuster.

Feasey, R. (1999) *Primary Science and Literacy*, Hatfield.: ASE.

Fuller, K. D. (1992) 'Innovation, Institutionalisation and Renewal in the Sixth Form Curriculum: A History of Nuffield A-level Physics', unpublished PhD thesis, University of Reading.

Garson, Y. (1988) *Science in the Primary School*, London: Routledge.

Harlen, W. (1992) *The Teaching of Science: Studies in Primary Education*, London: David Fulton.

Harlen, W. (1993) *Teaching and Learning Primary Science* (2nd edn), London: Paul Chapman.

Harlen, W. (2001) 'The Rise and Fall of Peripatetic Science Demonstrators', *PSR* 67, pp. 9–10, ASE.

HMSO (1988) *Education Reform Act (1988)*, London: HMSO.

Hodgson, B. & Scanlon, E. (eds) (1985) *Approaching Primary Science: A Reader*, London: Harper and Row.

Jenkins, E. W. (1979) *From Armstrong to Nuffield: Studies in Twentieth Century School Science Education in England and Wales*, London: Murray.

Jenkins, E. W. (1996) 'Historical and Policy-Related Research and the Practice and Rationale of School Science Education', a paper presented to the British Educational Research Association Annual Conference, 1996. www.leeds.ac.uk/educol/documents/000001027.html

Layton, D. (1973) *Science for the People*, London: George Allen & Unwin.

Longair, M. (1999) in Qualifications and Curriculum Authority, *The National Curriculum: Handbook for Primary Teachers in England*, p. 77, London: DfEE/QCA.

National Curriculum Council (1990) *Curriculum Guidance 3: The Whole Curriculum*, York: NCC.

Nott, M. (1992) 'The Nature of Science or Why Teach Brownian Motion', in Atlay *et al.* (eds) *Open Chemistry*, Milton Keynes: Open University Press.

Nott, M. & Wellington, J. (1993) 'Science Education Notes', in *SSR* pp. 109–112, September 1993, 75 (270).

Peacock, G. (1998) *Science for Primary Teachers: An Audit and Self-study Guide*, London: Letts Educational.

Qualifications and Curriculum Authority (1999a) *The National Curriculum: Handbook for Primary Teachers in England*, London: DfEE/QCA.

Qualifications and Curriculum Authority (1999b) *Early Learning Goals*, London: DfEE / QCA.

Richards, R. (1994) 'O tempora! O mores!', *PSR* 34, pp. 2–3, ASE.

Robinson, A. (1992) 'Forward', in Harlen, W. *The Teaching of Science: Studies in Primary Education*, London: David Fulton.

Russell, T., Qualter, A., McGuigan, L. & Ewart, M. (1992) 'A Project to Evaluate Implementation of the National Curriculum at Key Stages 1, 2 and 3', *PSR* 24, pp. 32–33, ASE.

Selley, N. J. (1989) 'Philosophies of Science and Their Relation to Scientific Processes and the Science Curriculum' in Wellington, J. (ed.) *Skills and Processes in Science Education*, London: Routledge.

Stenger, R. (2000) 'Scientists Discover Possible Microbe from Space', www.CNN.com

Sutton, (2001) 'Planning for the Future but Learning from the Past', *PSR*, March/April 2001, pp. 5–8, Hatfield: ASE.

Sykes, J. B. (ed.) (1982) *The Concise Oxford Dictionary* (7th edn), Oxford: Oxford University Press.

Waring, M. (1979) *Social Pressures and Curriculum Innovation: A Study of the Nuffield Foundation Science Teaching Project*, London: Methuen.

Wastnedge, R. (2001) 'When the Tide Began to Turn', *PSR* 67, pp. 11–12, ASE.

20

Science in the Primary and Pre-primary Curriculum

This chapter examines the requirements of the science curriculum in England and Wales, beginning with an introduction into the documentation on which a school's science curriculum is based. For the youngest children, those in the Foundation Stage, science is delivered alongside other subject areas under the heading of *knowledge and understanding of the world.* (DfEE/QCA, 1999b). The science coverage uses the natural curiosity of our youngest children, encouraging and enabling them to find things out for themselves and to make sense of their explorations through discussion. Schools and nurseries therefore assist pupils in making sense of the world by providing opportunities for the children to explore objects, materials and feelings in meaningful situations. The chapter considers how the *knowledge and understanding of the world* aspect of the Early Learning Goals can be used to enable young children to develop their awareness and understanding of the world around them and offers suggestions for science activities for this age group. The chapter acknowledges that the science offered in the Foundation Stage forms the basis for the children's learning in Key Stages One and Two of the National Curriculum, which is explored next.

Science is identified as a key subject in the National Curriculum and is thus one of the *core areas* of the curriculum, alongside English and mathematics. It has prescribed requirements within a National Curriculum Order, setting out the skills, knowledge and understanding that children are to be taught. The chapter outlines the requirements and offers examples of practice, to begin to illustrate how the primary science curriculum may be delivered in the classroom.

The chapter ends with a consideration of how science may be linked to the whole curriculum, particularly with respect to Literacy, numeracy and ICT. It is becoming generally accepted that the current curriculum in primary schools is a *pure and applied curriculum*. The *pure* aspect involving Literacy and numeracy, the *applied* aspect involving all the other subject areas. Within other subject areas, therefore, opportunities to apply the skills developed in the pure curriculum need to be identified and so the chapter looks at how science can provide contexts for the pure curriculum. The chapter also considers the role of science in delivering other key skills, as identified in the National Curriculum (DfEE/QCA, 1999a, p. 20). Within this section, the role of talk in learning within science will be explored in terms of what children may gain cognitively, personally and socially through talk. The use of ICT to develop knowledge and understanding in science will begin to be explored, together with the importance of thinking skills.

The Science Curriculum in England and Wales

The National Curriculum Order for Science and the Early Learning Goals are the documents that provide the outline for the science curriculum for the 3–11 age range. They do not prescribe the curriculum in terms of statutory activities to be carried out; they do, however, detail what is considered to be the experiences necessary for our pupils to be provided with, which will provide the basis for a relevant and satisfactory science education. It is a union of the aspects of science, identified in Chapter 1, and includes both the teaching of science and teaching about science, i.e., children are involved in their own science work and learn about the work of other scientists. It is important that the student or newly qualified teacher critically evaluates the curriculum offered in these documents, in order to continue to determine for themselves why, and how, primary science is taught and made relevant to the children they are teaching. It is obvious that judgements have been made centrally about what is relevant and meaningful to this age group, and thus decisions have been made about what is included and what is not. However, it must be remembered that the National Curriculum Order and the Early Learning Goals set out what is a minimum requirement; they do not therefore preclude other, additional scientific activities. Consequently, the staff involved within a 3–11 setting in designing a *school* science curriculum will have made decisions about the nature of the subject, the relevance of the aspects of science to the setting, the areas of science that should be studied in the school and those that should not. A school science curriculum should be viewed as a fluid entity, one that is to be developed, amended and improved over time, and so needs to be reviewed regularly. Reviews will include:

- The content of the curriculum;
- The relative weighting of each aspect of the curriculum;
- The relationship within the curriculum of the aspects of science;
- The curriculum time pupils spend engaged in science;
- How far children are introduced to a particular aspect of science.

The review will require a consideration of teaching methods. One school of thought is that all knowledge should be taught through investigation and practical work. Harlen (1992) warns against this by stating that although scientific facts emerge from observation, and are indeed part of science, observation does not involve an understanding of the facts. It does not necessitate interpretation or discussion and so teaching which involves only the discovery of facts reduces the learning to merely fact learning rather than science learning. An alternative view to the discovery model is to present science facts to the children, as if they are empty vessels waiting to be filled. In practice, the primary science curriculum falls somewhere between these two extremes. Scientific Enquiry is deemed central to the study of science but it is also accepted that some knowledge cannot be developed solely through investigation, and so research by the children, using secondary sources of information, is an integral part of the science curriculum. Primary science is therefore the interplay between content and enquiry; primary children engage in scientific activities and make progress in their scientific learning using their own experiences. This gives children ownership of their learning; it is not merely the teacher transferring their knowledge to the child with no active involvement of the child. Where investigation is appropriate, it is the role of the teacher to ensure that the child has had the opportunity to make sense of what they have observed through discussion between child and child, and teacher and child.

 A science education programme is incomplete if it neglects any of the following:

- Scientific knowledge
- The processes and methods of science
- Scientific activity
- Scientific attitudes
- The relationship between science and society

Early Learning Goals

In the maintained sector our youngest children, i.e., children aged between 3 and 5 years, work towards the Early Learning Goals (DfEE/QCA, 1999b). These children are deemed to be in the Foundation Stage of Learning. The guidance given within the Early Learning Goals (ELG) states that they both provide the basis for planning throughout the Foundation Stage, and establish the expectations for most children to have reached by the end of the Stage. Each ELG is broken down into stepping-stones, which show a path towards achieving the ELG. The aim of the ELG is to provide a secure foundation for future learning, consequently the curriculum is not to be viewed as separate to Key Stage 1 and

Key Stage 2, but is the precursor to learning in these subsequent stages. However, the Early Learning Goals are structured around six broad areas of experience rather than the narrower subject boundaries to be found in later phases of education: the learning here therefore feeds into the next stages of learning rather than being the first introduction of each subsequent curriculum subject.

The Early Learning Goals

The curriculum for children in the Foundation Stage is organized under six headings

- Personal, social and emotional development
- Communication, language and literacy
- Mathematical development
- Knowledge and understanding of the world
- Physical development
- Creative development

Science as a named subject, as a coherent body of knowledge and systematic process of investigation, does not exist in the Foundation Stage and yet young children are still experiencing science. The opportunities for early scientific learning across the Foundation Stage may be identified under a number of the headings, although the richest sources of ideas for early science work are to be found under the heading *knowledge and understanding of the world,* which encapsulates science alongside design and technology, history, geography and ICT. The area of *knowledge and understanding of the world* provides ample opportunities for developing early scientific skills, attitudes, a rudimentary scientific knowledge and scientific understandings, as in the following table.

Knowledge and understanding of the world

By the end of the Foundation Stage children should be able to:

- investigate objects using their senses;
- find out about and identify some features of objects;
- look closely at similarities, differences, patterns and change;
- record findings;
- ask questions about why things happen and how things work;
- model investigative work;
- find out about the place they live in.

(DfEE/QCA, 1999b)

Our youngest children are naturally curious, capable of asking questions and able to find things out for themselves, with and without adult support. These are basic skills and qualities needed for learning in science and are utilized in much of what already goes on in nursery and reception settings. The skill of the early-years

Scientific Activities	Examples
Encouraging younger pupils to investigate objects using their senses: What does it look like? What does it feel like? Does it have a smell? Does it make a noise?	Collecting leaves found on the ground in autumn during a walk around the outside of the Nursery. The children will use sight, touch, smell and hearing to investigate and sort the leaves.
Identify some features of objects: Explore using senses. Recall past experiences of their own and relate them to the objects being explored. Classify objects. Identify similarities and differences. Make comparisons such as dull and shiny, heavy and light, etc. Demonstrate awareness of cause and effect.	Investigating a range of musical instruments during structured play sessions. Finding out how to make sounds using the instruments, which have high/low sounds and how to make loud and quiet sounds.
Investigate similarities, differences, patterns and change: Observe habitats. Carry out weather investigations. Identify families, family members and growth of babies. Show sensitivity and empathy towards others.	Keeping a class log of frogspawn developing into tadpoles. The children will observe the spawn's habitat and share in looking after the developing tadpoles.
Record findings: Drawing Writing Audio/video tape Models Photographs	Investigating objects that float and sink and recording their observations as they occur, assisted by an adult. The tape to be played back to a group/class when reporting the results of their investigations.
Ask questions about why things happen and how things work: Why does it . . .? What will happen if I . . .? Could I try . . .? Will it . . .?	Investigating floating and sinking objects. Posing the question why does this plastic boat float? Will it sink if I push it down? Could I put something else in it to make it sink? Will this (object) make it sink?
Model investigative work: Discuss regularly occurring events Examine change over time Handle equipment	Observe sunflower seeds growing, firstly in a pot inside then in the ground. Using a hand lens to look for changes in the leaf/stalk/flower.
Learning about the place they live in: Investigate the local area Exploration of the wider local environment Observe and identify materials	A walk around the Nursery/school identifying the use of different building materials, i.e., brick, plastic, glass, etc.

teacher lies in identifying opportunities for learning in science, setting up suitable activities for the learning, directing the children in the activities and using the activities in the development of appropriate language and vocabulary during the activity. Nursery and reception teachers therefore encourage children to engage in finding out, problem solving, decision-making and critical thinking as much as the acquisition of knowledge.

Children find out information for themselves through exploring, questioning and/or consulting. The skill of finding out can be encouraged through involving children in:

- asking and answering questions;
- hypothesizing;
- suggesting possible solutions to problems;
- participating in group discussions, listening to the views and ideas of others, commenting on others' ideas;
- using all their senses to gather information;
- initiating interactions with adults as information sources, seeking knowledge, clarification and reasons;
- using books and other sources of information.

Teachers use challenging questions to encourage children to speculate, predict and explore. At the same time the teacher is encouraging and supporting children's speaking and listening. It is essential that children are able to articulate their thoughts, and the development of appropriate scientific vocabulary is one of the main aims of scientific learning at this stage. In turn, critical thinking needs to be encouraged, as it is an essential skill for future learning in science. Critical thinking can be taught, through modelling, i.e., thinking out loud with pupils is one way of illustrating the processes and strategies involved. Nurturing talk and discussion with children about *their world* contributes not only to their scientific learning, but also to language, literacy and personal and social development – as children are encouraged to take turns and listen to others. It also forms the earliest stages in making children both receptive to, and respectful of, different points of view. By actively encouraging debate and the exchange of ideas, teachers of young children use such activities to intervene and sensitively challenge assumptions regarding scientific ideas. Teachers are also able to model a sense of wonder, fascination and curiosity in objects and events, using first hand experiences with artefacts.

CS Case study

Miss R, the Reception teacher, brought into class a variety of ice shapes. She had frozen water in cubes, animal shapes and small balloons. She encouraged the small group of children working with her to observe the shapes. The children were able to look closely at the shapes and feel them. 'They're very cold!' was one remark, followed by 'They're slimy.'

Miss R asked the children why the shapes felt cold and for more words to describe the shapes. She wrote the children's words down on a large piece of paper. With Miss R's encouragement the children began to notice bubbles trapped inside the shapes and described the outside of the shape as 'frosty'. They could also hear cracking sounds as the ice began to melt. Miss R repeated the children's comments, qualifying or introducing *new* wording where necessary. Towards the end of the session Miss R read out the comments sheet and invited the children to choose the 'best' descriptive words. She then asked the children which shapes they thought would melt the fastest and why, thereby leading the children to make predictions about an everyday event. The use of various ice shapes provided for fascination and curiosity in the children.

The plan below shows an example of how the Early Learning Goals for Knowledge and Understanding of the World has been translated into a programme of work for a Reception class from which the above case study arose.

Year group: **Reception**
Unit of work: Winter
Main areas of learning: Knowledge and understanding of the world/Language and literacy
Links to National Curriculum – Science, English

Learning objectives	Activities	Organization	Resources
investigate objects using the senses.	Observation – using sight, touch, sound – of ice shapes.	Small groups, working at a table with the teacher.	Variety of ice shapes. Large paper and markers.
To record observations.	Group collaborative poem using words from observation.	Small group. Teacher to scribe collaborative poem.	Record sheet from activity above + paper and markers.
To look closely at patterns and change.	Observation of ice shapes melting.	Children looked at different shapes melting at intervals during a morning session.	Variety of ice shapes in separate dishes.
To find out about the natural world. To discuss features of an environment.	Use of pictures and large size books to identify animals that live in icy conditions.	Teacher to read large text to whole class. Class discussion of text and pictures.	Relevant books and pictures.
To ask questions about why things happen and how things work.	Large role-play area – the ice cave. Children to 'play' in ice cave. Through play to consider how animals and humans live in ice cave.	Paired/small group role-play. Focused play supported by an adult.	

Science in the National Curriculum 5–11

At the age of five, when children move from Reception to Year 1, the science curriculum follows the requirements of the National Curriculum Order for Science. The children follow the requirements of Key Stage 1 until the end of Year 2; the next stage – Key Stage 2 – is followed until the end of Year 6.

Time allowance for science in the National Curriculum

Science, as a core subject, requires a time allowance of approximately two hours at Key Stage 1 and $2^1/_2$ hours at Key Stage 2. Of the time allowance, 50% of the time at Key Stage 1 is to be spent on *Scientific Enquiry*, at Key Stage 2 this reduces to 40%.

The recommended time allowance for science in Key Stages 1 and 2 indicates a balance in the teaching of science skills, through scientific enquiry, and scientific content. This balance is essential to the science curriculum, as Harlen (1993) warns that a curriculum that is more content-based over-emphasizes the learning of individual facts, whereas a reliance on a skills-based curriculum may lead children to discover incorrect ideas through their investigations.

The National Curriculum was first made statutory in 1989 and although there have been subsequent reviews and alterations to the Order (see Chapter 1), the basic form has remained. At the time of writing, the Order may be found in two documents – Science Key Stages 1–4 (DfEE/QCA, 1999c), which sets out the science curriculum across four key stages, and The National Curriculum Handbook for primary teachers in England: Key Stages 1 and 2 (DfEE/QCA, 1999a) which sets out the primary curriculum for all subjects including science. The science requirements for Key Stages 1 and 2 are the same in both documents. The Order for science has two main sections:

1. The Programmes of Study;
2. The Attainment Targets.

The Programmes of Study are used for planning the teaching and learning of science, they set out the knowledge, skills and understanding that are to be delivered to the children. The Attainment Targets are used primarily for assessment purposes, they set out the knowledge, skills and understanding that pupils are expected to have *acquired* by the end of a Key Stage. The Attainment Targets are therefore used to base judgements about pupils' performance at the end of a Key Stage and to aid end of year judgements about pupils' attainment (see Chapter 6). They may also be used to aid the planning process, by indicating the level at which to pitch the teaching activities (see Chapter 3).

The following table shows the format of the Programmes of Study in the Order.

Structure of Programmes of Study

Sub-section of PoS	Content of sub-section	Examples – from KS 2 PoS Sc4 – Physical Processes
Summary of content	Found at the start of each key stage. Summarizes main things pupils will learn during the key stage.	During Key Stage 2 pupils learn about a wider range of living things, materials and phenomena . . . (p. 83).
Main column	Two sorts of requirement: 1. Knowledge, skills and understanding 2. Breadth of study Requirement 1 lists what has to be taught during the key stage. Requirement 2 lists the contexts, activities, areas of study and range of experiences through which the knowledge skills and understanding should be taught.	1. Electricity Pupils should be taught: • To construct circuits; • How changing components in a series circuit can make bulbs brighter or dimmer; • How to represent series circuits by drawings and symbols, and how to construct circuits on the basis of drawings and diagrams (p. 88). 2. Pupils should be taught through: • A range of domestic and environmental contexts familiar to them; • Looking at science and development of useful things; • Using a range of sources of information and data; • First-hand and secondary data (p. 89).
Examples – also within main column.	Non-statutory examples – given inside square brackets.	Using buzzers and motors when constructing simple circuits
Links to English, maths and ICT	Indicates connections between teaching requirements, suggesting how a requirement in science can build on the requirements in another subject (in the same key stage). Identifies opportunities for pupils to use ICT as they learn science.	ICT opportunity. Pupils could use simulation software to extend an investigation of components in a series circuit (p. 88).
Notes	Notes giving key information to be taken into account when teaching. May include definitions of words or phrases.	Note for 1b. Resistance does not need to be taught (p. 88).

(Adapted from DfEE/QCA, 1999a)

The Attainment Target section of the Order sets out the expected attainment in level bands, giving expected attainment alongside examples to clarify the statements made. Each level band – the Level Descriptions – corresponds roughly to the ages and stages set out below (Key Stage 3, for children aged 11–14 years, is given to illustrate the overlap of Levels expected between key stages).

Attainment Target 3: Physical Properties
Level 3

Pupils use their knowledge and understanding of physical phenomena to link cause and effect in simple explanations (for example a bulb failing to light because of a break in an electrical circuit, the direction or speed of movement of an object changing because of a push or a pull). They begin to make simple generalizations about physical phenomena (for example, explaining that sounds they hear become fainter the further they are from the source).

(DFEE/QCA, 1999a, p. 23)

Range of levels within which the great majority of pupils are expected to work.		Expected attainment for the majority of pupils at the end of the Key Stage.	
Key Stage 1	1–3	At age 7	2
Key Stage 2	2–5	At age 11	4
Key Stage 3	3–7	At age 14	5/6

(DFEE/QCA, 1999a, p. 1)

The National Curriculum Order acknowledges the need for both process and content, to be delivered through the primary science curriculum. The Programmes of Study and their Attainment Targets for science are therefore characterized by these two interrelated strands. The curriculum seeks to establish an iterative relationship between the scientific content contained in *Life and Living Processes, Materials and their Properties and Physical Processes,* and the skills necessary for *Scientific Enquiry*.

Scientific enquiry

There are many supporters for a curriculum that includes scientific method as an integral aspect of the subject, Selley (in Wellington, 1989) makes the statement that scientific enquiry is the only method by which children are able to develop a true understanding, a unique account of the natural world. However, Selley also cautions against the study of scientific processes for their own sake, i.e., context-free; it must therefore be considered that scientific method is primarily used in order for children to be able to appreciate and understand the workings of science. The skills of scientific enquiry thus aid children to make sense of their explorations and consequently develop their knowledge and understanding of science. However, Peacock (1998) warns that understanding in science is not developed simply by carrying out practical work, but is achieved through reflecting on the experience. Consequently, the role of the teacher is to structure the learning activity in order to incorporate time for discussing the results of practical work, both in small groups and as a class. It is hence a well-established practice in the primary school that scientific skills are used and taught explicitly, usually within a specified context from the content area of the National Curriculum Order. For our youngest children the skills are primarily used to enable children to investigate concepts for themselves, and thus to be actively involved in the process of science teaching and learning. In other words, teaching and using the skills in this way reinforces the acquisition of specified scientific knowledge. In this respect primary science does differ from the accepted view of science as a whole, as the use of scientific skills in this way relies on the pre-existence of scientific knowledge, which is not the case in the wider world of science. However, this way of working reinforces established knowledge, teaches about the methodology of science, i.e., teaching about science, and helps develop scientific attitudes, with respect to both an understanding of how science knowledge is arrived at and how scientists work. It must be remembered here that the majority of our children will not become professional scientists, and so an over-emphasis on this aspect of science is inappropriate to their needs. The ultimate aim of the study of scientific method is threefold:

- To enable children to have an understanding of how scientific knowledge is arrived at;
- To enable children to discern between competent, exciting science and poor or spurious science;
- To enable children to understand the relevance of science to their everyday life.

These aims are achieved both through the experience of carrying out their own science investigations and through the critical appraisal of work done by others, i.e., through the stories of scientists and their work. The need for children to understand the relevance of science to everyday life was included in the National Curriculum in response to a perceived need for the public to be aware of scientific issues. Traditionally, science had been taught, albeit in the secondary school, as a subject based on the acquisition of scientific facts, with little reference made to the relevance of the science work to the pupil's everyday life. This relevance has now been made an explicit part of the modern-day science curriculum, in order to encourage children, and consequently adults, to become scientifically literate. To be *scientifically literate* is defined as being able to question scientific explanations and discoveries, as explained by DfEE (1999a, p. 15) which states that by studying science, pupils begin to understand how major scientific ideas contribute to technological change, and impact on industry, business and medicine. Through this study children will develop the confidence and ability to question and discuss science-based issues that initially affect their own lives and then to issues which influence the direction of society and the future of the world in general.

Scientific enquiry draws heavily on children's ability to think as well as to remember, and as such teachers need to encourage children to exercise these skills by providing scientific activities that ask children to observe, measure, classify, compare and contrast, hypothesize, use reason and logic, and synthesize ideas. Children need to be made aware of different interpretations, and will need assistance in learning to appreciate and understand this diversity of opinion. Children are encouraged in science to use evidence critically, relating their evidence to previous science work and to critically appraise their findings, rather than merely accept their results. In the later stages of Key Stage 2 children should be encouraged to question and challenge the accuracy of their work and to begin to repeat measurements and observations.

Scientific Enquiry

Key Stages 1 and 2
Pupils should be taught:
- Ideas and evidence in science
- Investigative skills – planning, obtaining and presenting evidence, considering evidence and evaluating.

(DfEE/QCA, 1999a)

 ## Case study of a Scientific Enquiry activity

Miss J's Year 5 class was investigating the formation of shadows using classroom objects, a white screen and a torch. John suggested that when the torch was near to an object the shadow was bigger. Miss J encouraged John's group to investigate John's **idea**. The group turned John's idea into a **question to investigate** – What happens to the length of a shadow when the distance of a torch from an object is changed? The group **predicted** that the shadow of the object would get bigger as the torch gets nearer. They considered how to carry out their investigation and produced a **plan**. To make the **test fair** they would keep everything the same, i.e., object used, distance of object from screen, same torch, etc, and only alter the distance of the torch from the object. The group listed the **equipment** they would need, including a rule to **measure** the distance of the torch from the object and the length of the shadow.

Miss J looked at the children's plan and then the group carried out their **investigation**. They followed their plan and **recorded their results** on a chart, showing distance from the torch to the object in one column and length of shadow in the second column. They had decided to use distances from the torch every 5cm, i.e., 5cm, 10cm, 15cm, 20cm, 25cm, 30cm, etc., and to measure the length of the shadow in cm.

The group used their results chart to **draw a graph**, showing length of shadow against distance of the torch from the object. They used their graph to **look for a pattern** and discovered that John had been correct in his idea. They drew the **conclusion** that the nearer the torch to the object, the longer the shadow the object made.

Miss J talked to the group about their investigation and asked them if they were happy with the results and the way they worked. The children agreed that the hardest part of the investigation was measuring the shadow. They thought they should have **repeated**

this measurement to make sure it was accurate. The group also thought it was difficult to hold the torch in the same way each time and suggested that an **improvement** to the investigation would be to keep the torch on the table. Miss J suggested they **write up** their investigation and include their **evaluation at the end**.

Scientific enquiry provides pupils with the opportunity to involve themselves in the practical aspects of science. As most primary school children are naturally curious, this strand of the science curriculum offers teachers chances to capitalize on this thirst for learning by providing relevant opportunities for children to find things out for themselves. It is through their own enquiry that children gain experience of locating, examining and questioning scientific evidence. They begin by being directed in their explorations and by using their own experiences as a way of understanding their results. Their comprehension at this stage may be limited, but it is unlikely to improve if we deny them opportunities to extend and enhance it. Increasing maturity, experience and appropriate intervention all play a part in developing children's ability to understand, explain and interpret their findings. They are then able to progress to an understanding of how events and observations can be interpreted differently. Integral to this understanding of different interpretations is the study of scientists and their work. Through this study the child is able to build up an understanding of the work of the scientist and how the body of scientific facts is arrived at and added to. For this reason the study of the lives and work of scientists is now part of the science curriculum.

Progression from teacher directed enquiry to pupil directed enquiry

Teacher decides what to investigate and discusses it with the children

Children sometimes offer their own ideas in response to prompt questions

Children offer their own ideas for fair testing in response to prompt questions. They know there are different ways of getting evidence

Children sometimes offer suitable ideas for fair testing without prompt questions. They sometimes suggest ideas where evidence would need to be collected in different ways.

Adapted from Goldsworthy and Holmes (1999)

It is important to remember the role of the teacher as a source of information in science enquiry, as some degree of exposition will be needed to enable the children to access this aspect of the science curriculum. This does not mean lecturing children on the stories of scientists and how they worked; exposition is merely one way of ensuring that they have access to essential and interesting information and is a means of helping to explain and justify information. Such exposition may also have the added advantage of motivating and stimulating children's interest in the subject. Children can be helped further to find answers to questions about science and scientists from a range of sources, thereby drawing heavily on investigative skills that are not necessarily unique to science. Such skills include the ability to cooperate, to share ideas and information, to use all their senses, to apply existing knowledge, ask questions and deploy their research skills, including the use of ICT. An enquiry may also require children to employ empathy and imagination, both of which have to be informed by knowledge of the context and content.

Scientific content

The content aspect of the science curriculum for the 3–11 age range is a vital part of their scientific learning. Using the definition for science identified in Chapter 1 (p. 9), it is important that knowledge about science facts is included in the curriculum, in order for it to be termed science. A number of scientific facts are included in the National Curriculum Order for Science, organized under three headings – Life and Living Processes, Materials and their Properties and Physical Processes. These three headings basically equate to the known content of the disciplines biology, chemistry and physics. Summarized below are the requirements for both key stages in these three areas.

Life and Living Processes

Key Stages 1 and 2 pupils should be taught about:
- Life processes
- Humans and other animals
- Green plants
- Variation and classification
- Living things in their environment

(DfEE/QCA, 1999a)

Materials and their Properties

Key Stage 1 pupils should be taught about:
- Grouping materials
- Changing materials

Key Stage 2 pupils should be taught:
• Grouping and classifying materials
• Changing materials
• Separating mixtures of materials

(DfEE/QCA, 1999a)

Physical Processes

Key Stage 1 pupils should be taught about:
Electricity
Forces and motion
Light and sound

Key Stage 2 pupils should be taught about:
Electricity
Forces and motion
Light and sound
The earth and beyond.

(DfEE/QCA, 1999a)

The boxes above list the Areas of Study contained within the Order for science. Each of these is then broken down into statements specifying the knowledge, skills and understanding to be taught during the Key Stage. The statements referring to the knowledge, skills and understanding for one area of study are given below.

Science Key Stage 1 Sc2 Life processes and living things	**Science Key Stage 2** Sc2 Life processes and living things

Life processes
1 Pupils should be taught:
  a. the difference between things that are living and things that have never been alive
  b. that animals, including humans, move, feed, grow, use their senses and reproduce
  c. to relate life processes to animals and plants found in the local environment.
	Life processes
	1 Pupils should be taught:
	  a. that the life processes common to humans and other animals include nutrition, movement, growth and reproduction
	  b. that the life processes common to plants include growth, nutrition and reproduction
	  c. to make links between life processes in familiar animals and plants and the environments in which they are found.

(DfEE/QCA, 1999a, p. 79)	(DfEE/QCA, 1999a, p. 85)

Delivery of the science curriculum

At the time of writing, the National Curriculum documentation leaves the choice of when and how to tackle the various programmes of study to the discretion of schools. Consequently, different schools are free to introduce different concepts to pupils at different points during their primary education. Schools may opt to deliver them as a discrete science topic or, alternatively, as part of an integrated topic involving one or more of the other National Curriculum subjects. Unlike the other National Curriculum Core subjects of English and maths, science has not had a more prescriptive strategy brought into schools. It has merely had the advice regarding coverage (as noted earlier in the chapter) and a non-statutory Scheme of Work for Science (Standards and Effectiveness Unit, 1998). The published Scheme of Work provides a suggested framework for the delivery of the National Curriculum Programmes of Study. The document may be used in a variety of ways:

- As a resource bank of ideas;
- As a resource or teaching programme used to supplement a school's own Scheme of Work;
- As a template for a school to write its own science scheme of work;
- Adopted as written.

The delivery of the science curriculum, including scientific enquiry, and the use of the QCA Scheme of Work is discussed in more detail in Chapter 3.

Linking Science to the Whole Curriculum

The Early Learning Goals provide for science to be included in an integrated curriculum whereas the National Curriculum provides an Order for science as a discrete, core subject. However, science at all stages in the 3–11 setting has wider relevance for the whole curriculum. As noted in the introduction to the chapter, Ofsted is moving towards the notion of a *pure and applied curriculum*, and is currently looking for evidence during inspections of such a curriculum. Within this model, Literacy and Numeracy form the *pure* aspect of the curriculum; all other subjects form the *applied* curriculum. It is reported (Junior Education, 2000) that the requirements of the present primary curriculum potentially make it both overloaded and subject-specific, and suggest that it is more manageable to work from the Literacy Strategy, the Numeracy Strategy and the National Curriculum Objectives and to look for emerging links between them. In practice this means that skills, specific to English and maths, are taught during Literacy and Numeracy sessions and then used, i.e., applied, in other subjects. It is the application of skills that is expected to lead to coherence in children's learning, as it is believed that making links between subjects makes sense of the learning. The aim of a science lesson should therefore continue to be the development of a child's scientific knowledge, understanding and skills, but the teacher should also be mindful that science offers opportunities for applying learning from mathematics and language in a scientific context. In the same way, science offers powerful contexts to be used for the development of key skills during the Literacy and Numeracy lessons themselves. It is important to regard the use of the scientific contexts in terms of adding unity to the curriculum, for the subject areas to be complementary, as work during the Literacy hour must fulfil objectives taken from the Literacy Strategy, whilst work designated as science must have objectives taken from the Science Order, this is explored further in the section below.

Science and the Key Skills

Cross-curricular skills are those skills that are relevant in varying degrees to teaching and learning in all subjects, but which are not the preserve of any one subject. These skills are sometimes referred to as key skills and include communication skills, numeracy skills, ICT capability, problem solving, interpersonal skills, thinking and study skills.

(NCC, 1990)

The 1999 National Curriculum Handbook for Primary Teachers (DfEE/QCA, 1999a, pp. 20–21) reinforces the importance of these key skills, listing them as

- communication
- application of number
- information technology
- working with others
- improving own learning and performance
- problem solving

Science provides many opportunities for developing this range of skills, and so the chapter now concludes with a consideration of each of these key skills.

Communication within KS1		Communication within KS2	
Sc1g – communicate what happened in a variety of ways, including ICT. (DfEE/QCA 1999a, p. 78)	Breadth of study – 2a use simple scientific language to communicate ideas and to name and describe living things, materials, phenomena and processes. (DfEE/QCA 1999a, p. 82)	Sc1h – use a wide range of methods, including diagrams, drawings, tables, bar charts, line graphs and ICT, to communicate data in an appropriate and systematic manner. (DfEE/QCA 1999a, p. 83)	Breadth of study – 2a Use appropriate scientific language and terms, including SI units of measurement, to communicate ideas and explain the behaviour of living things, materials, phenomena and processes. (DfEE/QCA 1999a, p. 89)

Communication

Within the Scientific Enquiry strand of the National Curriculum Order and the breadth of study, emphasis is given to the communication of children's scientific enquiry and their ideas.

These requirements demonstrate the need for children to develop their ability to structure information and communicate their understanding. Teachers therefore must provide opportunities for children to

- listen to others
- describe their findings
- explain their ideas
- debate with others
- display their learning

Many of these communication skills are not restricted purely to science, but use and develop skills needed across the curriculum, thereby linking science to the whole curriculum. In order to communicate their information, pupils may record their findings in a variety of written, numerical or artistic ways. To aid children with the demands of organizing and communicating their information, writing frames (as below and overleaf) may be used. Such frames are used to direct pupils towards certain styles of writing, to ensure that written work is not just narrative or descriptive in nature, but is also analytical and explanatory. A writing frame gives a child a skeleton outline for a particular style of writing; often the framework gives differing key words and/or phrases, starters, connectives and sentence modifiers. These provide a structure within which children are able to concentrate on the information they wish to communicate rather than concentrating on the format itself. Using frames also ensures a child becomes familiar with the requirements of a particular writing structure.

Writing frame for developing a persuasive argument

We are debating . . .

Arguments for	Arguments against

After considering all of the evidence I think that . . .

(Feasey 1999, p. 103)

```
┌─────────────────────────────────────────────────────────────┐
│                Writing frame for comparison                   │
│                                                               │
│  ┌─────────────────────────────────────────────────────────┐ │
│  │ Although _____ and _____ are diferent _____ __ │ │
│  │ they are alike in some                                    │ │
│  │ interesting ways. For example they both _____.   │ │
│  │                                                           │ │
│  └─────────────────────────────────────────────────────────┘ │
│  ┌─────────────────────────────────────────────────────────┐ │
│  │ They are also similar in . . .                            │ │
│  │ The _____ is the same as _____.     │ │
│  │ The _____ resembles _____.          │ │
│  └─────────────────────────────────────────────────────────┘ │
│  ┌─────────────────────────────────────────────────────────┐ │
│  │ Finally they . . .                                        │ │
│  │                                                           │ │
│  │                                                           │ │
│  └─────────────────────────────────────────────────────────┘ │
└─────────────────────────────────────────────────────────────┘
```

When researching information, children are often tempted to copy chunks of text from various sources and persuading children to use their own words can be difficult. This obviously does not show that a child has learnt or understood anything about science and so teachers also need to spend time training children in how to take information from texts, without copying whole sections. This can be done in various ways, e.g.,

- By jointly reading a text with pupils and asking them to identify any key words or ideas;
- By structuring their work under certain headings and sub-headings;
- By presenting their work in note form, i.e., by substituting short phrases for long sentences and summarizing paragraphs (a note board may be provided which limits the space for copying text, as shown overleaf);
- Providing a question sheet to be completed (as overleaf);
- By using question boards, whereby children generate their own research questions, and answer boards (as overleaf).

Note board

When you have read your information, make a list of the key ideas, facts or things that happened.

1
_____

2
_____

3
_____

4
_____

5
_____

6
_____

7
_____

8
_____

9
_____

10
_____

(Adapted from Feasey 1999, p. 97)

Question sheet

Can you find out the answers to these questions about the life-cycle of a plant?

Question	Answer
1. What are the main stages in a plant life cycle?	
2. Why is the flower an important part of a plant?	
3. What is pollination?	
4. How are seeds produced?	
5. How are seeds spread?	
6. What is germination?	

Question board

Write down 10 questions

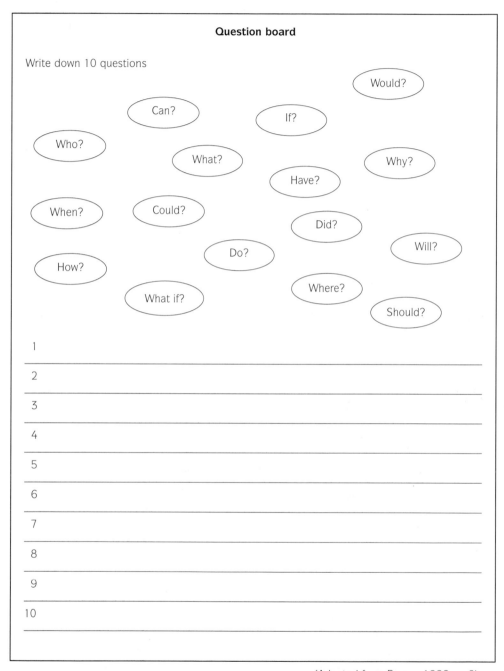

Would?

Can?

If?

Who?

What?

Why?

Have?

When?

Could?

Did?

Do?

Will?

How?

Where?

What if?

Should?

1 _____

2 _____

3 _____

4 _____

5 _____

6 _____

7 _____

8 _____

9 _____

10 _____

(Adapted from Feasey 1999, p. 9)

Answer board

Use this board to answer your 10 questions

1
_____

2
_____

3
_____

4
_____

5
_____

6
_____

7
_____

8
_____

9
_____

10
_____

(Adapted from Feasey 1999, p. 91)

Literacy and science

At the time of writing almost all schools in the maintained sector are delivering the National Literacy Strategy. (Although it is not statutory, if schools do not wish to use it they have to show that their method of Literacy teaching is as good as or better than the Literacy Strategy. The generally accepted criterion for this is the attainment of children within the Key Stage 2 SATs.) Consequently, the role of science in Literacy has to be considered when planning the curriculum. Feasey (1998, p. vi) states quite simply that science and literacy are '. . . inextricably linked'.

Without personal literacy individual children will find it more difficult to engage with science, and certainly doors to a range of literature, both fiction and non-fiction, will be closed.

Feasey 1999, p. iv.

When planning an activity, in science or literacy, the teacher must determine a tight objective for the activity, i.e., the reason for carrying out the activity. It is this objective that identifies the activity as either a science activity or a literacy activity, and so determines if science is being used as a context within literacy or if literacy skills are being used within science. Feasey (1998, p. vi) describes this as science offering '. . . natural contexts for the use and development of literacy skills and understanding whilst literacy helps to offer the individual access to the exciting and challenging world of science'. The tables below show:

1. the use of science as a context within a Literacy lesson
2. the application of Literacy skills within a science lesson

The use of science as a context within a Literacy lesson

Year group: 4
Term: 2

Literacy objective	Activity	Science context
To collect information from a variety of sources and present it in one simple format – a wall chart.	Children to use 3 sources of information about exercise to produce an informative wall chart. The 3 sources to be used are: 1. results from an investigation into the effect of exercise on pulse rate; 2. research into different types of exercise in books;	The effect of exercise and rest on pulse rate. The importance of exercise for good health.
Writing composition 23, NLS p. 41)	3. research into the pulse using the Internet.	(Life processes and living things – 2dh, NC Order for Science)

The application of Literacy skills within a science lesson

Year group: 1
Term: 1

Science objective	Activity	Literacy skills
To know that seeds grow into flowering plants.	Children to grow bean seeds. Children to observe/ compare/discuss features of plant at different stages of growth. Children to make own labels for plants, including different parts of the fully-grown plant, and provide	Write and draw simple instructions and labels for everyday classroom use.
(Life processes and living things – 3c, NC Order for science)	instructions for growing bean seeds.	(Writing composition 16, NLS p. 21)

The examples above demonstrate how easily the disciplines of science and literacy can be complementary. It must be appreciated that this is not an artificial connection, that both disciplines benefit from being studied together. Children do need to be able to express their ideas and understandings in science; this can only be achieved if they are confident in themselves and their ability to communicate accurately. Therefore there is a real need for the child to have a sound literacy base. It must be noted here that oracy is included in the National Literacy strategy, and so the spoken word is also to be considered. Feasey (1999, p. vi) states that the '. . . spoken word is central to literacy and science and should be afforded time in planning both literacy and science activities'. A child's literacy base will therefore also enable the child to organize their own thinking for themselves and provide the necessary scientific language for communication of ideas and understandings.

Application of number

As with the National Literacy Strategy, at the time of writing the majority of schools in the maintained sector are delivering the National Numeracy Strategy. (The justification for this is exactly the same as for Literacy (above) and the same criterion applies as regards the position of Ofsted.) Consequently, the role of science in Numeracy, and thus the application of number, has also to be considered. Again the relationship is a valid one, as Feasey and Gallear (2000, p. iv) report quite simply that 'At the heart of science is mathematics.' They also state (p. v) a '. . . key issue in science is that the teacher should raise the profile of the application of number in this curriculum area'. and suggest that only adults with both a sound science background and an understanding of the skills of a numerate person will be able to engage fully with an increasingly technological world.

Science relies on the use of mathematics to provide quantitive evidence on which scientists make comparisons, note patterns and trends, make generalizations and draw conclusions.

Feasey & Gallear (2000, p. vi)

Feasey & Gallear (2000) also state that the very success of primary science is dependent on the ability of a child to both transfer and apply knowledge and skills from mathematics into science. The student or newly qualified teacher must therefore plan for this transfer and application. As explained above with regards to science and Literacy, planning for science and Numeracy begins with the lesson objective. The objective denotes the activity as either a Numeracy activity in which science is the context, or a science activity in which Numeracy skills are being applied. The tables on the next page show this in action.

The use of science as a context within a numeracy lesson

Year group: Reception

Numeracy objective	Activity	Science context
To talk about, recognize and recreate patterns.	Children to look at brickwork pattern in the school grounds. Children to discuss the pattern using mathematical language – next to, above, below, etc.	Investigate objects and materials by using all of their senses as appropriate.
(Key objectives, NNS, p. 2)	Children to recreate the pattern using printing blocks on paper.	(Knowledge and understanding of the world, Early Learning Goals.)

The application of Numeracy skills within a science lesson

Year group: 6

Science objective	Activity	Numercay skills
To know how to measure forces.	Children to be introduced to Newtonmetres for measuring size of a force. Children to record size of force needed to carry out a range of movements including	Record estimates and readings from scales to a suitable degree of accuracy.
	• opening a drawer	
	• closing a door	
Physical Processes 2e, NC Order for science.)	• pulling an object across the table	(Teaching programme: Year 6, NNS, p. 27)

Information technology

New technologies are having a profound effect on science teaching and on children themselves. Children are becoming increasingly enthusiastic and proficient users of information technology, many now having access to some form of ICT in the home. The use of ICT in the nursery/classroom offers considerable potential for enriching and enhancing the science curriculum, through the provision of opportunities for interactive learning. It also provides opportunities to use science as a context for the development of

- fine motor skills
- personal and social skills
- reasoning skills

Using information and communications technology in this way will also aid children in becoming increasingly familiar, confident and positive about their skills as users.

ICT can provide valuable tools for

- reinforcing first-hand and practical scientific experiences, e.g., through the use of writing packages.
- recalling, selecting and organizing information.
- communicating their knowledge and understanding in a variety of ways.
- widening pupils' scientific knowledge and understanding.
- engaging in scientific enquiry.

Using ICT in science teaching

Themed software
Packages that set out to provide information in support of a specific concept, e.g., Space or to science generally. Speaking and listening can be enhanced through the use of audio-equipped scientific CD-Roms.

Eyewitness Encyclopedia of Nature (Dorling Kindersley, DK Multimedia, London).
The Way Things Work (Dorling Kindersley, DK Multimedia, London).
Riverside Explorer (Ordnance Survey).

Open-ended software
This software is not specifically related to any particular topic, but can be used to extend and enhance children's efforts to communicate and organize scientific information, e.g., data collection and handling packages and the use of word processing packages. Editing and redrafting benefit in particular (HMI/DES, 1991) from the use of open-ended software.

Clarisworks (Apple software).
Word (Microsoft software).
Office 2000 (Microsoft software).

The Internet
Numerous web sites exist with scientific content. However, many are not suitable for direct use by children, but may still offer teachers a considerable source of information with which to inform their teaching. It is important that sites for use by the children are visited first by the teacher and then bookmarked. Some schools have started to produce their own web sites in which scientific topics feature.

www.edleston.cheshire.sch.uk
www.ambleside.schoolzone.co.uk/ambleweb/localsch.htm
http://vtc.ngfl.gov.uk
www.askjeeves.co.uk
http://www2.edc.org/sciencequest/

It is important that ICT is used to assist, rather than replace, teaching and learning in science. It will not do the teacher's job for him/her, nor will it improve a badly planned or executed lesson. It is therefore a resource to be used only to improve attainment or make a lesson more accessible for the child/children. (The use of ICT in science teaching and learning will be covered further in Chapter 5.)

Working with others

Science provides many opportunities for children to work together, with and without the support of an adult, to discuss their work with others and to work with others to meet a challenge. They are encouraged to contribute to small group and whole-class discussions, about their work and the work of others. Through these activities the children are able to develop their social skills, their awareness and understanding of the needs of others. If structured well, scientific activities enable children to

- cooperate with others
- work effectively with others
- work together in formal and informal settings
- appreciate the experiences of others
- consider different perspectives
- benefit from others' thoughts, words and actions

(Group work in science is further explored in Chapter 4.)

Improving own learning and performance

The specific requirements of the Programmes of Study for Science 1 – Scientific Enquiry – cover the need for children to reflect on their investigative work, share their reflections with others and use their reflections to develop and improve their own learning and performance.

Requirements of Key Stage 1 – Sc1	Requirements of Key Stage 2 – Sc1
2j – review their work and explain what they did to others	2m – review their work and the work of others and describe its significance and limitations
DfEE/QCA 1999a, p. 78	DfEE/QCA 1999a, p. 84

Within scientific activities children are given the opportunity to develop and refine a wide range of skills. Through the activities they are encouraged to

- reflect on their learning
- critically evaluate their work
- critically evaluate what they have learned
- identify ways to improve learning and performance
- assess their progress in learning
- identify obstacles and/or problems in learning
- discuss ways to improve their learning

The skills of reviewing and improving learning and performance is thus inextricably linked with the delivery of scientific enquiry, as shown in the case studies overleaf.

Case study 1

A small group of children from Miss P's Reception class had been comparing how far they could jump in the playground. They had been supervised by an adult helper. The group then reported back to Miss P what had happened, and thus **reflected on their learning**. All the children could remember that Emma had jumped the furthest and Peter hadn't jumped very far at all. Most of the children were surprised at this because Peter was the fastest runner in the class. Miss P asked the children to line up in the order of who jumped the furthest, who came next, etc. Mary pointed out that Peter was the smallest in the group and Emma was the tallest. The group discussed this, supported by questioning by Miss P.

 Case study 2

Two children from Mr W's Year 3 class tidied up the sink area and returned all the containers they had used to the science resource area. They began to discuss their work. 'I was surprised the custard powder didn't dissolve in the water, I was sure it would,' Amy began. 'I didn't think it would because I've watched my mum make custard at home and she uses milk,' John replied.
'Do you think it would have made a difference then if the water was warm?' asked Amy.
'I think we could have stirred it more, I don't think we stirred it for long enough,' suggested John.
Amy and John's conversation demonstrates their ability to **critically evaluate their work**.
'We didn't count how many times we stirred each mixture did we?' Amy continued.
'It would have been a fairer test if we had,' replied John.
'Do you think our results are right then?' Amy asked.
'Some things dissolved and some didn't. I think the ones that dissolved are right,' said John quietly.
The children's continuing conversation demonstrates that they are able to identify ways to **improve learning and performance** and **critically evaluate what they have learned**.

Case study 3

Miss J sat with her group of middle ability Year 5 children. They were discussing the results of their investigation into the strength of different-sized springs. Miss J asked for Robert's conclusion to the investigation. Robert reported that the tightly coiled springs were stronger than loosely coiled springs. He felt he'd learned a lot through investigating the springs because he thought bigger springs were stronger but that wasn't necessarily true for the springs he'd used. Robert was therefore able **to assess his progress in learning**. Robert thought that the group hadn't used enough springs in their investigation, they had only used four, but Robert thought that to provide all the information they needed they would have needed to test at least eight different ones. Robert thus **identified obstacles in their learning**. Miss J suggested that they could repeat the investigation using more springs and asked the group if this would alter how they carried out the investigation. Alice thought they would have to record their results in different ways and suggested using Carroll diagrams to show how the length and tightness of coil affected the strength of the spring. Robert wasn't sure how that would work. Emma said she would show him and began to draw a Carroll diagram and explain it.

	Tightly coiled spring	Loosely coiled spring
Strong spring		
Weak spring		

The group thus demonstrated their ability **to discuss ways to improve their learning**.

Problem solving

The skills needed to engage in problem solving include

- identifying and understanding a problem
- planning ways to solve a problem
- monitoring progress in tackling a problem
- reviewing solutions to problems

Science naturally provides the opportunities to develop and use these skills through scientific enquiry. The requirements of the Programmes of Study for Scientific Enquiry ensure that children are encouraged to test, modify and review progress during their explorations.

Problem solving skills in science

Problem solving skill	NC Sc1 requirement		Example
	Key Stage 1	Key Stage 2	
Identifying and understanding a problem	2a – ask questions.	2a – ask questions that can be investigated scientifically	How does the type of exercise affect the breathing rate?
Planning ways to solve a problem	2a – decide how they might find answers to questions 2c – think about what might happen before deciding what to do	2a – decide how to find answers to questions. 2c – think about what might happen or try things out when deciding what to do	Children decide whether the answer to a question needs a classroom investigation or is to be researched in a book.
Monitoring progress in tackling a problem	2e – follow simple instructions to control risks 2f – explore and make observations	2e – take action to control risks 2g – check observations and measurements, repeat if necessary	Evaluating evidence from an investigation and deciding if a pattern can be drawn or if it needs further evidence to be collected.
Reviewing solutions to problems	2h-j – consider evidence and evaluate work	2i-m – consider evidence and evaluate work	Children reviewing how they worked together and if their results are valid.

Adapted from Dfee/QCA (1999a)

Thinking Skills

In addition to the key skills explored above, emphasis is also given to the promotion of thinking skills across the curriculum (DfEE/QCA 1999a, p. 22). The National Curriculum Handbook for primary teachers states that the use of thinking skills aids children in learning how to learn and are naturally embedded in the primary curriculum, and thus in the science curriculum. Five aspects of thinking skills are identified – information processing skills, reasoning skills, enquiry skills, creative thinking skills and evaluation skills. The five aspects are considered in the following table.

Thinking skills

Skill	Explanation	Example – in science
Information processing skills	Pupils locate and collect relevant information. They sort, classify, sequence, compare and contrast, analyse relationships.	Use Internet to search for relevant information regarding investigative work.
Reasoning skills	Pupils give reasons for opinions and actions, draw inferences and make deductions. They use precise language to explain thoughts and make judgements and decisions informed by reasons or evidence.	Using results to formulate a conclusion to an investigation.
Enquiry skills	Pupils ask relevant questions, pose and define problems, plan what to do and how to research. They predicate outcomes and anticipate consequences, test conclusions and improve ideas.	All skills used in investigations.
Creative thinking skills	Pupils generate and extend ideas, suggest hypotheses, apply their imagination and look for innovative outcomes.	Drawing conclusions from investigative work.
Evaluation skills	Pupils evaluate information, judge the value of what they read, hear and do. They develop criteria for judging the value of their own and others work or ideas. They have confidence in their judgements.	Children judge the value of information when carrying out research using books and/or ICT. They reflect on their own, and others', practical work.

Science and the Cross-Curricular Elements

Although often used as a collection of easily definable subjects, in reality the National Curriculum comprises much more than just these. The Education Reform Act of 1988 placed a statutory responsibility upon schools to promote the spiritual, moral, cultural, mental and physical development of pupils. The Act also made it clear that schools were expected to prepare children for the 'opportunities, responsibilities and experiences of adult life' (NCC, 1990). To support schools in meeting these requirements, the curriculum outlined in the 1988 Act also contained a set of cross-curricular elements including themes, skills and dimensions as well as the subjects. The inclusion of these elements was intended to offer schools opportunities to pull together the broad education of individuals and augment the basic curriculum as outlined in the core and foundation subjects (NCC, 1990).

The **cross-curricular dimensions** included equality of opportunity for all including preparation for life in a multi-cultural society, and equality of access to the curriculum for children with special educational needs

(NCC, 1990)

The cross-curricular dimensions were centred on the belief that all children have an entitlement to equality of opportunity in education. Although the National Curriculum Order for science may seem to indicate to the student or newly qualified teacher that teachers are simply involved in the delivery of prescribed content and then assessing children by reference to standard norms, teaching is in fact a much more complex task. Schools and nurseries have a duty to work positively for equality of educational opportunity and to ensure science teaching encourages this ideal. The provision of an equal opportunities science curriculum is considered in Chapters 7 and 8, the contribution of the cross-curricular themes to equality of opportunity is considered below.

The **cross-curricular themes** offered pupils contexts within which they can begin to think about and reflect upon values and beliefs as well as acquiring additional knowledge and understanding important for their future lives as adults. The themes covered economic and industrial understanding, careers education, health education, citizenship and environmental education.

(NCC, 1990)

The requirements of the cross-curricular themes have been simplified with the introduction of the 1999 National Curriculum Handbook for Primary Teachers. The handbook (DfEE/QCA 1999a, p. 11) sets out two broad aims for the school curriculum:

1. to provide opportunities for all pupils to achieve and learn,
2. to promote pupils' spiritual, moral, social and cultural development and prepare all pupils for the opportunities, responsibilities and experiences of life.

Sccience activity	Science objective	Aim 2 reference	Aim 2 notes
Investigating habitats in the school grounds.	To know about the different plants and animals found in different habitats (KS2, Sc2, 5b).	Distinguishing between right and wrong.	Know that it is wrong to disturb the habitat and to follow instructions given for observing a habitat.
Researching diets in different cultures.	To know food is needed for activity and growth and the importance of a varied and adequate diet (KS2, Sc2, 2a).	An understanding of beliefs and cultures.	Know that some religions and cultures have specific dietary requirements but their diets are adequate for health.
Looking at different houses in the locality. Discussing who lives where.	To find out about the uses of a variety of materials. (KS1, Sc3, 1d).	Values	Recognize that people choose to live in different areas and different houses and that the choices they make are dependent on their values, e.g., to be near family or friends.
Discussions of a topical science issue, e.g., the outbreak of foot and mouth disease.	To look at the part science has played in the development of many useful things (KS2, Breadth of Study, 1b).	Citizenship	To be able to express a point of view. To discuss science knowledge given by 'experts' and the effect on the public's views of the outbreak.
Sort leaves into two groups using own criteria.	To investigate objects/materials using all the senses as appropriate (ELG, Knowledge and Understanding of the World).	Equal opportunities	Children to use senses as appropriate, therefore not discriminated against if not all the senses can be used. Using own criteria ensures all children can access activity.
Sorting litter found in the playground.	To care for the environment. (KS1, Sc2, 5c).	Respect for the environment – both local and global.	To know that some litter is more harmful to the environment than other types of litter. To know effects of litter on environment.
Carrying out an investigation into cars rolling down a ramp.	To find out about, and describe the movement of, familiar things (KS1, Sc4, 2a).	Decision-making	Deciding how high the ramp should go, if the car should be pushed or held, etc.
Working within a group to design an investigation.	To carry out a whole investigation – planning, obtaining and presenting evidence, considering evidence and evaluating work (KS2, Sc1, 2a–j).	Respect for self and others	Respecting all ideas. Working together to refine ideas.
Working with a partner to test the relationship of exercise to pulse rate.	To know about the effect of exercise and rest on pulse rate (KS2, Sc2, 2d).	Relationships	To be able to work effectively with a partner.
Listening to a visitor about their studies in science.	To ask questions about why things happen and how things work (ELG, Knowledge and Understanding of the World).	Further education	To know that education doesn't stop at 16 years.
Visit to a sports centre	To know that taking exercise helps humans to keep healthy (KS1, Sc2, 2c).	The world outside school, including work and leisure.	To know sports centres have people working there and that people go to exercise for leisure.

It is easy to see how teaching and learning in science makes a cont[...]
of these aims. Aim 1 relates to the subject areas defined i[...]
Curriculum of which science is a core area. Aim 2 can also be ass[...]
delivery of the science curriculum. The aim includes reference to[...]

- distinguishing between right and wrong,
- an understanding of beliefs and cultures,
- values,
- citizenship,
- equal opportunities,
- respect for the environment – both local and global,
- decision making,
- respect for self and others,
- relationships,
- further education,
- the world outside school, including work and leisure.

The table opposite gives examples of activities that support learning in science and cover aspects of aim 2.

Summary

Science in the primary curriculum is based on the requirements of the Early Learning Goals and the National Curriculum. The documents detail the experiences, knowledge, skills and understanding that children in the 3–11 age range need to be taught and to learn. It is the role of the teacher to interpret the content of the relevant document and use it as a base for science teaching. Science for the under 5s is mainly found under the heading of Knowledge and Understanding of the World, whilst for the over 5s much of the science to be taught is detailed under the subject heading of science. Therefore, for the under 5s, the integration of science with other subjects is almost assured, as the curriculum in the Foundation Stage is not planned under subject headings. For children in the 5–11 age range the integration of science with other curriculum subjects – specifically English, maths, ICT – is centred on the requirement for key skills to be covered in all the curriculum subjects. Such integration is needed to provide coherence in the teaching and learning of the 3–11 age group. The implication for the teaching of science is that it should not be delivered in isolation from the rest of the primary curriculum.

REFERENCES

Department for Education and Employment (1998) *The National Literacy Strategy*, Cambridge: Cambridge University Press.

Department for Education and Employment (1999) *The National Numeracy Strategy*, London: DfEE.

Feasey, R. (1999) *Primary Science and Literacy*, Hatfield: ASE.

Feasey, R. & Gallear, B. (2000) *Primary Science and Numeracy*, Hatfield: ASE.

Goldsworthy, A. & Holmes, M. (1999) *Teach it! Do it! Let's get to it!*, Hatfield: ASE.

Harlen, W. (1992) *The Teaching of Science: Studies in Primary Education*, London: David Fulton.

Harlen, W. (1993) *Teaching and Learning Primary Science* (2nd edn), London: Paul Chapman.

National Curriculum Council (1990) *Curriculum Guidance 3: The Whole Curriculum*, York: NCC.

'On Target for Literacy' (1999) *Junior Education*, February, pp. 29–36.

Qualifications and Curriculum Authority (1999a) *The National Curriculum: Handbook for Primary Teachers in England*, London: DfEE/QCA.

Qualifications and Curriculum Authority (1999b) *Early Learning Goals*, London: DfEE/QCA.

Qualifications and Curriculum Authority (1999c) *Science: Key Stages 1–4*, London: DfEE/QCA.

Peacock, G. (1998) *Science for Primary Teachers: An Audit and Self-study Guide*, London: Letts Educational.

Selley, N. J. (1989) 'Philosophies of Science and Their Relation to Scientific Processes and the Science Curriculum', in Wellington, J. (ed.) *Skills and Processes in Science Education*, London: Routledge.

Standards and Effectiveness Unit (1998) *A Scheme of Work for Key Stages 1 and 2*, London: DfEE/QCA.

SECTION 2

Planning, teaching and class management

Planning for Science

Chapter 3 is the first chapter in the section of the book focusing on planning, teaching and class management of science for the 3–11 age range. This chapter considers the planning process in detail, in order to aid the reader in understanding the need for clear, concise, effective and thoughtful planning. The chapter explores the notion that such planning underpins effective teaching in science. Planning is a process that begins with whole school long-term planning, which is developed into medium-term planning and then to short-term planning. The chapter begins by exploring the development through the three levels of planning and details the requirements of each level. In order to illustrate this continuum of planning, one concept area in science is tracked through the three levels.

Chapters 1 and 2 have established the rationale for including science in the curriculum for the 3–11 age range and have introduced the reader to the documents on which the science component of the curriculum is based. The next section of this chapter considers how planning, using the documentation, is made relevant to the school in which it is being delivered. Consequently, although the planning of science must fulfil the requirements of the Foundation Stage, by using the Early Learning Goals (ELG), for children aged 3–5 or the requirements of the National Curriculum Order, by using the Programmes of Study for children aged 5–11 years, it must also reflect a school's overall aims, objectives and policies. Each school will therefore interpret the requirements (i.e., the Programmes of Study, the Early Learning Goals) in different ways. This section of the chapter seeks to demonstrate how the documentation is used to plan interesting, relevant and effective teaching sessions. Within this consideration the features of a good lesson are discussed. A good lesson is like a story, having a clear beginning, a gripping middle and good ending! The student and newly qualified teacher must be able to plan these three aspects of a lesson equally well and so this section ends with an overview of how the three aspects may be shown in a short-term plan.

Finally, the chapter goes on to demonstrate how the three levels of planning contribute towards continuity and progression in the subject across the 3–11 age range, to ensure the advancement in children's learning whilst ensuring a coherent science curriculum. Examples of good practice from across the foundation and primary phases will demonstrate how continuity and progression is shown in planning. The examples will also illustrate different approaches to the delivery of science. Chapter 2 established the requirement for science to be taught alongside other curriculum subjects and explored how connections need to be made between the subjects. This need is further considered and the case is made for science teaching to take place within discrete units of work, cross-curricular activities and continuing work.

The Planning Process

Good, effective planning underpins good teaching and purposeful learning. To be effective, planning needs to be thoughtful, clear, concise and relevant to the children and to the school in which it is to be delivered. The three recognized levels of the planning process used in schools are – long-term, medium-term and short-term planning:

- long-term – planning for science across the Foundation Stage, across Key Stage 1 and/or 2,
- medium-term – the planning of units of work,
- short-term – the planning of individual lessons or activities.

The three levels are related and so are not mutually exclusive. Each level is a development of the previous level, as shown in the figure below.

Long-term plans

The National Curriculum and/or Early Learning Goals are allocated to Year groups and/or Topics

Medium-term plans

The Long-term planning is given more detail. Contexts for the science work and activities are decided

Short-term plans

Fine detail is added to the science planning – resources needed, differentiation and assessments

The figure above shows long-term planning as the first stage in the process that gives an overview of science coverage over the range of year groups in the institution that it covers. Medium-term plans are derived from the school's long-term plan and show how the science coverage is to be delivered in termly or half-termly blocks to a specific Year group or class. Short-term plans are then developed from the medium-term plan and show how a teacher is to deliver a particular session of science. Each level of planning hence provides more detail about the science teaching to be delivered than the previous level. The three strands of planning thus form a continuum of planning.

Whole School Long-term Planning for Science

Long-term planning covers the delivery of science across a school as a whole; this may be the Foundation Stage, Key Stage 1, Key Stage 2, or a combination of Stages. It is used to ensure that the school science curriculum provides children with worthwhile, non-repetitive experiences of science throughout their schooling. Long term plans, also known as a school's Scheme of Work, provides a mechanism by which teachers can build in continuity and progression into the curriculum, both within and between Key Stages, in terms of knowledge, understanding and skills, and breadth of scientific study – this will be considered in more detail later in the chapter and is shown below.

 *Case study*

Taking one concept area in science, the coordinator responsible may initially allocate the National Curriculum Programmes of Study to different Year Groups. This allocation will be mindful of the perceived development of knowledge, skills and understanding within the concept area. The long-term planning sheets are then completed to indicate how the concept is delivered at different points across a Key Stage. The long-term plan may also indicate where the learning in this area begins in the Foundation Stage. The allocation below shows a progression in the study of habitats, beginning with children in the Foundation Stage becoming aware of where they live and that they share their environment with other animals and plants. This awareness is developed in Year 1 and built upon in Year 3 when the children begin to compare habitats. Year 5 children are then made aware of how the plants and animals co-exist and the relationships between the species in a habitat.

Area of study: living things in their environment (Sc2 Life processes and living things).

Foundation Stage: ELG, – To observe, find out about, and identify features in the place they live and the natural world.

Year 1: KS1, 5a, – To find out about the different kinds of plants and animals in the local environment.

Year 3: KS2, 5b – To know about the different plants and animals found in different habitats.

Year 5: KS2, 5d – To use food chains to show feeding relationships in a habitat.

Long-term plans thus take into account the requirements for the Stage (or Stages) covered and allocates these to individual Year groups. At Key Stages 1 and 2 long-term planning must meet the statutory requirements of the National Curriculum in terms of the knowledge, skills and understanding stated within the Order, together with the prescribed breadth of study. The long-term plan therefore outlines both the science content to be covered across the school and the organization of its delivery. A coordinator usually leads the development of the long-term planning of the school curriculum. The coordinator leading the development may be the curriculum coordinator, the Key Stage coordinator or the relevant subject coordinator. There are various interpretations of the role of the coordinator in the 3–11 age range, these will covered in more detail in Chapter 9, but it is most likely that the student and newly qualified will encounter one or more of the following coordinators:

- Curriculum coordinator – who has the overall responsibility for the whole curriculum within the school, of which science is one area, and all curriculum issues within the school. The coordinator may be responsible for one or more Key Stage;
- Key Stage coordinator – who may oversee the planning, delivery and assessments of the school curriculum across a Key Stage;
- Subject coordinator – who has the responsibility for all issues regarding the planning, delivery and assessment of one subject area only, although in practice the primary teacher often coordinates more than one subject;
- Year group coordinator – who leads all planning, ensures the effective delivery of the school curriculum and assessments for one year group only.

The long-term plan sets out all the *planned* science to be covered in the school. The written plan must however be regarded as detailing the minimum science to be taught; further opportunities for science, either planned for at the short-term planning stage or incidentally arising, are also to be encouraged. The plan thus requires the involvement of the whole staff, by adding their ideas and other contributions, by reviewing the plans and ultimately the agreement of the long-term plan. The plan is then updated and modified at regular intervals, in order to ensure its continuing relevance.

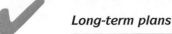

Long-term plans

Long-term plans include brief details of:

- the science to be taught to each year group;
- the learning objectives to be delivered;
- suggested activities to deliver the objectives;
- when the science is to be taught;
- in what depth the science is taught;
- whether it is taught separately or linked with other subjects;
- the resources needed;
- the assessments which may be made.

For Key Stages 1 and 2, the long-term plan maps out how the statutory requirements have been used to develop Units of Work, which are manageable and coherent. Each unit will have a specific science focus that is clearly stated. The broad content of each unit, together with any links to other subjects, or aspects of the curriculum, are also clearly stated in the long-term plan. At the Foundation Stage, this level of the planning process should indicate a range of experiences that will enable children to work towards the Early Learning Goals. The table below demonstrates the features of long- term planning, using an example for a Year 1 class.

Unit of Work for Year 1 – Term 3

Focus: Living things
Links to other subjects: Literacy, P.E., Art, DT.
Resources: 'Hungry Caterpillar' – big book, photographs of a family, life cycle jigsaws.

NC PoS	Objective	Suggested Activities	Children's recording	Link to Sc1
LPLT 2a	To be able to name all the external body parts.	Observation of partner. Matching words to a life-size picture.	Labelled drawing of partner – label body parts.	Make comparisons – class chart of shoe sizes, hair colour, etc.
LPLT 2a	To compare the external body parts of humans with those of other animals.	Compare partner to an animal studied on a visit.	Pictures + list of body parts.	Collecting evidence.
LPLT 2b	To know humans and other animals need food and water to live.	Class read of 'The Hungry Caterpillar'.	Class discussion of story.	Identify associations – class data on what their pets eat and drink.
LPLT 2c	To know that humans need to take exercise and eat healthily.	1. Discussion of different ways to exercise. 2. Discussion of favourite meal. Identify healthy/unhealthy foods.	1. Draw pictures of different ways + a sentence about each one. 2. Sort foods into groups. Draw favourite meal.	Observation – of breathing before, during and after exercise.

LPLT 2d	To know the role of drugs and medicines.	Reporting to the class about a visit to the doctors'/hospital.	Safety poster about taking medicines.	Using firsthand experience.
LPLT 1b	To know that humans have babies.	Sorting/describing family photographs.	Picture of own family.	Identify patterns – discuss heights of different family members.
LPLT 2f	To know that babies grow.			
LPLT 1b	To know that animals move, feed, grow and reproduce.	Life cycle jigsaws and games. Discussion of stages and how they occur.	Draw the life cycle of a butterfly.	Identifying patterns – all animals have a life cycle of birth, growth, reproduction.

In order for long-term planning to reflect the individuality of the school, the requirements of the Order need interpretation, set within the context of the school. The plan must therefore be written with regard to:

- a school's particular circumstances;
- its location;
- the interests of the children,;
- the expertise of the teaching staff;
- the resources available.

As noted in Chapter 2, schools may make use of commercially produced schemes of work to assist in long-term planning for science. However, published schemes should always be scrutinized carefully – teachers need to examine them critically and ensure that they take the above points into consideration when deciding which materials are relevant and appropriate. Such schemes are most useful as a bank of ideas for activities to deliver the statutory science requirements for the age range; the suggestions contained in many of the schemes may be adapted to become more meaningful to the children in a specific location. Particularly with respect to accompanying teaching resources, e.g., worksheets, these will not be appropriate to all institutions and to all circumstances, indeed they are likely to have been produced with for use with *a typical child* of a certain age, and so these too may need modifying or even replacing.

In addition to commercially produced schemes of work, an exemplar Science Scheme of Work has been produced by the QCA (QCA/DfEE, 1998) to aid schools in developing their own Scheme of Work for science. It is a non-statutory document that may be used in various ways:

- as a bank of resources;
- as a format or basis for a school's scheme of work;
- alongside a school's scheme of work, i.e., to supplement the school's own ideas of planning.

QCA Unit 3D Rocks and Soils

The unit focuses on the characteristics of rocks and soils. Children are taught that underneath all surfaces is rock, which may not be seen, and that rock is broken down into pebbles and soils that we often see. It establishes that different rocks have different characteristics.

Guidance is given regarding:

- where experimental and investigative work fits in;
- where the unit builds on earlier units in the Scheme of Work;
- links to other subject Schemes of Work;
- specific vocabulary to be used;
- resources needed;
- end of unit expectations;
- a series of learning objectives, related teaching activities, expected learning outcomes and explanatory notes.

Medium-term Planning for Science

Medium-term plans usually detail a term or half-term teaching programme. Year group staff use the school's long-term plan to formulate these plans. There are various models for developing the medium-term plans:

- one teacher working alone;
- a number of staff working in a Year group teaching team;
- cross-year planning teams;
- individual teachers or teaching teams supported by the relevant subject or Key Stage coordinator.

Medium-term planning should set out a logical progression of a scientific concept, using teaching objectives derived from the Early Learning Goals or National Curriculum Programmes of Study. The plans add clarity to the long-term plan with respect to contexts for the science work and more detail about suitable activities through which the objectives can be met. Medium-term plans also begin to consider assessment opportunities for the pupils. The activities through which the objectives will be delivered must be interesting, motivating and relevant to the children's circumstances. The plans therefore detail:

- Specific activities;
- Resources needed to support the teaching and learning;
- The teaching methods, classroom organization and ideas for differentiation to be used (see Chapter 4 for further details);
- The context for the science teaching – in the Foundation Stage this may be *where* the science learning will take place, e.g., a role-play area or outdoor play area. In the later years the context may be *how* the science learning is to be addressed, e.g., as an independent science unit or within a cross-curricular topic. (The different contexts for scientific activities are discussed later in the chapter.)

Medium-term plans usually therefore also indicate where the planned activities link with another subject or area of the curriculum and, increasingly, where there are opportunities for teaching and learning in science to contribute to children's learning in literacy, numeracy or ICT (as addressed in Chapter 2). The medium-term plans below show how one concept area from a long-term plan is given more detail and is delivered across the Foundation Stage and Key Stages 1 and 2.

Science Medium-term Plan for the Foundation Stage

Year Group:Reception
Term: 1
Topic title – My Home
Main area of learning: To observe, find out about, and identify features in the place they live and the natural world.
Linked areas of learning: Knowledge and understanding of the world, language and Literacy.

Learning objectives	Activities	Organization/resources	Assessment Opportunities
To observe features of where they live.	Walk around locality, pointing out their own house, the shops, the park, etc.	Class activity.	Observation/discussion.
To identify features of where they live.	*Make a large floor-map of local area. *Use small world role-play area to set out a locality.	Photographs. Art materials. Roamer. Small world play equipment + spot tray. Children to work in pairs (structured play).	Observation.
To know features of part of an area where they live.	Outdoors play. Children to set out their version of the park.	Outdoor play equipment. Children to work in small groups.	Observation/questioning.
To identify features of the natural world.	*Class stories of animals in natural settings. *Role play area to be set out as a home for a specific animal.	Relevant stories. Role-play area and equipment. Whole class story reading + small group work.	Observation/questioning

Science Medium-term Plan for Key Stage 1

Year Group: 1
Term: 3
Topic title: The Park
Main area of learning: To find out about the different kinds of plants and animals in the local environment.
Linked areas of learning: Literacy, Art, Geography.

Learning objectives	Activities	Organization/resources	Assessment Opportunities
To identify plants and animals found in the local environment.	Field study of green plants and trees in local park. Observation of animal life in park.	Class visit.	Observation of children/ questioning.
To compare two plants found in the local environment.	Study closely two plants from park. Describe similarities and differences.	Plants collected on visit. Hand lenses.	Mark work/pictures and captions.
To relate life processes to plants and animals found in the local environment.	Discussion of needs of plants and animals. How do they survive in the park?	Pictures/photographs taken on visit.	Questioning to elicit thoughts.
To describe an environment.	Describe the part of the park where a particular plant and/or animal was found.	Pictures/photographs taken on visit.	Assess children's comments.

Science Medium-term Plan for Key Stage 2

Year Group: 3
Term: 3
Topic title: Habitats
Main area of learning: To know about the different plants and animals found in different habitats.
Linked areas of learning: Literacy, Art, Geography.

Learning objectives	Activities	Organization/resources	Assessment Opportunities
To know there is a variety of living things.	Compare pictures of minibeasts, domestic animals, wild animals, etc.	Pictures of a variety of living things. Children to work in pairs.	Observation of children working.
To be able to use a key to identify plants and animals.	Collaborative use of keys to identify minibeasts, plants, etc.	Prepared keys + pictures. Children to work in small groups.	Mark work.
To be able to assign plants and animals to groups using keys.	Give simple statements about plants and animals, using given pictures. Use statements to form own plant/animal key.	Pictures of a variety of living things. Children to work in groups.	Observation/mark work.
To know there are different plants and animals in different habitats.	1. Minibeast hunt in the school garden. 2. Pond dipping.	Prepared map of school garden. Pond dipping equipment. Class activities.	Questioning to elicit thoughts and knowledge.

Year Group: 5
Term: 2
Topic title: Our Environment
Main area of learning: To use food chains to show feeding relationships in a habitat.
Linked areas of learning: Literacy, Art, Geography

Learning objectives	Activities	Organization/resources	Assessment Opportunities
To identify animals and plants in an environment.	Observe a small area of school garden – using a hoop – identify range of plants and animals seen.	Hoops. Clipboards. Reference books. Children to work in groups.	Observation of children's organization.
To know how animals and plants in two different habitats are suited to their environment.	Comparison of 2 habitats – local + a residential visit in a contrasting locality. Consider adaptation of species to environment.	Visit books. Children to work in pairs.	Mark written reports of habitats observed.
To know the language of food chains.	Introduction of language. Produce own glossary. Relate language to own food chain for lunch.	Class discussion. Individual recording.	Questioning to elicit children's knowledge.
To know that food chains show feeding relationships in a habitat.	Identify food chains from given pictures. Role-play of a garden food chain.	Relevant pictures of contrasting habitats showing main plants and animals. Class activity.	Questioning to elicit children's knowledge.
To know that nearly all food chains begin with a green plant.	Discussion of food chains derived from pictures. Introduce energy flow through food chain and importance of sunlight. Identify green plants as originator of most food chains.	Relevant pictures of contrasting habitats showing main plants and animals. Class activity.	Mark recorded work, look for evidence of importance of green plants to a food chain.

Short-term Planning for Science

Short-term lesson or session plans are drawn from a teacher's medium-term plans. Again further, finer detail is added. All teachers produce a written session plan in some form. More experienced teachers may commit less to paper than the student or newly qualified teacher, but will nonetheless have notes to refer to.

The notes need to be written in a style or format that is easy for the teacher to use and refer to throughout the lesson. A note style of writing is essential – for ease of reference and also for time management purposes. However, this level of planning, whether for a lesson or an activity, should be sufficiently detailed to indicate clearly to others what is to be taught. A good maxim to follow is that the plan should contain enough detail for another teacher to be able to teach directly from the plan. The plan needs to make clear:

- The objective of the lesson – taken from the medium-term plan;
- The activity/activities to be carried out – taken from the medium-term plan and given more detail;
- The resources needed to carry out the activity (see Chapter 5);
- The key points of the teaching session;
- Key questions to be addressed;
- The organization of the lesson, i.e., the use of whole class teaching and/or group work, the use of first-hand experience and/or research, etc. (see Chapter 4);
- How the teaching and learning is to be differentiated to take into account the range of ability (see Chapter 4);
- The recording method the children will use;
- The assessment opportunities the teaching will provide, including what is to be assessed and how it is to be assessed (see Chapter 6).

The features of good short-term planning are demonstrated on the lesson plan overleaf. The plan details a single lesson for a Year 3 class that is taken from the medium-term plan shown in the preceding section of this chapter. The plan shows three sections to the lesson – the introduction, development stage and the plenary. These relate to the beginning, middle and end of the lesson.

A lesson must be considered to be like a story and have three parts:

A beginning – the introduction to the lesson/activity.
The middle – the main body of the lesson, where children are finding out for themselves.
An ending – the plenary, where the children report back on their learning and the teacher is able to reinforce the learning objective.

At this stage of planning a lot of thought needs to go into each section of the lesson. Each part is different in terms of time but is essential to the success of the lesson.

Lesson plan
Subject area: Science
Year: 3
Term: 3
Date: 14. 6. 01

Learning objective: To be able to assign plants and animals to groups using keys

Resources:
Set of pictures of common animals – rabbit, mouse, cat, dog, hedgehog and hamster.
Set of pictures of common flowers – poppy, rose, daffodil, carnation, bluebell and pansy.
1 set of pictures per table.

Introduction:
Whole class introduction. Children seated in ability groups.
Recap on use of keys to identify minibeasts, etc.
Choose one child to lead the class through one key.
Introduce task.
Share learning objective – that the children will be designing their own keys for either a set of plants or a set of animals.
Show children a large picture of an animal. Ask children to make a statement about the animal. Write responses on board. Discuss statements made.
Repeat with plants.
Ask the children to work together to make statements about 4 of the pictures in front of them.

Development:

Pupil activities:
Children work together to generate various statements, e.g., it has spines. Statements to be written on strips of paper.
Teacher to monitor all groups. Ensure children know what to do.
When all groups have provided a set of statements, CT to introduce second part of activity.
Show children how to take one statement and group animals/plants to show if they do or do not fit the statement.

Differentiation:
Less able children – physically sort the four animals/plants under one statement. Sort each pair using 2 other statements. LSA to support.
Able children – turn the statement into a question; sort 4 animals/plants into 2 groups. Repeat to give a key for 4 plants/animals. Record on paper.
More able children – use statements to make a key, on paper, for 6 animals/plants.

Extension activity:
Test each others' keys.

Teaching points:
Clarity of statements
Non-repetition of statements
Share good examples as lesson proceeds
Use observable features only

Plenary/conclusion

Ensure all children complete task to their ability.
Share keys made. Discuss features/clarity of statements or questions.
Recap on lesson objective.

Assessment: Are the children able to assign plants and animals to groups using keys?
Criteria: to sort at least 4 plants or animals correctly using statements or questions.
Mode: observation/marking of work.

Session plan

ELG: Knowledge and understanding of the world
Nursery
Term: 1
Date: 7.9. 01
Context: The Beach
Learning objective: To observe materials, objects and textures.

Resources:
Role-play area
Sand, water, pebbles, shells, buckets, spades, range of plastic objects including containers, boats, etc.
'Junk' materials – cardboard boxes of different sizes, yoghurt pots, corrugated card, etc.

Introduction:
Whole group introduction on the carpet
Sing seaside rhymes together
Talk about seaside holidays
What do you see?
What do you do on the beach?
Talk about the role-play area
Encourage children to begin work on one of the structured activities

Role-play area	Wet sand	Dry sand
–set up as a beach hut with chairs, table, sun hats, buckets, spades, etc.	Put in pebbles, shells, buckets, etc.	Put in pebbles, shells, buckets, etc.
Children's talk encouraged by Nursery nurse.	Children to explore shapes, textures, etc.	Children to explore shapes, textures, etc.
		Teacher to work with children in sand.
		Is it easier to make sand shapes in wet or dry sand?
Water	**Mark making**	**Construction**
Put in pebbles, shells, buckets, etc.	LSA to supervise writing area.	Children to combine 'junk' materials to make a lighthouse.
Children to explore floating and sinking.	Children to write postcards home from a beach holiday.	Adult helper to support.
		Discuss shapes, colours, textures, etc., of materials used.

Plenary/conclusion

Children return to carpet at end of session.
2 pairs of children to talk to group about the activity they have worked on.

Assessment:
Are the children able to discern different objects and textures?
Criteria: to identify at least three different objects. To describe at least 2 different textures.
Mode: observation.

A good beginning

The introduction of a lesson or session plays an important part in the success or failure of the learning experience. Through the introduction, the enthusiasm and involvement of the children are harnessed. It is important that the children know at the outset what they are going to be learning and why, as they are more likely to learn effectively if they are told the purpose and plan for the lesson or activity. Also, by sharing the purpose of the session in this way the children will be better able to reflect on their learning at the end of the session during the plenary. The student or newly qualified teacher must therefore be prepared to spend time beforehand thinking how he/she is going to gain the children's attention and interest them in what is to follow. There are various ways to achieve this, as in the examples below.

Ideas for gaining children's attention and interest at the beginning of a lesson.

Context: The body

Idea	Example
Artefacts on the tables to look at	A piece of old medical equipment
A story or piece of text to listen to	Story of an athlete
A question	How could you clean your teeth if you hadn't got any toothpaste?
Reference to a display	Display of footwear from different sports
A game	Matching pictures of body parts to their function

Once the children's attention is gained, the teacher then needs to maintain their attention and enthusiasm. This may be achieved by discussing the activity they have just completed, asking another question related to the task or by using a group of children to assist in the introduction to the main body of the lesson. This part of the lesson is where key teaching points, questions, and new vocabulary are introduced, and where previous experiences are recalled and recapped upon. Time is also provided here for children to ask questions, clarify points and to ensure that they are clear about what they have to do. There is a lot to cover in this section of the lesson and yet it must not be over-long, or children's attention and concentration may be lost.

 ### Case Study: introduction to a group in a Foundation setting.

Mrs L put out a selection of photographs on the table and asked John, Jenny, Emma and Peter to look at the photographs and choose their favourite one. After a few minutes Mrs L asked children in turn to point to their favourite photograph and say why they had chosen that one. John pointed to a photograph but didn't have a reason for choosing it. The other children gave reasons related to hair length, hair colour and eyes. Miss L asked the children questions about their choices, using them as a focus for eliciting information about **how people are the same and how they are different**. John then said he liked 'his' photograph because the boy had short hair; Mrs L praised John for his contribution to the discussion. Mrs L then introduced the task to the children. She asked them to point to a baby, then to a mummy or daddy and then to a grandparent. Mrs L then asked the children to put the photographs into families, with one baby, one mummy or daddy and one grandparent.

 ### Case study: introduction to a whole class in KS2.

Mr G had written on the board:

> **Can you draw a picture to show how the earth orbits the sun and how the moon orbits the earth? You are not allowed to write on your drawing. You may work with a partner. You have 2 minutes to complete the task.**

He had provided large pieces of paper and marker pens. The children worked quickly together. After a few minutes Mr G asked the children to put down their pens. He chose Sam and David to hold up their picture, saying they had worked well together and had put down their pens first. All the children sat up and listened to Sam's explanation. Mr G praised their work and chose another group to show their picture. Mr G then told the class they were going to investigate what happens when there is an eclipse of the sun. He wrote 'eclipse' on the board and invited the children to explain what it meant. He responded positively to each comment made. He then instructed one group to draw what they think happened, one group to research information about eclipses using books and the computer, one group to design a model to show an eclipse and he was to work with a fourth group using a torch and various spherical objects.

The main body of the lesson

The main body of the lesson or session plan then outlines how the science activity introduced at the beginning will develop. Again, thought needs to be given to the organization of this section of the lesson – the task(s) in which the children will be engaged, how the tasks and children will be organized, the differentiation (other than by outcome) to be offered, together with the nature of any adult intervention. Teachers need to consider very carefully both their role and that of the children during this time. It is important for children to be encouraged to work independently in science and yet direction needs to be given, in order for the children to succeed at the task. The amount of adult direction and intervention will be dependent on the skills of the children and their maturity. The teacher must therefore be able to recognize when children need support to continue their learning. Although the teacher may work specifically with a particular group or child, or may monitor all the groups within the class, their main role is in maintaining the pace and direction of the lesson. This may be achieved by providing more input and/or information when and where it is needed, or by encouraging effort and extending learning through asking appropriate questions.

It is also in this section of the lesson that an extension activity may be needed, in order to cater for the needs of the very able pupils or those who finish early. The extension activity must be considered in terms of how the children's learning is to be extended; it should not merely be a repeat of the main activity. An extension activity may involve applying a newly acquired skill in a different context or using different reference sources to increase the children's knowledge.

CS *Case study*

Natalie, a Year 5 child, completed her healthy living poster. She had included references to the importance of a varied diet that was low in fat, to the importance of exercise and its effects on the body, and to avoid cigarettes, drugs and too much alcohol. Her work was beautifully illustrated. Mr H, her class teacher, was pleased with her poster. Natalie was a capable girl who always worked to the best of her ability. Mr H discussed Natalie's poster with her and talked about low fat foods. He asked Natalie what this meant. Natalie knew some fatty foods such as sausages and meat pies and knew that fruit and vegetables were low in fat. She referred to an advert for cereals and low fat yoghurts. Mr H asked if there were different types of fat or were they all the same. Natalie wasn't sure. Mr H asked Natalie if she could find out more about fat in food using the Internet. Natalie found some information to share with the class during the plenary of the lesson.

The plenary

A science lesson or session plan needs to allow sufficient time at the end for resources to be put away and for a plenary session. It is here that the teacher reinforces the teaching objective, reviews and consolidates the children's learning. Again this section may take many forms, as shown on the next page.

Ideas for the plenary

Context: Sorting materials according to properties.

Idea	Example
Playing a game	20 questions – the teacher thinks of one object in the classroom. The children ask questions to which the teacher answers 'Yes' or 'No'. The children have to identify the object in less than 20 questions.
Sharing and discussing their learning	Children to show their work and explain it to the class.
Connecting the present work to future activities	Explain how the next lesson will focus on comparing different materials for one property, e.g., waterproofness.
Asking similar questions in a different context	Introduce a 'new' set of materials to sort. Work through collaboratively.

Summary

This section of the chapter has considered how short-term plans are devised, using the medium-term planning and taking into account the structure of a good lesson. It is worth while spending time on the short-term plan as a good plan underpins an effective lesson. Detailed planning provides a mechanism for the student or newly qualified teacher to consider all aspects of the teaching and learning to be carried out during a session. The list below summarizes the points made regarding the features of a good lesson or session plan.

Features of a good lesson or session plan:

- A clear, specific learning objective,
- Clarity on the the purpose of the lesson,
- Clarity over what will be assessed (linked to the learning objective) and how.
- Key teaching points noted,
- Key questions to be asked, and desired responses.
- Where ICT is to be used,
- How the children will be organized,
- Details of the interesting, relevant activities to be carried out,
- Resources needed, matched to children's experience and ability,
- An indication of previous learning,
- Information regarding previous assessments,
- Provision for differentiation.
- Time built in for feedback to the pupils,
- Time for plenary discussion in order to check on and reinforce pupil learning,
- Clear progression from the introduction to the conclusion,
- Indication of pace and timing throughout the session.

Planning for Continuity and Progression

Continuity and progression are often used as a single term, to indicate that the learning experiences must build upon each other. However, continuity and progression are two separate terms with quite distinct meanings. At the simplest level continuity is *what stays the same* and progression is *what changes*. A better interpretation of the terms is given by the Zeneca publication 'Bubbles' (1997) where it is stated that continuity is '. . . maintaining progression so that learning is not perceived as a fragmented experience', and progression is '. . . moving children forward by building on existing skills and knowledge . . .'. The terms are therefore to be considered separately as the presence of one does not necessarily indicate the presence of the other. In other words, children may regularly be engaged in practical work in science, and so there is continuity in their experiences, but the children's skills in scientific enquiry may not develop (and thus progress) unless specifically taught. It may also be that scientific skills are taught in some year groups but not in others, thereby providing progression across the key stage but without continuity of experience.

In long-term planning it should be evident where continuity is occurring. This will be in terms of skills to be taught and scientific content re-visited throughout the 3–11 age range. Most science schemes of work are written with reference to the 'spiral curriculum' (Wood, 1998). This is the term used to indicate that the children revisit key elements of the curriculum throughout their school experience, each time at a higher level of understanding or refinement.

Example of the spiral curriculum – from DfEE/QCA Scheme of Work (1998)

Science focus: Grouping and classifying materials
Year 1, Unit 1C – Sorting and grouping materials.
Year 2, Unit 2D – Grouping and changing materials.
Year 3, Unit 3C – Characteristics of materials.
Year 4, Unit 4D – Solids, liquids and how they can be separated.
Year 5, Unit 5C – Gases around us.

Continuity is also considered within the range of learning activities presented to the children throughout the Key Stage programme, in order to ensure the provision of investigative, research based, creative and imaginative approaches to the teaching of science. To ensure continuity within learning activities, it is important that all staff have a shared understanding of science as an active and investigative pursuit, and not simply a collection of facts about various concepts. Finally, continuity can be sought in the provision of resources; schools try to ensure that all children have access to high quality equipment for investigative work, appropriate reference material and the opportunities to work with relevant artefacts, documentation, visual material, and ICT. Progression should also be evident in planning involving the development of knowledge, skills, understanding, values and attitudes. Planning for progression therefore takes place through the content and sequence of learning activities being structured through long-term and medium-term plans, and also with reference to individual children's records, assessments of children's learning and capabilities, in order to enable the children to make progress. These issues will be addressed further in Chapters 4 and 6.

Continuity in science

Continuity in science across the 3–11 age range is dependent in part on a shared understanding between the staff. It is providing a science curriculum that is coherent and has a uniform approach to its delivery. A long-term plan, which details the science to be covered through practical work, investigative work and research, will provide continuity in the children's experiences and ensure that the learning is not a fragmented experience.

Progression in science

Progression in science across the 3–11 age range ensures that children move forward in their learning. Long-term plans that show related scientific work across a Key Stage (or Key Stages) where the children's knowledge, skills and/or understanding are developed are necessary for progression. It involves learning by building on existing skills, knowledge, understanding, values and attitudes.

Approaches to the delivery of science

The final section of the chapter begins to consider approaches to the delivery of science, Chapters 4 and 5 will build on this consideration. Chapter 2 established a rationale for science to be taught alongside other curriculum subjects, however, it may also be delivered as a stand-alone science topic. The stand-alone topic approach is used where the majority of lessons focus on science, with few or no links made between this and other areas of learning; a cross-curricular topic is where two or three areas of the curriculum are taught through a common theme. Both these approaches to teaching science have advantages and disadvantages that must be considered when planning the delivery of a unit of work.

Discrete science

Discrete science work is taken from one area of learning and is taught within a short period of time, possibly only two weeks or up to half a term. Each unit of work will have a tight subject focus with a distinct, coherent body of knowledge, skills and understanding. The children may be taught science intensively for the duration of the unit, but then may not experience science again for some time and so a limitation of this approach is that the children may 'forget' the key aspects of the learning in the interim period between the units of science. A second criticism of this approach is that the children may not develop an understanding of the relevance of science to everyday life, as the work is taught in isolation from the rest of the curriculum. However, although the science content covered in the units will vary, core aspects of scientific method will feature irrespective of whether the children are learning about electricity or the conditions for growth of a green plant. As a result, children will revisit core skills at regular intervals, irrespective of the topic heading, and so will advance their knowledge and understanding towards a higher level. Consequently, although science is taught in discrete units, with the concept involved being likely to alter in order to achieve coverage of the National Curriculum study units, the children's experience of science will be continuous through the study of some aspect of science in each year. The following example illustrates how one area of study from Sc4 – Physical Processes – can be delivered as a short, two-week topic of discrete science.

Discrete science unit: Springs

Year: 4
Term 3: 2 weeks

Objective:
To know that when a spring is pushed or pulled an opposing push or pull is felt.

Activities:
*Comparison of 4 springs. Compare length, diameter, tightness of coil, metal used.
*Compare effects of pushing and pulling 4 different springs.
*Identify 'best' spring for a Jack-in-the-box toy.
*Record results of spring comparisons on a leaflet advertising the sale of the springs.

Cross-curricular planning

This is an approach to planning whereby several subjects are taught through a common topic, e.g., Our Environment, People Who Help Us. It is becoming less used as a vehicle for teaching in the primary school, but is effective if planned well. The approach should not be confused with integrated lessons, where more than one subject is being taught simultaneously. The purpose of cross-curricular planning is to increase the coherence of the curriculum by capitalizing on common or complementary knowledge, skills and understanding contained in different subject areas and by providing a relevant context for the work being delivered. The advantages and disadvantages of this approach to the primary curriculum have been debated for many years. Those in favour of the integrated approach argue that a well-planned, carefully structured, linked approach provides relevance to the learning being presented. It is believed that the approach reflects the holistic way in which children learn and in which they view the world around them. The approach allows children to construct their own meanings, using the full range of their learning experiences in the various, linked activities, thereby focusing on the process of learning rather than on the acquisition of facts, which may be attributed as a disadvantage to the discrete delivery of science. The approach also embraces the areas of the curriculum, which do not fit readily into subject 'boxes', and so the cross-curricular approach is a useful way of building these areas into the teaching and learning. However, the integrated approach has been criticized as undemanding and failing to provide for progression, with subjects losing their identity and characteristics within it. It has been reported that breaking the curriculum down into subjects has resulted in 'the most powerful tools for making sense of the world which human beings have ever devised' (Alexander et al., 1992 p. 17). And yet with thoughtful planning, recognizing the need to retain the individuality of each subject area, several subjects can be effectively delivered in this way. No longer does the approach in the primary age range require the linking of several National Curriculum subjects into one topic, which was the practice criticized for failing to provide sufficient clarity and rigour in terms of teaching and learning.

Linked work

Subjects can be taught in a linked unit when:

- they contain common or complementary knowledge, understanding or skills;
- the skills acquired in one subject or aspect of the curriculum can be applied or consolidated in the context of another;
- the work in one subject or aspect of the curriculum provides a useful stimulus for work in another.

Case study of linked work

Cross-curricular topic: The Garden Centre
Year: 5
Term: 1
Focus: Instructional texts (NLS, p. 45)

Subject Area	Objective	Activity
English	To read and evaluate instructional texts.	Read instructions for planting bulbs. Evaluate for purpose, layout, language and clarity.
	To write instructional texts and try out.	*Write instructions for caring for a winter flowering plant. *Write instructions for making a terrarium.
Maths	To measure accurately, using cm and mm.	Measure wood and plastic accurately for terrarium.
	To know the properties of 3D shapes.	Choose 3D shape for terrarium and describe shape.

(continued opposite)

Science	To know life processes common to plants.	*List life processes and explain *Instructions for caring for a plant *Grow bulbs *Research use of terrariums *Instructions for using a terrarium *Use terrarium to care for plants
DT	To design and make a product.	Design and make a terrarium.
Geography	To use atlases and globes.	Locate countries of origin of plants observed at Garden Centre and bulbs to be grown in school.
Art	To record from experience.	Field sketches at Garden Centre.
	To collect visual and other information.	Record terrarium designs.
	To communicate ideas and feelings.	Illustrate instructional texts.
		Illustrations to add information to texts.

Continuing work

Both the approaches to teaching science considered thus far may result in science being taught intensively for a short period of time, and then not revisited for a further period of time. A further approach to science teaching is the continuing or ongoing approach. This can ensure both continuity and progression in the delivery of the science curriculum. It requires ongoing teaching and assessment to be planned across a Key Stage and is characterized by a progressive sequence of learning objectives, in order to provide for progression in pupil's learning (SCAA, 1995). This approach to science teaching is particularly valuable where aspects of the curriculum – whether skills, knowledge or understanding – require time for their systematic and gradual acquisition, practice and consolidation (SCAA, 1995). It ensures that the skills, knowledge and/or understanding already acquired are not lost through being forgotten over time. However, due to the present demands of Literacy and Numeracy in the primary curriculum, planning for continuing work in science does need to consider the time available. There are two ways to ensure time is available for continuing work – one is to timetable science weekly, in the same way that Literacy and Numeracy are timetabled. This would replace the need for time intensive topics at intervals throughout the year and spread the science coverage more equally. This approach would therefore provide a different format for teaching the topics. The second way to ensure continuing work in science is to make good use of the small pockets of time usually available in the overall weekly timetable. The pockets of time, possibly as small as ten minutes only per week, may be used to reinforce concepts, ask and answer questions, practise skills, as well as extending the children's scientific knowledge and understanding.

Foundation Stage: *play a matching game – matching pictures of offspring to the adult, i.e., kitten/cat, puppy/dog, etc.
*singing songs and rhymes – e.g., 'Them bones', 'Toddlerobics' (Newcome, 1998)

Key Stage 1: *give verbal instructions on how to look after own pet
*'I'm thinking of a fruit . . .' game
(20 questions to identify a fruit using its characteristics)

Key Stage 2: *question given to find answer in a reference book, e.g., who discovered penicillin?
*Read a classroom thermometer accurately
*Time an event accurately, e.g., a piece of paper dropping to the floor

Opportunities for continuing work are most likely to be found in the Foundation Stage, where teachers plan for early science but children do not necessarily make subject distinctions. Activities based on Knowledge and Understanding of the World will be a regular feature of the children's experiences. The children in the Foundation Stage may also contribute to continuing science work by asking questions about their environment, about the wider world and by discussing significant events in their own lives and the lives of their families, thereby increasing their use and knowledge of scientific vocabulary.

Summary

Having identified different approaches to the planning and delivery of the science curriculum, it can be appreciated that the student or newly qualified teacher will encounter a variety of science curricula and schemes of work. In practice, the most effective approach for delivering science is most likely to be the one that is planned to incorporate both the teaching of science as a separate subject and the teaching of linked topic work, thereby exploiting the advantages of both approaches where appropriate. In this way, children's learning can be kept focused by restricting the numbers of subjects or aspects of the curriculum that are linked, and by avoiding contrived or artificial connections. The learning will be supported by ongoing work that reinforces concepts, skills and understandings taught in the main teaching activities. The main consideration of effective planning is that the subject's basic concepts and skills are clearly identified and incorporated into relevant activities that enable children to progress from one level of knowledge, understanding and skill to the next.

80

Year: 4
National Curriculum allocation of areas of study:
Sc2, 5bc – Adaptation
Sc3, 3ab – Separating mixtures of materials
Sc4, 3abc – Everyday effects of light.

81

Discrete unit of science	Linked unit of science	Continuing science
Separating solids: *separating particles of different sizes, including soils, by sieving. *separating solids in a liquid by filtering. *investigating evaporation as a way of separating a solid from a liquid.	Investigating plants and animals in a habitat. Links with: *English – reporting; *Maths – coordinates; *Geography – map work, land use, features of an environment; *Art – field sketches.	Recap on use of scientific equipment – hand lenses, thermometer, etc.
	Investigating solutions and mixtures. Links with: *English – reading and writing captions; *Maths – measuring accurately using standard and non-standard measures; *DT – food technology; *R.E. – food requirements in different cultures and religions.	Recap on sorting objects/materials/living things into groups. Play 20 questions, 'Guess who' using all children in the class, sorting cards in a set time, etc.
	Investigating effects of light. Links with: *English – 'light' poems; *DT – designing and making a shadow puppet theatre; *Art – drawings of puppets; *Music – to accompany puppet theatre show.	Response to a natural object brought in by a child – a shell. Discussion of what it is, what its function is, etc.

Reflective questions

Questions to be considered when writing, or referring to the school's long-term plan, include:

- Have the statutory requirements for science been consulted?
- Have the school's circumstances been considered?
- How can the long-term plan reflect the school's aims, objectives and policies – for example the use of first-hand experience, equal opportunities, etc?
- How much time is to be allocated to the teaching of science?
- How is the time to be allocated – weekly, in blocks?
- What opportunities are provided in the local environment for teaching and learning in science?
- What opportunities for teaching and learning science do the school buildings and grounds offer?
- What opportunities are provided beyond the local environment for teaching and learning in science?
- What resources are currently available or easily purchased?
- To what extent can science contribute to the whole curriculum?
- What historically has each year group covered in the science curriculum?
- What are the needs, abilities, and achievements of the children?
- What previous experiences, in science, do they have?
- How do children learn in science, i.e., how do they acquire knowledge, skills, attitudes and understanding in science?

Questions to be considered when writing short-term plans include:

- Does your planning contain clear learning purposes based on National Curriculum Programmes of Study or Early Learning Goals?
- Is your planning for science part of a whole school approach set out in long- term plans?
- Do you use a variety of planning approaches, including continuing, blocked and linked science work?
- What would you expect to see in terms of continuity in science in the Key Stage you are currently working in?
- What would you expect progression to look like from the Foundation Stage to the end of Key Stage 2, in terms of children's knowledge and understanding of science?
- Have you consulted books and other texts for ideas for activities?
- Do you know what related activities the children have carried out in previous years?
- Do you know the knowledge, skills and understanding the children already have?

REFERENCES

Alexander, R., Rose, J. & Woodhead, C. (1992) 'Curriculum Organisation and Classroom Practice in Primary Schools: A Discussion Paper', London: DES.

Carle, E. (1986) *The Very Hungry Caterpillar*, London: Hamish Hamilton.

Cheshire County Council (1997) *Bubbles: Bridging the Gap, KS2/3 Liaison*, Zeneca.

Department for Education and Employment (1998) *The National Literacy Strategy*, Cambridge: Cambridge University Press.

Newcome, Z. (1998) 'Toddlerobics', in *Stories and Fun for the Very Young*, London: Walker Books.

Standards and Effectiveness Unit (1998) *A Scheme of Work for Key Stages 1 and 2: Science*, London: DfEE/QCA.

Qualifications and Curriculum Authority (1999a) *The National Curriculum: Handbook for Primary Teachers in England*, London: DfEE/QCA.

Qualifications and Curriculum Authority (1999b) *Early Learning Goals*, London: DfEE/QCA.

Qualifications and Curriculum Authority (1999c) *Science: Key Stages 1-4*, London: DfEE/QCA.

Schools Curriculum and Assessment Authority (1995) *Planning the Curriculum at Key Stages 1 and 2*, London: SCAA.

Wood, D. (1998) *How Children Think and Learn* (2nd edn), Oxford: Blackwell.

Effective Teaching Methods in Science

Chapter 4 is concerned with the use of teaching methods in science, in order to ensure that all children have access to a relevant science curriculum. Every nursery and school has a responsibility to provide a broad and balanced curriculum for all their pupils; the Early Learning Goals and the National Curriculum provide starting points for planning a curriculum that is both relevant and interesting. However, children learn in different ways and at different rates, and have diverse levels of attainment, interest and confidence. Harlen (1993) makes the point that the teacher's view of how learning takes place determines what experiences he/she provides for the pupils, the role the teacher takes in the children's learning and the role the teacher expects the pupils to take in their learning. It is therefore important for the student or newly qualified teacher to have an overview of the theory of how children learn; this is needed to appreciate how the theory of learning is related to the practice of teaching, and so the implications of the theories for teaching in science are explored.

The chapter continues with an outline of a variety of teaching methods in science, considering the relative merits of whole class teaching and group work approaches in science lessons. The methods are thus explained and illustrated with examples of activities from the Foundation Stage and Key Stages 1 and 2. The purpose is to make the case for why various teaching methods are justified in science teaching, and how teachers utilize a mixture of the methods. The content of this section of the chapter should be viewed as a summary only, for there is little space within the book to cover the various theories of learning in detail or to do justice to the interplay between children's cognitive development and their development in other areas, for example social and emotional development.

The chapter then goes on to consider various strategies for differentiation in science. Differentiation is the term used to describe how the teacher uses the teaching session to cater for all individual needs. The chapter will therefore explore the choices made by the teacher prior to the teaching of a science activity, with respect to the most appropriate method of delivery for each child. It will be noted that when considering differentiating the curriculum, it is usual to do so by grouping the children by ability, to give groupings of similar ability, or to ensure mixed ability groups. Case studies are used to illustrate how differentiation is provided in practical settings, including differentiation in science by outcome, by task and by support. This section of the chapter also considers children's misconceptions in science, the ideas about science which children hold that are not the recognized scientific ideas, and how these may be dealt with by the teacher.

Finally, the chapter is concerned with the crucial skill of reflection. It offers guidance on self-evaluation as a mechanism for improving the quality of teaching and learning in science. The chapter also suggests sources of information and research that can be used to inform science teaching. The chapter therefore concludes with a consideration of how honest self-appraisal of strengths and weaknesses in the teaching of science, coupled with attention to research evidence, are vital if planning and teaching skills are to improve.

Children's Learning in Science

Learning is a developmental process whereby ideas are developed and changed until they conform to a universally accepted norm. Harlen (1993) describes this as changing ideas, rather than taking in ideas from scratch whilst Pines and West (1986, p. 587) define learning as '. . . a process in which learners make sense of the inputs from their environment'. This definition is at the heart of what is termed constructivism. Driver *et al.* (1993) portray the constructivist position of learning as knowledge acquisition being the result of a learner actively building on previous knowledge, rather than through transfer of information from teacher to pupil. The theory does point to learners being willing partners in the acquisition of knowledge, as it centres on learning as an active process (Driver *et al.*, 1993), and so teachers must consider how they are to encourage and stimulate the children to be active in the teaching sessions.

CS *Case study*

Mrs C's Year 5 class had spent some time on the concept of solids, liquids and gases. Mrs C had used instruction, discussion and drama to investigate the differences of the three states. The children were recording their understanding under the three headings of solids, liquids and gases as an information sheet for someone who didn't know what they were. Asia included references to 'liquid is like water' and 'we cook with gas in our house'. Asia then described condensation as 'trapping a gas to turn it into water'.
Asia was demonstrating through her work how her learning was developing, by relating the new information to what was already familiar to her.

Piaget is credited with developing our understanding of how children learn (Donaldson, 1978). It was his work that suggested that children were not merely passive learners but actively constructed meaning and ideas about how the world works. He used the concepts of assimilation, disequilibrium and accommodation to explain this process of learning.

Piaget's model of learning:

- Assimilation – children assimilate knowledge about the world around them through firsthand experience.
- Disequilibrium – such experiences require a re-evaluation, by the children, of their original ideas in the light of new information. This causes lack of equilibrium or disequilibrium, as the new data does not conform to, or extends, their old model (schema) of the world.
- Accommodation – the children incorporate the new knowledge, data and experience into their existing models, thus having improved and enhanced them in order to accommodate the new reality.

Piaget's model suggested that intellectual development was the result of the loss of equilibrium followed by its restoration at a new, higher level. He suggests that the older and more mature the child the more able they are to take into account increasing quantities of information. Older children are also able to problem-solve using increasingly more complex strategies and develop their thinking on a more abstract level.

One basic tenet of Piaget's work was that knowledge is '. . . constructed by the individual by individual means;' (Bliss, 1995, p. 154). This implies that what a child learns is not necessarily that which the teacher wishes the child to learn, and suggests that learning is an individual pursuit that does not necessitate the intervention of others. However, Vygotsky put forward the theory that knowledge is constructed through social means (Bliss 1995). This theory suggests that children develop as learners through social interaction between children and adults and between children themselves. He suggests a developmental process of learning, beginning with the child taking on the role of spectator, observing work carried out by an *expert* – the parent or teacher. He/she then starts to take over the work, under the close supervision of the expert. As children mature they assume greater responsibility for their work with the expert continuing to act as a guide. Eventually they assume full responsibility for the task, with the expert present in the role of a supportive audience.

Teacher modelling/demonstrating

⇓

Joint activity

⇓

Scaffolded activity

⇓

Independent activity

Both Piaget and Vygotsky held the principles of the learner constructing knowledge for him/herself and the process being a developmental one. The difference in the theories lies in the method by which this is achieved. Piaget believed in the construction of knowledge on an individual level whereas Vygotsky stated the need for social interactions with others for learning to take place. Later in the chapter the use of individual work, group work and whole class teaching will be explored, thus considering the theories of learning of Piaget and Vygotsky in practice.

The constructivist theory of learning hence indicates that the role of the teacher is to provide a range of experiences that encourage discussion, reflection and cognitive conflict (Driver et al., 1993). Davydov (1995) interprets the Vygotskian approach to teaching and learning as a partnership between teacher and child; where the teacher's role is to guide, direct and encourage the child's learning. Learning in practice should therefore be neither didactic nor purely discovery learning by the child. It should offer opportunities to experiment with, and try out, feelings and behaviour in an attempt to make sense of them. Schools and nurseries therefore assist pupils in making sense of the world by exploring objects, materials and feelings, in meaningful situations. Such experiences thus harness children's natural curiosity, as they are encouraged to ask why and how things are as they are and investigate their own ideas. Through this, their existing ideas are challenged and developed through their own evidence.

Effective Teaching Methods in Science

It is the responsibility of the teacher to ensure all children have access to the science curriculum. Thus, the curriculum needs to accommodate the many differences between children, and match learning opportunities with individual learning needs. It is essential to develop good daily practice in the classroom, which facilitates effective teaching; a general checklist of good practice follows.

Features of good daily practice:

- a clear, crisp start to each lesson;
- specific lesson objectives that are shared with the children;
- direction in the children's learning;
- known, planned learning outcomes;
- high expectations of the children;
- clear instructions and explanations;
- appropriate, sequenced questions leading towards learning objectives;
- use of recapping on previous knowledge;

- learning is consolidated – through time at the end of a session used to reinforce the objective and the main points of the activity;
- use of resources that are appropriate and easily accessible for the children;
- appropriate language is used to ensure every child understands what is being asked of them;
- a balance of teacher exposition with times when children are working independently or collaboratively;
- the use of interesting and exciting displays that encourage learning and reflect the teacher's high expectations;
- children's responses, not just correct answers, are valued and discussed;
- positive, high quality feedback is given to the children, both on their progress in science and their way of working;
- feedback is given promptly, is written or verbal, and gives the child points for improvement;
- the classroom appears supportive and focuses on the use of positive discipline and praise.

Chapter 2 demonstrated how the Early Learning Goals provide guidelines on how young children should be taught and that the National Curriculum contains particulars of what to teach (the content of teaching) but not how to teach the content (the process of teaching). Accordingly, teachers need to be able to use a range of teaching and learning strategies to make certain that science is both accessible and of interest to all pupils. In the early stages of their teaching, students or newly qualified teachers may focus their attention on the content of lessons and the delivery of that content in the time available, and yet it is equally important to consider what the children are actually learning and how this is to be organized. It is important, therefore, for teachers to be comfortable with a range of strategies but, more importantly, to be able to match a strategy to both the activity and the children being taught. Many of the choices of strategies for delivery are made at the short-term planning stage and will be identified on the teacher's short-term planning notes.

Organizing the children

Teachers organize the children in a variety of ways in response to various needs; these needs include the learning objective, the activity being delivered, the availability of resources and the teaching environment. The children may work together as a whole class or large group, in small groups, in pairs or individually. Effective teachers are able to match the most appropriate form of organization to the task in hand.

Organization	Task
Whole class/large group	• Direct teaching – exposition, questioning • Introducing new work • Recalling and recapping on previous work • Giving instructions • Checking learning • Summarizing, reviewing and consolidating learning
Small group	• Promoting language and social skills • Promoting more active learning • Interpreting evidence • Sharing ideas • To support, challenge and extend peer group learning
Paired teaching	• Computer work • Research • Collaborative reports
Individual teaching	• Developing children's ability to take more responsibility for their own learning • Developing children's independence • Assessing children's ability – by providing evidence of individual attainment

In practice all the forms of organization may be used within one teaching session, as in the case studies that follow.

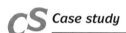 *Case study*

Miss D sat with the Nursery **class** on the carpet. The afternoon session began with the children answering to their names on the register and then singing a selection of rhymes. Miss D then pointed out the different activities set out in the Nursery. She asked James, Attiya, Alexander and Ellie if they would like to go outside with Mr P (the Nursery nurse) to investigate some objects in the water tray.

Mr P helped the children to put on aprons then asked them about the objects in the water. He encouraged the children **individually** to look at an object, feel it, listen to it, push it under the water, hold it under the water, etc. He talked to the children as a **group**, to encourage the children to listen to each other and to test out different ideas. When James and Attiya had finished the activity they asked if they could tell Miss D about it together. As a **pair** they told her what they had found out.

Case study

Miss L's Year 6 class are investigating the effect of canopy size on the drop of a parachute. The session begins with Miss L sharing the objective of the lesson with the children, to be able to observe and measure accurately. As a **whole class**, the children recall previous work on forces, the names of forces and the effects of different forces. The session continues with a whole class discussion of forces involved in parachutes – air resistance and gravity. Miss L then introduces the task to the whole class —to make and test a parachute.

Following the introduction, children work in **small groups** to assemble equipment, make and test their parachutes. The children work together to make observations and accurate measurements, and make notes about their work.

The **whole class** then comes together, with Miss L, to discuss individual findings. Miss L leads a discussion to compare findings and discuss the children's conclusions. The class also considers ways to record the investigation.

The children then work in **pairs** to record their work.

Whole class teaching in science

Whole class teaching is used at some point in a great many science activities at Key Stages 1 and 2. It may be a less appropriate strategy in the Foundation Stage of learning where children are encouraged to exercise choice and decision-making (Early Years Curriculum Group, 1989). Whole class teaching is often used during the introduction and the plenary sessions in primary classrooms, and may be used in the main body of a science lesson. As a method of organizing the children, it relies on a high level of communication and presentation skills on the part of the teacher. It also requires good exposition skills, in order to explain concepts in different ways, thus challenging the most able and ensuring the participation of the less able children. The method requires the teacher to be aware of all the children in the room and to engage them all. The teacher, therefore, must not focus only on a particular part of the class or certain children, or this can lead to other pupils feeling excluded and risks causing disruption. A further consideration is that of resources, as whole class activities may require a large quantity of resources to be available for all the children to participate in a task. In addition to the amount of resources it also needs to be considered how they will be made available. It may be disruptive to the flow of the lesson if the children need to collect resources at a certain point in the lesson and so it may be appropriate to set the resources out beforehand but, in other instances, the resources may distract pupil attention and so a method of introducing them part way through a task may need to be found.

Whole class teaching must engage all the pupils' attention. One of the most important factors in the success of this method is the interest and enthusiasm of the teacher and their ability to motivate the children. A good introduction to the task is essential and must be supported by the use of appealing and relevant resources. Pacing and timing throughout the session are crucial. O*ver-dwelling* on a subject can result in the children fidgeting and becoming disruptive, rushing through an aspect of the lesson may result in confusion and lack of learning.

Miss H had prepared her Year 2 classroom for science before the children came into the room. On each table was a set of pictures that together would form the life cycle of a flowering plant or an animal. There was also a set of pictures 'hidden' on the carpet area. The children came into the room and on to the carpet area as directed.

As the children sat down four of them 'found' a picture and put up their hand to say what they had 'found'.

'Yes, Thomas?' Miss H said.

The children around looked at Thomas and listened to what he had to say.

'I've found this on the floor, Miss.'

'What is it, Thomas?'

'A picture of a yellow flower.'

Three more hands went up.

'Have you got a picture too, Amy?'

'Yes Miss H, it's a picture of a bowl.'

The other children described their pictures – a watering can and an onion.

'Come and stand next to me,' Miss H instructed the children with the pictures.

James put up his hand. 'I think Emma's picture is a bulb not an onion Miss H,' he volunteered.

'Why do you think that, James?'

'Because all the pictures are the same.'

'Do you mean the same?'

Other children put up their hands.

'They're all to do with growing,' offered Gemma. 'You need a bowl to put the bulb in and it grows into a flower.'

'Well done, Gemma, but what is the watering can for?'

'You need water to make the bulb grow,' stated John.

'Well done, children.'

Miss H collected in the pictures and told the children they were going to look at the changes a plant or an animal goes through in their life. She explained the group task was to look at the pictures and decide together what order they were to go in. She asked the children to put the pictures in a circle on the table. Each group was then sent to its table to begin its task.

Miss H gained the interest of the children using pictures 'hidden' on the carpet area. The use of the pictures began the lesson immediately without having to call the children to order. Miss H used their interest to steer them through the lesson introduction. She maintained the pace of the introduction by using skilful questions to elicit their ideas and by standing them with pictures together to give the class clues about the connections. Miss H did not overdwell on the introduction. She did not immediately correct Emma who thought her picture was an onion but let the introduction flow until James worked it out that the picture must be a bulb. After the initial introduction Miss H then shared the purpose of the lesson with the children – *to look at the changes a plant or an animal goes through in its life*. The setting of the task – *to order pictures to form a life cycle*, followed the introduction seamlessly.

91

Using group work in science

Group work is especially important in science. The children are able to carry out investigations for themselves and use the group to help make sense of their work. There are, however, numerous ways in which groups can be formed and used. Each method of using groups has its own advantages and limitations.

Grouping of pupils	Advantages	Limitations
Mixed ability	Mixed ability groups can be useful where different roles within the group can be assigned to each child, for example carrying out practical work, recording and reporting findings. The group can use its participants as role models and provide support for less able pupils. The group can promote tolerance of others – from more able pupils for the less able pupils and vice versa.	More able pupils may 'coast' through the planned work. More able children may be used as substitute teachers, thereby instructing others but learning little new themselves. The slow pace of their peers may frustrate the more able children. The more able children may take over the running of the activity, which results in their peers being left behind.
Similar ability	Enables the use of specific differentiated tasks. Allows for extending the learning of the more able children. Enables the teacher to identify groups of children who require closer attention or additional help. Enables the teacher to work with a group that has reached a particular stage in their learning.	May lead to children viewing themselves as good or bad at something, particularly if the grouping is used permanently or inappropriately. Groups may be determined on the basis of the children's ability in literacy and numeracy, rather than on their scientific ability. May result in teachers under- or over-estimating pupil ability in science.
By age	Easy to organize. Suitable for mixed year classes. Allows for teaching of different objectives within one class.	Children of one age are not of the same ability. May not be appropriate for all children, due to widely different levels of ability, interests and needs.
By friendship	Popular with pupils. Can be motivating for the children. Encourages sharing of learning.	May be divisive. May isolate certain children. May reinforce stereotypes, e.g., boys may only choose to work with other boys.
By interest/ enthusiasm	Used for independent study. Not all children need undertake the learning experience. Results in the achievement of high goals and high levels of commitment and perseverance.	Not practical for study by all class. Children's interest not always sustained.

Group work has been the subject of much research. It is believed that the opportunity for the children to engage in discussion and collaborative inquiry enables them to challenge and extend their understanding; Vygotsky (1978) put this notion at the centre of learning. In this way the children *scaffold* each other's understanding in a way that they would have been unable to do alone. However, the student and newly qualified teacher must be able to distinguish between group work, where the children work together as a group, and working seated in a group, where children work as individuals within a collective setting. Group work requires children to be able to relate well to their peers, to observe recognized classroom procedures and be able to work collaboratively by accepting differences of opinion and to deal with these in a positive manner. Group work of this nature has to be developed over time, as the children need to understand the conventions of the technique. The children may also need to be taught the social skills necessary for this degree of collaboration and cooperation, as it may be that the children being taught have had only limited opportunities to experience sharing, taking turns, discussing with peers and listening to the ideas of others. The teacher also needs to have an understanding of group dynamics; this will enable them to identify the roles for each child within the group, to help him/her to get the most out of the group work. By ensuring each child has a role, either self-chosen or suggested, the teacher is reducing the opportunity for a child to withdraw from the task either mentally or physically. In addition to the consideration of group structure, the use of group work with respect to the activity to be carried out must also be given due regard. The table below explores the advantages and limitations of the use of group work in practice.

Group organization	Ádvantages	Limitations
All groups working on the same task	*Easy to plan *All children presented with same experience *Resources can be provided before the lesson begins *Use of firsthand experience *Task can be matched to the ability of the group	Large quantity of resources needed Extension activity needs to be planned
Each group working on a separate task, which contributes to the lesson objective	*Less demanding on **same** resources *Use of firsthand experience *Task matched to group ability *More areas of same concept can be explored in a limited amount of time *Each group needs to report back to the whole class therefore communication skills are developed and the children have an audience for their work	*Not as easy to monitor the learning by each group *May not lead to coherence in learning *Does not ensure all children share the same experiences over time *Does not ensure understanding through exposition

(continued from page 91)

Group organization	Advantages	Limitations
Each group rotating round different activities (circus of investigations)	*Provides interest and motivation *Less demanding on **same** resources *Provides a range of experiences	*Large quantity of resources needed *Requires a lot of planning and organizing *Children may compete to finish task without developing their knowledge and/or understanding *Less opportunity for reporting back *Activities not covered in a set order, therefore not hierarchical
Each group working on an area chosen by the group	*Motivating for the group *Variety of interest and experience *Tailored to needs of group	*Cannot be resourced in advance *Demanding on teacher knowledge *Not structured by teacher

Small group work in Foundation settings

The Early Years Curriculum Group (1989) stress that the younger the child the more important it is to identify individual learning needs and plan for these, that it is less appropriate to expect the youngest children to learn within a large group. Small group work is thus the main organizational strategy. Within group work there should be opportunities for children to be involved in activities planned by adults and in activities initiated by themselves (DfEE/QCA 1999b). The use of appropriate adult intervention in both types of activity will promote the learning process. Activities should be planned for the youngest children so that one learning objective is delivered in a variety of ways and the learning objective is revisited many times. This will aid consolidation of the children's learning and coherence in their development. (DfEE/QCA 1999b, p. 16).

 ### Case study – Reception

The routine in Mrs D's Reception class is for Mrs D to be available to talk to parents as they bring their children into school. Most parents stay in the classroom for the first few minutes of the day, helping their children to put his/her things away and choose which activity to become engaged in first. Whilst Mrs D speaks to parents, Mr J (Early Years Practitioner) works with the children. The whole group then moves to the carpet for register and the introduction to the day.

On Monday Mrs D asked the children to say if they had noticed anything different about the school garden that morning (a lot of flowering plants had been planted by the caretaker over the weekend). John had told Mrs D that he had seen a ladybird that morning and asked if he could draw a picture of the ladybird; Mrs D agreed. John had worked with Mr J and two other children to draw the ladybird then make up a story about it. Other planned activities for that day included drawing a flowering plant and labelling parts of a plant. At the end of the day John and his partners showed their work to the class and Mrs D asked all the children to look for a ladybird on the way home. The introduction to the day on Tuesday began with a discussion about what the children had seen the previous day. The class then shared an information text about minibeasts.

The case study demonstrates the opportunities provided in this class for group work that is planned by the teacher and that which is initiated by a child. Both activities required the children to look closely at a living thing and to record their observations in words and pictures. Mrs D used skilful intervention – initially by Mr J and then herself, to guide the children's learning through both activities. She also used John's enthusiasm and interest to move the learning of the whole group forward.

Paired and individual work

The use of paired work in science is similar to group work, in that there is the opportunity for shared understanding to develop through discussion of the learning experience. The choice of pairings needs to be made with reference to the advantages and limitations noted above for group work and maybe mixed ability, shared ability or friendship pairings. One advantage of paired work over group work is that group dynamics do not apply in the same way, and so the division of work within the task should be more equal. There may be less opportunity for disagreements to occur as there are only two children involved, although disagreements may be potentially more difficult to resolve, as there cannot be majority decision-making. In practice paired work is very demanding on resources and so is used most effectively for computer work, where the pair are able to share the work or take on the role of author and secretary, for research work and the recording of science work, where the same roles may be adopted.

Individual work in theory is an excellent approach for matching work to individual ability, however, in practice this is very hard to achieve, as it potentially requires the teacher to formulate thirty individual lesson plans for one objective. For the older child this may be possible, if the activity is open-ended, thus giving the child an opportunity to take more responsibility for his/her own learning – as in the case study below – and for developing a child's independence. The individual approach is also ideal for assessing children's abilities in science. Individual work is therefore used most often alongside other approaches to teaching science, rather than being used throughout a teaching session.

 Case study – a paired research task

Jamie and Marie, both Year 3 children, were researching the needs of a rabbit. The teacher had provided a range of books for the children to access and a prepared fact sheet. They began to look through the books, focusing on the pictures. They both found information and wanted to record it. Jamie wrote his piece of information down first, Marie started to look at another book. Jamie found copying the information difficult and asked the teacher for help. The teacher suggested that the children worked together on one piece of information only. He suggested Jamie tell Marie the information and Marie write it down. Jamie would be able to hold the book and Marie could concentrate on writing. Then Marie could read out her piece of information for Jamie to write down. Before the teacher intervened the children were not really working together and supporting each other's learning. They were working individually on a shared task. By acting as author and scribe the children were able to discuss the information they had found, decide which information was relevant and which words to use to record it.

 Case study – an individual task

Mr P had set the children their homework – to find out facts about the rainforest. He had specifically asked for information about the plants and trees to be found in the rainforest. Robin had used the books he had at home and his older sister had helped him. The task in school was to write up the homework as an advert. for living in the rainforest. Robin wanted more information before he wrote his advertisement and so went into the school library as soon as school opened, before the teaching day began. He found the information he required using the Internet. In class Robin used his notes to write an advert. and a description of the rainforest.

Selecting an approach

The majority of science lessons, in Key Stages 1 and 2, are likely to begin and end with the whole class working together with the teacher; whole class situations are used less often within the Foundation Stage. In the interim time, children will be working either individually or collaboratively, or indeed through a mixture of the approaches. Effective teachers aim to achieve a balance between the different teaching methods; the main criterion for choice of method is that of efficiency, for example introducing a task to each group in turn within a class requires the teacher to deliver the same instructions to each group and to maintain their own enthusiasm for the task throughout the time taken to work with each group in. A focus on individual work calls for similar points to be repeated many times, thus children may make less progress, lack the stimulus of other children, and have limited contact with the teacher (Dean, 1993). In order to be efficient with available resources, children may have to work in groups on different tasks; this takes careful planning and again instructions may have to be repeated. In reality, true group work can be a slow process, as children have to work collaboratively and therefore manage the group dynamics, as well as complete the task. Whole class teaching ensures all children have the same experience, but may not be understood by all children. By using a range of methods, the teacher is able to balance the efficiency needs of the lesson with the needs of the individual children.

Learning about Science through Play

Bruce (1997) regards play as central to young children's learning. It enables the integration of children's learning making it deeper, broader, and more relevant than might otherwise be the case. In science, firsthand experience through play offers the chance to manipulate, explore, discover, practice and apply knowledge and ideas. Exploratory play of this sort can help children to gain a deeper understanding of science through firsthand experience of artefacts. Play is the forerunner of structured investigative work and can offer children opportunities to increase their understanding and their ability to express thoughts and ideas. Although it is believed that most children will play spontaneously in an educational setting, teachers will need to structure some play opportunities to make the most of the potential for scientific learning. Teachers may take on various roles in the play situation, as shown in the table below.

The role of the adult in the play situation

Role	Example
• Mediator – intervening sensitively to advance children's play by modelling, explaining and promoting cooperation and consideration.	• Suggesting the children take on individual roles within the play, e.g., one child a zookeeper and other children animals he is looking after, rather than all the children being animals running around.
• Active participator – a co-player offering suggestions and information that will help to sustain the play.	• Becoming a visitor to the zoo and helping the zookeeper to look after the animals.
• Assessor – the teacher makes assessments of children's learning in science.	• Observe the play. Ask questions about what each animal is doing and noting the responses.

Learning about science through play is particularly important for the 3–5 age group (The Early Years Curriculum Group 1989, p. 2). It is through play that our youngest children '. . . practise and consolidate learning, play with ideas, and develop what they know'. However, it is important to realize that play continues to be a valid approach to learning for older pupils. At this stage the play will be much more structured by the teacher, usually through role-play situations. It will be necessary to establish a physical environment to promote play – the learning environment is explored further in Chapter 5.

Planning drama and role-play

Drama and role-play activities can develop scientific knowledge and attitudes by underpinning the child's own scientific interpretations. Adequate preparation by the teacher is crucial for drama and role-play activities in science to be focused and effective. The approach has to be based on evidence and not on uninformed ideas, it is therefore important to plan whether the information (evidence) with which to inform their drama or role-play will be provided by the teacher or located by the children themselves. Such activities therefore offer children an exciting and stimulating context within which to both draw upon and apply their previous learning, bringing together evidence arrived at through consulting literature, visiting environments outside school, exploring artefacts, using ICT and various interactions with others. Drama and role-play activities can thus be most effective in consolidating learning; however, the techniques needed for effective drama and role-play do need to be taught explicitly. Until children are used to working in this way the rewards will be minimal. It is therefore important for the teacher to first assess the ability of the children with the technique being used, and consequently not to make unrealistic demands of the children for their stage of learning.

Types of role play in primary science	Examples
Hot-seating	A child researches (with or without assistance) a scientist and takes on the role of this individual. Other children then ask questions, e.g., Alexander Fleming being asked about his discovery of penicillin.
Role-play	Children working in teams as scientists would work, recreating their conversations.
Role-cards	Children are given cards produced by the teacher which give information on a scientific theme. Children take on the role in a debate, e.g., the placing of a wind farm near a school.
Modelled role-play	Children acting out a model in science, e.g., the parts of an electric circuit or the molecules in water in three states.
ICT simulation	Some software packages offer children a simulated experience requiring them to engage with a scientific model or dilemma. These can be useful where direct experience may not be possible or to supplement and/or reinforce firsthand experiences. Simulations of this sort can also provide starting points for further study.
Predicting what happened next	The teacher provides a problem or tells part of a story about a discovery and the children suggest what they consider to be the likely outcome or ending. The teacher then provides the actual outcome and initiates a discussion about the similarities and differences between the actual outcome and the children's predictions.

Differentiation in Science

Differentiation is the term used to describe how the needs of individual children are met within the classroom. It involves providing all children with work at an appropriate level, thus ensuring that all children participate in a lesson and are able to learn, demonstrate what they know, understand or can do and make appropriate progress. Differentiation is therefore an essential element in effective teaching across the curriculum as it provides all children with access to the curriculum and with opportunities to fulfil their potential. It is also arguably one of the hardest aspects of teaching, particularly for student and newly qualified teachers, as it requires an in-depth knowledge of the children. However, this knowledge is only the first stage in differentiation as, after having identified individual differences between children, the teacher then needs to structure the work in order to deliver the science curriculum to each child. However, although differentiation is about catering for individual needs, it is not about creating 30 lesson plans for 30 individual children. This would be impractical and may also isolate children and prevent them from gaining the many benefits of working within a group.

It is at the medium-term planning stage that teachers need to begin to address the issue of differentiation. There are a number of steps that can be taken at this stage to ensure that all children are able to achieve and make progress:

- identify a range of teaching and learning strategies, i.e., organize the children in a variety of ways, provide a variety of approaches to teaching and learning;
- plan to use a wide range of stimulating resources, e.g., books, videos, artefacts, etc.;
- plan a range of methods for the children to record their work, in order to ensure all children are able to record their experiences;
- identify different methods for assessment of objectives, in order to enable all children to demonstrate their learning.

Further deliberation is given at the short-term planning stage. It is here that an individual lesson or session is considered in terms of how to ensure participation for all. There are a number of ways in which children's needs can be catered for, both in classroom based work and work beyond the school, the three major strategies for differentiation are described below.

Differentiation by outcome

This is probably the most common form of differentiation. It is one of the simplest to plan and organize as the same instructions are given to all children; they will demonstrate their level of ability by interpreting and completing the task to their own satisfaction. Children all use the same resources and have a common task that is sufficiently open-ended for all children to achieve success at their own level. Activities and materials need to be equally accessible to all pupils and should not be dependent upon knowledge and skills that only some pupils have.

Examples of children's work showing differentiation by outcome

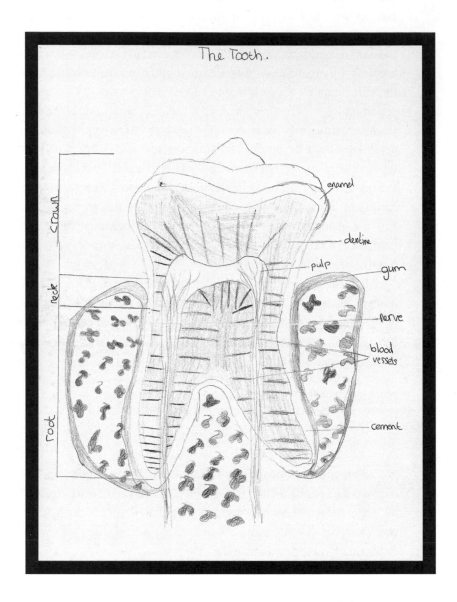

The Tooth.

enamel

dentine

pulp

gum

nerve

blood vessels

cement

crown

neck

root

Teeth

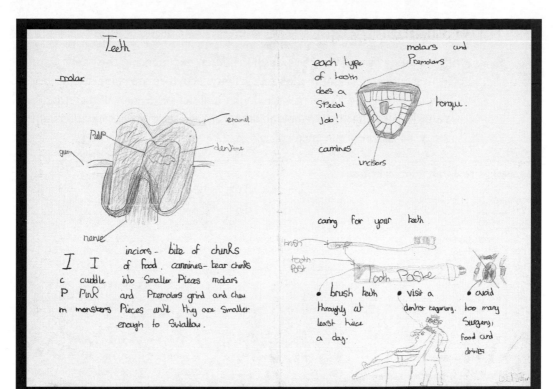

molar

pulp

gum

enamel

dentine

nerve

each type of tooth does a special job!

molars and premolars

tongue

canines

incisors

		incisors - bite of chunks of food. canines - tear chunks into smaller pieces molars and premolars grind and chew pieces until they are smaller enough to swallow.
I	I	
C	cuddle	
P	Pink	
m	monsters	

caring for your teeth

brush

tooth paste

Tooth Paste

• brush teeth throughly at least twice a day.

• visit a dentist regularly.

• avoid too many sugery, food and drinks

Teeth - care poster

Names - Incisors, Canines, Premolars, Molars.
   (I cuddle Pink monsters)

Number - A child has got 24 teeth.
    A Adult has got 32 teeth.

Function - You teeth can do 3 things
    Bite, tear, chew.

Care of teeth -
1. Brushing teeth at least twice a day helps remove plaque.
2. Flossing the teeth also helps remove plaque and bits of food which bacteria feed on.
3. Tooth decay is also prevented by visiting the dentist every 6 week.

Isw Pink

Differentiation by task

Differentiating by task involves all the children experiencing the same learning objective but not necessarily the same activity; activities are planned that vary in difficulty to complete. Children with similar abilities or needs will therefore carry out a task that is matched to their ability. There are various interpretations of this strategy, as shown in the table below.

Approaches to differentiation by task

Approach	Example	
	Lesson objective	Activity
Three different activities provided for *The less able children *The average ability children *The more able children	To know the part played by evaporation in the water cycle	*Observe over time a dish of water left on a radiator *Observe a puddle in the playground *Boil water in a kettle. Discuss what is happening to the water
One task may be made open-ended for some children, and more structured and clearly sequenced for the less confident or less able children.	To know magnets attract some materials but not others	*Objects provided by class teacher, children to sort into 2 groups. *Wider range of objects provided. Children to sort and offer explanation for magnetic/non-magnetic. *Children challenged to test materials in the classroom and identify magnetic/non-magnetic materials + explanation.
The introduction of stepped tasks, in which the pace and depth of learning will vary. A series of increasingly demanding tasks are thus provided, with some children completing all tasks, and others completing only some. *All children work on an initial activity. *The more able children then work on an extension activity, which further develops learning. *The most able children then move on to a second extension activity.	To know some materials dissolve in water	*Stir sugar into water. Observe. Describe observations. *1st extension activity – Investigate different substances in water. Observe. Describe observations. *2nd extension activity – Investigate the solubility of different sugars (icing, granulated, caster.) Observe. Describe observations.
The resources and/or materials differentiate the task provided. Resources can be provided which are more or less demanding, whilst materials can be varied to allow for a wider range of skills.	To know the life cycle of a human	*Set of pictures to order. *Books provided to research life cycle order. *Children to relate life cycle to own family.

Differentiation by support

Differentiation by support depends upon the level and quantity of adult support. This may be achieved by planning to work with particular children during a lesson or part of lesson in response to a specific need. This may not always be planned in advance, but may be made in response to pupil progress within a lesson. Accurate judgements about the apparent level of understanding or ability amongst the children during a session must therefore be made at the point of need to enable the child to progress. The additional support is employed to ensure progress is made throughout the lesson. It may include support with carrying out the task; with recording the task; with reporting their understanding of the task. Questions may be directed towards different children in order to reinforce and recap learning during plenary sessions, and be the focus of discussions regarding feedback and target setting for future learning.

CS **Case study**

The topic for Mr K's Year 1 class this half term is Growth and Change. He is planning for the children to observe the life cycle of a frog, from spawn to young adult. Various other activities will reinforce this work. The activities will include drawing the life cycle, playing a matching game and putting together a life cycle jigsaw. Amy has underdeveloped fine motor skills and Mr K expects that she will be unable to physically put the jigsaw together. In response to this need Miss J, the learning support assistant, will work with Amy. Miss J will discuss the activity with Amy and help her to complete it. Mr K has asked her to let Amy try the task for herself but be available to put the jigsaw together if needed, following Amy's instructions.

Children's Misconceptions in Science

Children come to science with an understanding of science concepts of their own. Scott *et al.* (1987) describes this as children already holding their own ideas about natural phenomena. Although the science curriculum develops learning through building upon children's ideas, children also build up their knowledge from a range of sources outside the school environment, knowledge that may be very different to that which we would wish them to develop. These different understandings are often referred to as pupil's misconceptions in science. Some misconceptions are quite common and children may hold any number of them; it is therefore important that the teacher is aware of them and is able to respond appropriately when they occur. The misconceptions may be extremely resistant to change and so it is not merely a case of instructing a child that their beliefs are wrong, the child needs to have their knowledge and understanding challenged and developed. Much research work has been carried out in the field of pupil misconceptions and teacher responses. Harlen (1993) reports that research work into children's ideas in science began in the 1970s in New Zealand. The main work into this area at primary level was carried out by the Science Processes and Concepts Exploration (SPACE), which was a joint project based at Liverpool University and King's College, London. The research involved children from the 5–11 age range and resulted in revealing the nature and extent of different ideas held by children across the whole range of concepts relevant to the primary level. McGuigan and Russell (1997, p. 15) write that such research not only catalogues 'lists of children's naïve ideas in science'; but also forewarns teachers about the range of commonly occurring ideas and suggests ways of managing teaching and learning in science. The list below records a sample of five of the common misconceptions held by children.

Some common misconceptions in science

- the 'active seeing' model of vision
- the 'clashing current' idea of electric circuits
- plants are not living things
- gravity acts more forcibly on massive objects than on lesser ones
- heavy things sink, light things float

(Adapted from McGuigan and Russell, 1997, and Edwards and Knight, 1994)

Misconceptions held by children in science need first to be identified through observation and assessment of a pupil's existing knowledge and understanding (see Chapter 6). Once teachers have established the nature of the misconception held by a child they can then develop their ideas. It is therefore through the accurate appraisal of where a child's learning *is* that assists the teacher in taking the child *to* a higher level of understanding. Misconceptions should not be viewed as wrong as they fit the child's own view of the world; it is the teacher's responsibility to work with this existing knowledge and understanding and to develop it.

Steps to develop a misconception

- identify the concept to be improved
- know the alternative concepts likely to be held by the child
- provide situations in which children may be encouraged to notice discrepancies
- encourage children to explore their explanation
- provide experiences for children to apply and consolidate their learning.

(Adapted from Edwards and Knight, 1994)

Reflecting on Teaching Methods

Trainee and newly qualified teachers who reflect critically about their own practice in teaching are more likely to increase their repertoire of effective teaching methods in science than those who do not. Reflection enables the teacher to review the effectiveness of what has been taught and learned. It involves teachers in considering their teaching critically. Edwards and Knight (1994) state that effective teachers reflect on their teaching and modify their teaching on the basis of their reflection; it is therefore a crucial skill to develop, and invariably leads to improved practice. The ability to become a reflective practitioner, by using evaluation, and then revising practice is thus an important aspect of teaching.

Checklist for a lesson evaluation

- learning objectives – to what extent they were achieved
- teaching methods – how appropriate the teaching methods and structure of the lesson were
- lesson content – how appropriate was the content of the science lesson for the range of ability in the group/class
- organization – how effective was the organization and timing of the session, including the effectiveness of groupings
- resources – the quality and use of resources
- activities – were the activities used suitable for the delivery of the lesson objective?

Evaluation involves the deliberation of both the positive and negative aspects of a lesson, and then a consideration of how the information can improve future practice. It is therefore purely a mechanism for improving the quality of teaching and learning in science; however, the teacher must not dwell only on the negative but must accept what went well and, more importantly, why it went well. Equally, where an aspect of the lesson did not appear to go well, the teacher must be able to determine why this was. At every stage of the evaluation process there should be a careful consideration of *how do you know*, and so appropriate criteria for determining this need to be employed. The teacher then needs to apply this knowledge to future teaching, by considering what could be approached differently next time, to improve the lesson. It is also important to use the evaluation to identify what the children need to learn or experience next, in order to move their learning further. Evaluation where the performance of the teacher is reviewed critically takes many forms. It occurs throughout a lesson, at the end of a lesson, during a unit of work and at the end of a unit of work. It is thus a continuous process, with formative and summative aspects. It is rarely a formal activity; teachers develop the ability to continually reflect on what is happening informally. The main source of evidence is therefore classroom observation but may also involve practitioner feedback.

Activity

Read the commentary below of a science lesson on the topic of The Earth in Space. Evaluate the lesson, identifying its strengths and weaknesses.

A review is provided at the end for you to compare with your own ideas.

Science lesson – The Earth in Space
Year group – 4

Following morning break the children quickly entered their classroom and sat at their usual tables. The teacher, Miss B, was ready at the blackboard and waited for the children to settle. When almost all the children were ready and looking attentively Miss B coughed quietly. She began the lesson by writing the word 'space' on the board. The children quickly started to put their hands up to offer information about 'space'. Miss B put many of the ideas/information given on the board, repeating what each child had said and asking him or her to qualify their comments through questioning. When the board was full of the proffered information she then instructed the children to copy down the information on to a prepared fact sheet, which the teacher handed out as she was speaking.

There was a few minutes of activity as the children collected pens, pencils and crayons but the children soon set to work on the task. Miss B moved around the groups of children praising their efforts and answering the children's questions. She assisted one child who regularly experienced difficulties copying from the board and moved another less able child to sit with, and work alongside, a more able peer.

As the children finished the task Miss B read out their work and showed it to the class. The children were asked to illustrate their work then read quietly until the lunchtime bell. Three children remained in the room after the bell finishing their work and assisting the teacher in clearing away ready for the afternoon session.

Review of science lesson – The Earth in Space

Miss B has in place good organizational strategies as the children knew where to sit, knew to look at the teacher by the blackboard and knew the response required to the teacher writing the prompt word 'space' on the board. Miss B responded to the proffered information and thoughts by using relevant questioning and putting the children's ideas on the board. At this point, if not earlier in the lesson, she ought to have shared the objective of the lesson with the children. This would have helped the children to understand what they were expected to learn from the activity. Miss B had a blank fact sheet prepared for the children to record their work on but interrupted the flow of the lesson by expecting the children to collect other equipment, i.e., pens, pencils and crayons. Miss B did not clarify that the children understood the task but did monitor all the children working and ensured they knew what they were doing by answering the children's questions as they arose. This part of the lesson merely consolidated what the children already knew – they had been given the information to be copied down – and thus did not extend their knowledge or understanding of the concept, although the less able children will have benefited from the information given by the more able children. Miss B worked with one special-needs child to ensure he completed the task, and yet, as he regularly experienced difficulties copying from the board, his needs would have been catered for more effectively through providing table top prompts and a differentiated activity. Miss B also ensured a second special-needs child was catered for, by seating him with a more able child for peer support. The activity itself was not differentiated as all children completed exactly the same task, differentiation was therefore planned to be through outcome, some children completing it early and some remaining through lunchtime. A more effectively differentiated task may have avoided this situation. Miss B celebrated the work of children who finished early and used it to motivate the other children. An extension activity was needed to further learning, the use of quiet reading 'until lunchtime' was not an appropriate ending to the activity. The lesson itself ended abruptly with the lunchtime bell. Miss B did not use the last few minutes of the session to recap on the focus of the lesson and to review the children's learning that had taken place.

Reflection based on reading and research

There are various further sources of information and research available to students and teachers, which can be used to inform science teaching. It is important to make use of the experiences and learning of others through the information included in professional journals, documentation from government departments and agencies, commercially produced curriculum materials and ideas located through the Internet. It is important to use such sources critically, particularly the Internet, as the quality and suitability of material can vary widely. A further source of information can be derived from Ofsted inspection reports that can also be accessed through the Internet. Such reports may set out what is considered to be good practice in teaching and learning in science in a range of schools.

Sources of information to support high quality teaching and learning in science:

Journals and other publications
Education in Science – issued by the ASE (Association for Science Education, Hatfield).
Primary Science Review – issued by the ASE (Association for Science Education, Hatfield).
Primary Maths + Science – published by Questions Publishing Company, Birmingham.

Books
Loughran, J. J. (1996) *Developing Reflective Practice: Learning about Teaching and Learning through Modelling*, London: Falmer.
Ovens, P. (2000) *Reflective Teacher Development in Primary Science*, London: Falmer.
Pollard, A. & Tann, S. (1993) *Reflective Teaching in the Primary School: A Handbook for the Classroom*, (2nd edn), London: Cassell.
Reagan, T. G., Case, C. W. & Brubacher, J. W. (2000) *Becoming a Reflective Educator: How to Build a Culture of Inquiry in the Schools*, Thousand Oaks, California: Corwin Press.

Government agencies and departments
Qualifications and Curriculum Authority – www.qca.org.uk
National Grid for Learning – www.ngfl.gov.uk
Department for Education and Skills – www.dfes.gov.uk/index.htm
Ofsted – www.dfes.gov.uk/index.htm

In order to develop primary practice further, teachers should continue to question their approach to teaching and learning, with respect to the reading, research and the theories of how children learn. Good practice should therefore persist in being the subject of debate and argument. Alexander et al. (1992) pointed out that if *practice is introduced from a sense of obligation rather than conviction,* it is likely to have adverse effects on children's learning. Consequently, teachers continue to need to be innovative in their teaching, whilst being mindful of current ideas about teaching and learning in science. The argument that children's learning is influenced and affected by experiences involving interaction with others, children and adults, combined with the importance of first hand experience, supports innovation in science, as does the abstract nature of science. This requires acts of imaginative reconstruction, albeit based on scientific models, in order to make sense of the world. Imagination, in science, can take a number of forms that require children to make use of their cognitive, emotional and communication abilities. Memory and learning can be enhanced in creative and imaginative approaches to science that heighten children's interest and enjoyment in the subject.

Reflective questions

Further considerations regarding teaching and class management include:

- How to avoid a queue of children asking the following questions during a science lesson – What do I do? What do I do next? Where is . . .? How do you spell . . .? Can I . . .? Is this right?
- The use of alternative ways of organizing and grouping the children.
- The effectiveness of presentation skills when introducing new science work.
- The effectiveness of pacing and timing throughout the lesson.
- The provision of opportunities for all the children to engage in debate, discussion, questioning and hypothesizing.
- The appropriate matching of activity to individuals, groups or whole class.
- Differentiation of the science teaching, for the range of ability in the class.
- The effectiveness of questioning the children, as a way of eliciting information about their understanding.

REFERENCES

Alexander, R., Rose, J. & Woodhead, C. (1992) 'Curriculum Organisation and Classroom Practice in Primary Schools: A Discussion Paper', London: DES.

Bliss, J. (1995) 'Piaget and After: The Case of Learning Science', *Studies in Science Education*, 25, pp. 139–72.

Bruce, T. (1997), *Early Childhood Education* (2nd edn), London: Hodder & Stoughton.

Davydov, V. (1993) 'The Influence of L S Vygotsky on Educational Theory, Research and Practice', *Educational Researcher*, 24 (3), pp.12–21.

Howe, A. (1996) 'Development of Science Concepts within a Vygotskian Framework', *Science Education*, 80(1), pp. 35–51.

Dean, J. (1993) *Organising Learning in the Primary School* (3rd edn) London: Croom Helm.

Donaldson, M. (1978) *Children's Minds*, London: Fontana Press.

Driver, R., Asoko, H., Leach, J., Mortimer, E. & Scott, P. (1993) 'Constructing Science Knowledge in the Classroom', Draft paper by the Children's Learning in Science Research Group, for submission to *Educational Researcher*. Mimeo.

Early Years Curriculum Group (1989) *Early Childhood Education: The Early Years Curriculum and the National Curriculum*, Stoke on Trent: Trentham Books.

Edwards, A. & Knight, P. (1994) *Effective Early Years Education: Teaching Young Children*, Buckingham: Open University Press.

Harlen, W. (1993) 'Children's Learning in Science', in Sherrington, R. (ed.) *Primary Science Teacher's Handbook*, Hemel Hempstead: Simon & Schuster.

Mcguigan, L. & Russell, T. (1997) 'What Constructivism Tells Us about Managing the Teaching and Learning of Science', *PSR* 50, pp. 15–17, ASE.

Pines, L. & West, L. (1986) 'Conceptual Understanding and Science Learning: An Interpretation of Research Within a Sources-of-Knowledge Framework', *Science Education*, 70(5), pp. 583–604.

Pollard, A. & Tann, S. (1993) *Reflective Teaching in the Primary School: A Handbook for the Classroom* (2nd edn) London: Cassell.

Qualifications and Curriculum Authority (1999a) *The National Curriculum: Handbook for Primary Teachers in England*, London: DfEE/QCA.

Qualifications and Curriculum Authority (1999b) *Early Learning Goals*, London: DfEE/QCA.

Scott, P., Dyson, T. & Gator, S. (1987) 'A Constructivist View of Learning and Teaching in Science', Children's Learning in Science Project, Centre for Studies in Science and Mathematics Education, University of Leeds.

Vygotsky, L. S. (1978) *Mind in Society: The Development of Higher Psychological Processes*, Cambridge: Harvard University Press.

The Learning Environment in Science

Chapter 5 is concerned with the provision of an effective, safe learning environment, which supports and encourages learning in science. Edwards and Knight (1994) describe the learning environment as crucial, as it is where the curriculum is *located*, therefore an environment that stimulates the children, is accessible to them and which contains high quality resources is likely to greatly enhance, support and encourage learning. The chapter thus examines how the learning environment can be used to foster pupil interest in science. It begins by considering health and safety issues regarding this provision and looks specifically at the responsibilities of the teacher to ensure that children's health and safety is addressed in line with the Health and Safety at Work Act 1974, as well as their common law duty of care to act *in loco parentis*.

The chapter goes on to explore the features of the learning environment – the areas to be used, displays within the environment and resources for teaching and learning. The areas to be used include both indoor and outdoor areas, as the outside environment is particularly relevant for children in the Foundation Stage of learning. The outdoor environment enables our youngest children to work with real experiences in the world around them and to work on a large scale, e.g., through construction and physical play (QCA/DFEE 1999b). The chapter hence considers how teachers may use the space available to them to support and encourage learning in science. An integral part of the learning environment is the display of children's work, scientific information and resources; different ways to create exciting and attractive displays are therefore explored. The section ends with a review of a broad range of resources, including physical resources, ICT and adults as a resource for supporting pupils' learning in the science. There is a vast array of physical resources that may be used to enhance both the learning environment and children's learning in science, the chapter thus informs the reader of a range of resources necessary to deliver an effective primary science curriculum. The chapter identifies both specialist equipment and everyday resources that may be useful and discusses the methods of storage and accessibility of resources.

ICT is considered here as a teaching and learning resource, identifying ways in which ICT supports the science curriculum and establishing when, and when not, ICT should be used. Within this section the use of adults in the classroom as a resource for learning is considered. The student or newly qualified teacher will no doubt encounter a range of adults in the classroom, from parents volunteering their help to trained support workers and specialist teachers. The management of adults in the classroom is the responsibility of the class teacher and so the chapter explores how this most valuable resource is organized effectively. Within this exploration the ways of incorporating scientific learning into partnerships between home and school will be noted.

The chapter concludes with a consideration of the use of the wider community in supporting learning in science. The role, and management, of environments and resources beyond the nursery or school is thus explored. It will be established that the wider community is used to both stimulate and interest children in the world around them and beyond.

Health and Safety

Teachers are legally responsible for providing an effective, safe learning environment in the classroom, an environment where children can feel secure and confident, and in which they can operate safely and purposefully. It is not realistic to suggest that a classroom can be totally risk free, but there is an expectation that teachers ensure they are knowledgeable about both the likely actions of their pupils in a given situation and the risks associated with a particular science activity. With respect to their pupils' actions, teachers are expected to be able to exercise a degree of foresight, as the failure to prevent injury or harm to a child in the classroom, when the dangers could be reasonably foreseen, constitutes negligence. The term *reasonable foresight* is important as all environments, including the 3–11 settings, inevitably carry some risks to safety. There is always a risk that children may fall over, trap their fingers or mishandle objects from time to time and so it is risk avoidance, risk awareness and risk management that are important skills for the student and beginning teacher to acquire. It is also desirable that our children acquire these skills, as they cannot be supervised 24 hours a day. The expectations on children to take some responsibility for their own safe working practices will become more demanding as children mature. However, although children's abilities in these areas will develop over time, it remains at all times the responsibility of the teacher to make every effort to ensure their children's safety. This requires the teacher to have an understanding of the children themselves, to make certain judgements about the children and consider the extent to which children are:

- able to handle the given equipment safely
- able to make sensible choices regarding the equipment available
- able to take responsibility for themselves and their actions
- able to understand and observe nursery/school rules and conventions.

In addition to a teacher's responsibility to ensure the safety of the pupils, the teacher is also bound by the provisions of the Health and Safety at Work Act 1974. The provisions of this Act dictate that all employees, including teachers, must not meddle or interfere with anything provided for the purpose of ensuring people's health and safety. They have a duty to care for their own safety at work and for the safety of others that might be affected either by their actions or their failure to act. Teachers must also cooperate with other members of staff who have duties under the Act, e.g., school/nursery health and safety representative and the first aid specialist. In response to this, all schools and nurseries have health and safety policies (often based on LEA policies) with which the staff are expected to be familiar. An invaluable reference source for carrying out risk assessments related to activities in science is *Be Safe: Health and Safety in Primary School Science and Technology* (ASE 2001, 3rd edn). ASE reports that many LEAs have adopted this publication, using it to form the basis for general risk assessments.

Ensuring the health and safety of pupils in science

- a risk assessment to be carried out before an activity takes place
- the learning environment in the classroom must be properly cleaned following science activity
- activities involving potentially hazardous materials need very careful supervision
- it may be necessary to restrict the usage of some resources to adults only
- in some cases adult intervention/supervision may be necessary
- it is advisable that teachers try out all activities before presenting them to the children
- it is advisable that teachers carry out preliminary visits to areas to be used outside the classroom, to try to anticipate any potential hazards

 ### CS Case study

Year group: 2
Activity: Observing litter left in an area. Counting litter, sorting litter.
Learning objective: To know that litter is a pollutant. To know that some litter is biodegradable and some is non-biodegradable (the technical vocabulary will not be used with the children).
Safety issues:
*Children should not touch litter with the naked hand; the teacher cannot know what is contained in litter.
*The children should wear plastic gloves.
*Anything sharp could cut a child through the bag.
*Even when using gloves the hands must be washed immediately after handling litter.

*Young children may put litter near to their face and mouth.

An alternative to collecting and handling litter would be to use hoops to cover an area of ground and to observe and count litter. The identification of biodegradable and non-biodegradable litter may then follow in the classroom, using 'litter' provided by the class teacher.

Creating an effective, safe learning environment in the classroom is crucial to the teaching and learning of science. The learning environment can be thought of in terms of:

- the use of the available space
- the use of display
- the use of equipment
- the use of human resources and climate setting.

The Use of Available Space

The creation of an effective learning environment is possible in all classroom situations but is dependent on both the available space and how the space is to be used. The layout of the classroom needs to be mindful of the types of activity that may be carried out by the children. Some scientific activities, for example those requiring children to investigate sound, may be quite noisy and dynamic, while others, such as investigating dissolving, are potentially messy. As a result, it may be necessary to plan and establish a mix of clearly defined areas and general purpose spaces in the nursery or classroom, with sufficient and varied space for a range of activities. It is an accepted practice to use furniture to mark out and define areas such as quiet areas and ICT areas, however it is important to make sure that these arrangements do not hinder your ability to observe and monitor children's learning.

Classroom layout – a checklist

- use bookcases and drawer units to section areas of the classroom
- use labels to indicate the focus of the area, e.g., ICT Corner, Science Bay, etc.
- keep noisy activities away from quiet areas
- keep 'messy' activities near to the sink area
- establish class rules about moving from one area to another
- include a role-play area for the Foundation Stage and Key Stage 1 (Role-play areas are less well-established in Key Stage 2 but may have a part to play in the school curriculum)
- be prepared to move furniture to change the layout if the mix of activities requires a different layout
- ensure that you are able to monitor children in all areas, i.e., do not obstruct your view

Outdoor space

Outdoor space may be used to extend the learning environment across the age range and is especially important for the younger child. It may be appropriate to set up science activities outside the classroom which require a large area or are 'messy', e.g., when investigating floating and sinking. Outdoor space is also invaluable for children to observe living things in their natural environment, e.g., minibeasts in a playground habitat or the range of plants in the school garden. Children may also be able to observe the effects of weathering by observing stone walls in the school or immediate locality, in preference to researching the effects using books or CD Roms. At the Foundation Stage of learning the outdoor area is an essential part of the learning environment (QCA/DFEE, 1999b). These children have less previous knowledge on which to build their ideas and understanding of the world and therefore need many opportunities to encounter living things, including people, and objects in a natural environment. It is therefore through observation and exploration that the children are able to develop their knowledge of the world they live in. Using outdoor space in the Foundation Stage also allows the children to work on a large scale, e.g., using large construction materials, water play, which may lead to smaller-scale, indoor explorations. Children also learn through play situations (see Chapter 2) and these can be structured using an outdoor area or garden.

The Use of Display

Within the learning environment display is an essential consideration. The main purpose of display is twofold:

1. To provide scientific information;
2. To celebrate the achievements and experiences of children within science.

Display can be used to communicate scientific information to children by displaying scientific equipment alongside relevant questions and research material (i.e., books, information sheets, pictures, website addresses). Such displays encourage the children to start talking and thinking about science, to ask questions and begin working scientifically. Displays may also communicate scientific information to parents and other visitors to school, e.g., the work currently being carried out by the children, the children's thoughts and ideas, special events in school, etc. A display of children's work demonstrates the value you place on the children's work in science. It shows praise for the work, recognizes achievement and encourages the children in their scientific work. Careful, well-presented displays can be used to motivate all children and sets the standards required in recorded work.

An attractively displayed room can help to create an effective learning environment by bringing the environment *alive* and stimulating interest in the children; poorly presented displays can have the opposite effect, by portraying science as a boring or uninteresting subject. A thoughtful display can thus persuade children of the excitement and interest to be found in science and may provide opportunities for children to engage in the communication and organization of scientific information and interpretation. Children's involvement in some of the decision-making about what and how to display, both resources and the results of their work in science, can help to ensure that a display is used and referred to.

There are various considerations when planning a display for science including:

- The use of both wall and tabletop displays.
- 3D as well as 2D images and artefacts on display.
- There needs to be a balance of hands-on interactive displays, where the children are actively encouraged to handle the display work, and static ones which are for viewing only.
- Science displays ought to be changed on a regular basis if they are to fulfil their potential for inspiring and motivating pupils. Whereas a new, well-presented display can provide an exciting stimulus for children, a tired, well-used display from a past topic may be largely ignored.

The assembling and maintaining of attractive and worthwhile displays does take a considerable amount of time and effort. Some teachers may have a natural flair for display, for others the required skills may need to be learned. Many schools have guidelines for display to be adhered to, e.g., about mounting work, the use of commercial display materials, the colours for backing paper, etc. It is worthwhile for the student and newly qualified teacher to take the opportunity to look at displays around school, to get a feel for the style of the displays that are expected.

There are many forms of display, as described in the following table and illustrations.

Form of display	Example
Science resources Displaying science resources enables children to: • become comfortable with handling scientific equipment; • to get to know the names of equipment; • to know the use of different pieces of equipment. This type of display is useful for developing confidence in the practical side of science. It is also useful for introducing whole investigations (see Chapter 2) where children are encouraged to select their own equipment from a range of alternatives. The display requires the teacher to accurately label the equipment and provide information notes for the children.	Table display of weather equipment to be used in a weather survey.
Science information This may be in the form of a poster, information cards or books. It enhances the children's work in science by providing information that they can access and may need to interpret. It is useful for encouraging children to search for information, during a structured activity or 'free' time in the school day	Wall display of the water cycle, using words and pictures or a poster of information. Table display of topic related books.
Children's work It is essential when displaying children's work in science that both *effort* and *outcome* are used as criteria for judging which pieces of work are put on show. By taking care to present children's work well, you are giving the message that their work is of value to you and to the learning environment. It is important that all children have an opportunity to display their work not only the more able children or the neat writers. By including pieces of work from all the children you are providing motivation and success for all. The criterion for selection must be that the piece of work chosen reflects that child's ability, this ensures that the resulting display will be of the highest quality whilst meeting the needs of all the children.	Wall display of quality mounted work completed by the children.
Combination of above The displays should reflect the variety and breadth of the science curriculum, showing the results of practical activities and the acquisition of knowledge. They may include photographs of work in progress, diagrams and pictures, models and written work. There may be written comments by the children showing their development of attitudes as well as skills and knowledge.	Table display of science information on cards together with children's recorded work in booklets.

Display of science resources

Table top display in a Year 2 classroom.
A variety of magnets – magnetic wand and marbles, bar magnets and horseshoe magnets.
Selection of magnetic and non-magnetic materials – wood, paper, fabric, feather, paper clips, metal discs, glass marble, nails.
A magnetic fishing game.
Labels – showing words of all items on table.
Books – giving information, in words and pictures, regarding magnetism.
Activity cards – inviting children to test which objects are magnetic and which are not, and to try the magnetic fishing game.

Display of science information (Year 4 classroom)

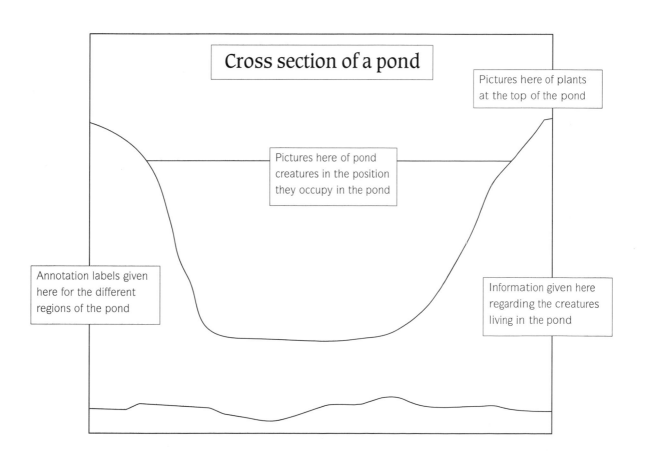

Cross section of a pond

Pictures here of plants at the top of the pond

Pictures here of pond creatures in the position they occupy in the pond

Annotation labels given here for the different regions of the pond

Information given here regarding the creatures living in the pond

Display of children's work

Sound *by Year 3*

Pictorial representation of children whispering, speaking quietly, speaking loudly and shouting in the playground. Use of speech bubbles to describe different sounds

Independent research on sound

Independent research on sound

Annotated model of a recorder made from wood and plastic

Model of a glockenspiel using wood and plastic

Combination display

The Water Cycle
Year 5

Glossary of terms provided by the teacher

Satellite picture of a similar scene

Large painting, by two children working together, of a hillside and lake. The children have written their version of the water cycle on cloud-shaped paper, which they have displayed on the completed picture

The Use of Equipment

Science for the 3–11 age range requires the use of resources that enable children to experience science firsthand, through investigating, exploring and handling objects. Feasey (1998, p. 7) lists a number of benefits to children of using equipment in science, as listed below.

Through using equipment in science children should:

- appreciate the importance of equipment in science
- become aware of scientific tools that aid science work
- know that different kinds of scientific equipment have specific jobs, e.g., a Newton meter
- appreciate that equipment must be used with care, and safely
- develop the ability to decide when equipment is necessary
- develop the ability to choose appropriate equipment
- develop the ability to use equipment accurately
- be aware that there is a range of one type of equipment, e.g., thermometers, and that they have to decide which thermometer is best for the job
- understand that measurement is important in science
- know that equipment can help provide accurate measurements
- appreciate that equipment used in the classroom often has an equivalent in real life
- appreciate that the skills developed through using equipment in science can be used in everyday life

The provision, storage and organization of equipment for scientific activities are therefore important considerations when creating an effective learning environment. This section of the chapter will examine the range of resources that may be used, how they may be stored and makes suggestions for their accessibility. The use of ICT as a resource for science teaching and learning will be discussed, together with the use of resources beyond the nursery/school.

Range of equipment

Equipment for primary and foundation stage science activities can be categorized as specialist equipment or everyday resources. In addition to the primary (hands-on) resources needed to deliver an effective science curriculum, secondary sources of information are also required. Such resources may be used before, during or after an investigation, to support children's learning through firsthand exploration.

Specialist equipment for primary science

A definitive list cannot be given here, but a good selection may include:

o Weather equipment – anemometer, barometer, compass, hygrometer, rain gauge, weather board
o Water equipment – aquarium
o Viewing equipment – binoculars, range of magnifiers, range of sample boxes (with magnifying lids), microscopes, viewing boxes, range of lenses
o Thermometers – range of thermometers
o Measuring equipment – callipers, height chart/measurer, metre sticks, tape measures, trundle wheel, Newton metres, measuring beakers, measuring cylinders, measuring jugs, measuring spoons, syringes, range of stopwatches/clocks/timers, range of scales and balances, metal masses, plastic masses, slotted masses and hangers
o Flower equipment – flower press, gardening tools, propagator
o Animal equipment – nets, pooters
o The body – human torso, body models, e.g., ear, eye, brain, teeth, skeleton, stethoscope, X-rays
o The earth – globe, pH meter/probe, quadrats, rocks and fossils, soils, soil meter, sieves
o Light – light meter/sensor, coloured acetate sheets, colour paddles, mirrors, concave/convex mirrors, lenses, lens holders, kaleidoscope, light ray box, periscope, prisms, torches
o Sound – musical instruments, plastic tubing, metal pipes, slinky, sound meter, tuning forks
o Mixtures – droppers, litmus paper, pH paper, funnels, filter papers, hob unit, metal rods, night lights, pestle and mortar, stands, goggles, tongs
o Electricity – batteries, battery holders, bells, bulbs, bulb holders, buzzers, crocodile clips, LEDs, motors, switches, chocolate block connectors, screw drivers, wire, wire strippers
o Magnetism – bar magnets, horseshoe magnets, polo magnets, fridge magnets, magnetic strip, magnetic tape, magnetic discs, magnetic marbles and wand, iron filings (encased), soft iron rods

Everyday resources for primary science

A definitive list cannot be given here, but a good selection may include:

o Aluminium foil
o Balloons and balloon pump
o Range of different sized balls
o Range of building equipment, e.g., bricks, tiles, slates, pebbles, sand, guttering
o Marbles, beads
o Bubble mixture and bubble blowers
o Range of card and card pieces
o Candles
o Pegs, cotton reels
o Compost, seeds, bulbs, plant pots, seed trays
o Jam jars

o Range of threads and strings
o Range of spoons
o Sponges
o Springs
o Straws
o Corks, rubber bungs
o Disposable cups
o Disposable gloves
o Range of wood – different size, shape, type (including bark)
o Rubber bands
o Range of paper
o Paper clips, paper fasteners
o Range of fabrics
o Range of toys – magnetic, electrical, wind up
o Range of metal samples, nails
o Range of plastic bags, plastic sheets, plastic containers, plastic bottles
o Plasticine

Range of secondary resources for science

- Video and photographic resources, e.g., video footage of the first man on the moon, photographs taken in space;
- TV programmes, e.g., Stage Two Science (ages 7–11, Channel 4), Science Zone (ages 9–11, BBC.);
- Non-fiction publications form an important resource and can be obtained in many bookshops or through specialist educational publishers, e.g., *1000 Things You Should Know About Science* (Farndon, 2000);
- Fiction, e.g., *The Very Hungry Caterpillar* (Carle, 1986);
- Biographies, e.g., *Archimedes* (Green, undated);
- Internet sites, e.g., www.naturegrid.org.uk/explorer
- Museums, e.g., *Eureka!* (The Museum for Children, Discovery Road, Halifax, HX1 2NE).

It is essential that all equipment is maintained in good condition and is both safe to use and child friendly. The equipment must also be up-to-date, stored appropriately and monitored for use. If equipment is not being used regularly it may be inappropriate or out-of-date and should be discarded. Consideration must also be given to the provision of suitable quantities of equipment; this will be discussed later in the chapter. School or class collections of scientific equipment may be augmented through the use of museum loans, loans from parents, loans from a secondary school and the local community. It is obviously important that a record is kept of all resources, from whatever source. Items that are on loan will need to be returned to the rightful owner at the end of a topic or the school year and so a detailed, up-to-date record is important. Parents need to be cautioned about loaning valuable items given the fact that children will be handling them.

Storage and accessibility of equipment

It is important that all children develop independence in their learning; one simple way to encourage this is to label the storage of equipment in an appropriate, age-related way. The children can then be directed to refer to labels and/or pictures on storage containers to identify the equipment stored within, thus enabling them to engage in selecting and handling some of the resources needed for their work. Children should be encouraged to make informed choices about appropriate equipment and materials; through this they will develop their own resource management skills and begin to take responsibility for the classroom environment.

Systems for the storage of equipment for science vary widely from school to school. Equipment may be stored centrally for use by the whole staff, stored in an area which is available to a team of staff, e.g., the nursery team, Year 3 only or a Key Stage or assigned to an individual class or teacher. It may be that resources are stored under a mixture of systems, as listed below.

Storage system for science equipment:

stored centrally – for use by the whole school	e.g., electrical equipment to be used at different times by classes in Key Stages 1 and 2
available to a team of staff	e.g., a water cycle model to be used only in Key Stage 2 kept in the Key Stage 2 science area
assigned to an individual class or teacher	e.g., everyday resources such as hand lenses and viewers

Containers for storing equipment range from plastic trays and boxes to fixed wall units and moveable trolleys. *Primary Science Equipment* (Feasey, 1998) is an invaluable reference source for ideas regarding the storage of equipment and the use of storage containers. Where there are shared resources and loans a booking system is often in operation in order to track the use of resources and their whereabouts at any one time.

Children may or may not have direct access to the storage areas for science resources. It may be the system in school that the teacher chooses the resources needed for an activity and takes them into the classroom. Alternatively, it may be that a child or group of children, who may or may not be supervised by an adult, are allowed to take resources from the storage area to the classroom themselves. Student and newly qualified teachers will be expected to become familiar with, and adhere to, the systems in use. Decisions regarding the issue of access to resources are influenced by:

- the storage system in place;
- the types of available resources;
- an awareness of suitability of the resources to the Year group;
- an awareness of the constraints of the classroom;
- a commitment to children's health and safety.

Within the classroom it is most likely that some resources may be teacher controlled whilst others are open-access for children. This system will ensure that there is safe provision of a wide range of interesting objects, materials and equipment in the classroom, which together will contribute to the creation of a stimulating learning environment, whilst being mindful of the age of the children and their developing resource management. The table below summarizes the suggested progression in choosing and using equipment in science by Feasey (1998, p. 9), which demonstrates the moving of the responsibility for choosing the equipment gradually from the teacher to child.

Progression in choosing and using equipment in science

	Choosing equipment	Using equipment	Safety/Care
Nursery	*teacher provides range of equipment for use in real life and play situations. *children encouraged children to try out equipment.	*teacher demonstrates and explains use of equipment to children. *equipment displayed and available for use in play situations.	*teacher introduces children to safe use of equipment. *children taught routines for getting equipment out and putting it away. *pictures and/or silhouettes used to help children put equipment away. *children taught how to share equipment.
Year 2	*children now familiar with basic range of equipment. *able to choose equipment with limited help from the teacher.	*children should be able to use basic range of equipment unaided. *children begin to appreciate need to use measuring equipment accurately.	*children should be able to use basic range of equipment safely. *children responsible for collecting and putting equipment away. *children able to inform teacher when equipment is damaged or pieces are missing.
Year 6	*children able to choose most appropriate equipment for the task. *able to suggest substitute equipment if most appropriate equipment is not available.	*children use equipment confidently. *children know accuracy is important. *children expect others to use equipment appropriately and accurately. *children able to set up computer sensors unaided.	*children recognize safety implications of equipment. *children offer own strategies for managing safety. *children understand that they are responsible for own safety and safety of others.

ICT as a resource in Science Education

ICT (Information and communications technology) is having an increasing effect on the delivery of the primary science curriculum. Its growth in recent years has been phenomenal. It is now the norm for nursery bases and classrooms to have more than one computer, with some primary schools having a dedicated ICT suite. Both the access to ICT equipment, including computers, calculators, video, tape recorders, etc., and the technology itself has thus greatly improved. The Internet is now regarded as a key to providing both teachers and children with a considerable source of information to support science teaching and learning. Grey (1999) suggests that the Internet now provides such a wealth of information that the problem facing schools has changed from *how do we get information?* to *how do we cope with all the information that's available?* The concern for the student and newly qualified teacher is therefore the management of the use of the Internet. Advice should be sought initially from the ICT coordinator and subject coordinator regarding the use of ICT in science; in addition there are many websites of interest to teachers and children, some of which are listed below.

Ten websites as starting points for using the Internet in teaching and learning:

www.dfes.gov.uk
www.ngfl.gov.uk
www.ase.org.uk
www.letsdiscover.org.uk
www.preschoolrainbow.org
www.welltown.gov.uk
www.mape.org.uk/kids/index.htm
http://grin.hq.nasa.gov/
www.nhm.ac.uk/education/quest2/english/
www.shu.ac.uk/schools/sci/sol/contents.htm

Storage and accessibility of ICT equipment, including software and accompanying documentation, needs to be kept in an efficient and organized manner, which is suited to the age of the children. Establishing a permanent place in the classroom for the computer can reduce disruption to the learning environment. An effective computer area will need:

• a range of software relevant to the current learning taking place,
• information that children might need, in order to use the software effectively,
• support equipment or materials, e.g., note-taking materials.

Audiovisual materials and equipment are also resources that come under the umbrella term of ICT. It is becoming more commonplace for children in the

3–11 age phase to have access to audio tape recorders, digital cameras and videos and materials produced using this equipment. Children therefore need to be taught the skills to use the equipment to record their work and the skills of listening and looking critically at audiovisual materials. An important part of using audio and visual material concerns critical appraisal of the content by the child. Visual material in particular can provide a rich and vivid insight into scientific theories and so children must be encouraged to question what they see and hear. Younger children begin to develop the necessary skills through a descriptive discussion of the content. This leads on to judgements about what people might be thinking or feeling. Older children should begin to question if the audio and visual material may provide only one interpretation and that there may be other, equally or more valid, interpretations. Teachers will wish to preview the resources, in order to assess their suitability for use by the children.

Audio material

Taped accounts
Taped broadcasts
Radio programmes

Visual material

Photographs
Cartoons
Posters
Film/video
ICT simulations

The use of ICT may be considered under two distinct headings – ICT as a teaching resource and ICT as a learning resource – i.e., it is used by teachers to provide teaching materials and by children to enhance their learning.

ICT as a teaching resource

Teachers use ICT as a teaching resource in a variety of ways, e.g., accessing information from the Internet and CD Roms, accessing lesson plans from the Internet, writing lesson plans, making resources for use by children, e.g., card games, access to professional support and for making worksheets and work cards. Worksheets and work cards when well designed, can be a most useful resources to support teaching and learning in science. The distinction between work cards and worksheets is quite clear and shown in the following table.

Work cards	Worksheets
Work cards are laminated and may be used to: • give instructions to the child • reinforce the instructions of the teacher • record observations, notes, etc., during an activity using a wipe on/wipe off pen Work cards are not used as a permanent record of a child's work; any notes made may be used by the child to write up the activity, the work card is then wiped clean and used again. Work cards are more likely to be used in Key Stages 1 and 2 rather than in the Foundation Stage.	Worksheets are printed on to paper and are designed for the child to complete as a permanent record of their work. They can be a useful tool for enabling younger or less able children to record their work on paper, and may be retained for assessment purposes

126

To be most effective, the use of a work card or worksheet must be considered as a part of the teaching strategy used, and not as a replacement for it. They can be used to:

• start and promote talk and discussion amongst pupils,
• help foster children's enquiry skills,
• help foster children's study skills,
• support practical activities, requiring pupils to follow instructions, or acting as an *aide-mémoire* for children,
• stimulate enquiry,
• provide a structure for recording.

Teachers need to ensure that the children easily understand work cards and worksheets. Attention should be paid to the readability of the card or sheet, and to the use of picture clues. The layout and presentation must be of a sufficiently high quality to encourage the children to take care in their completion. Using ICT to produce worksheets ensures that they can be of high quality and may include imported pictures or scanned photographs, in order to be attractive and motivating for children to use.

Although a high quality work card or worksheet can enhance learning in science, this is not assured. In order to ensure the effectiveness of them, students and newly qualified teachers must be aware that:

• Poorly thought out sheets, or an over-reliance on commercial worksheets, is unlikely to lead to high standards of attainment amongst children in science.
• Where worksheets and work cards are used merely as a means of keeping children occupied, or where there is little thought given to what might be learnt through their completion, the resulting work will most likely be meaningless to the children.
• They are no substitute for quality interactions between pupil and teacher, between pupil and pupil and between pupil and equipment.
• The worksheet or work card cannot be questioned, and cannot rephrase or explain things further to children, nor can they praise or recognize effort and/or the eventual outcome.
• Where the majority of science lessons involve the children in completing worksheets, no

matter how well designed and produced, there is a very high likelihood of frustration and boredom setting in for some children.

Work card for the use of a less able Year 3 child

Which objects do you think you can see through?

Hold each object up to the light and record your results with a tick in one of the boxes

---

Object/material	I can see through clearly	I can see through a bit	I cannot see through at all
A brick			
A coloured bottle			
A piece of card			
A piece of tracing paper			
Black plastic			

When you have completed the workcard, copy on to paper with illustrations.

Which objects do you think you can see through?

Make your prediction for each object first. Record with a tick in one of the boxes
Then hold each object up to the light and record your results with a tick in one of the boxes

Object/ material	Prediction/ Test result	Can see through clearly	Can see some light through	Cannot see through at all
A brick	I predict			
	Test result			
A coloured bottle	I predict			
	Test result			
A piece of card	I predict			
	Test result			
A piece of tracing paper	I predict			
	Test result			
Black plastic	I predict			
	Test result			

When you have completed the workcard, copy on to paper with illustrations.

What is the taste?

Plate number   What did it taste of?   Were you correct?
                      Draw a picture of the food

1

2

3

4

5

Worksheet for the use of a more able Year 1 child

Can you find out what these things are by using your senses?

What do you think it is?	What is it?	Were you right?
1		
2		
3		
4		
5		

What senses have you used?_____

Checklist for producing effective work cards and worksheets.

To be effective work cards and worksheets must

- be well laid out and clear
- be motivating to use, with some graphics included
- be easy to understand, with straightforward vocabulary
- not be overloaded with text
- have a clear purpose
- be open-ended or graded to provide for differentiation
- provide for independent and collaborative working
- ask questions such as *how?*, *why?* and *which?* that promote higher order thinking as well as questions which require a factual response

In addition, worksheets for use during visits should

- include questions which involve thinking rather than simply doing
- require different types of response, such as drawing, deciding or estimating
- not contain too many directions
- encourage children to use their senses where appropriate and safe

130

Three key principles for the use of ICT in subject teaching:

1. Decisions about the use of ICT should be based on whether its use supports good practice in teaching the subject;
2. Decisions about the use of ICT in a particular lesson must be related to the learning objective of the lesson;
3. The use of ICT should either allow the child to achieve something they could not have achieved without it or learn something more effectively and efficiently.

Adapted from 'Using ICT to meet teaching objectives in science' TTA (1999)

The use of ICT can enrich and extend learning in the science curriculum, at the same time aiding children to acquire the confidence to use the technology. ICT can be a particularly valuable resource when teaching science to pupils with special educational needs, (see Chapter 8). The term *ICT* is used primarily to refer to the use of the computer, although it also encompasses audio-visual equipment, e.g., tape recorders, cameras etc., these will be considered later in the chapter. ICT offers children opportunities for:

- communicating information and ideas,
- gaining access to information,
- capturing, storing information,
- changing and interpreting information.

There are very many advantages to using ICT in science; however, the basic question that must be asked when considering whether to use ICT is 'is the use of ICT a better method than pencil and paper?' The method therefore being considered must offer advantages over other approaches, if it does not then the use of ICT should be questioned. ICT has the potential to make a significant contribution to children's acquisition of scientific knowledge, skills and understanding. The table overleaf shows where the use of the computer can aid learning in science.

Use of the computer to aid learning in science:

Produce tables, charts and graphs.	Handling data from scientific investigations. Show trends in information.
Spreadsheets	Order information. Show trends in information.
Databases	Handling information.
Data logging	Collecting data.
E-mail	Reporting to an audience. Collecting information.
Internet CD Rom	Researching information. Responding to information.
Graphics	Pictorial record of information.
Word processing	Recording information for a specific purpose, e.g., published in school newspaper.
Digital camera/video	Recording investigations. Recording observations.
Audio tape	Recording/reporting findings to a specific audience.

The Use of Human Resources and Climate Setting

Perhaps the most important resource in teaching and learning in any area of the curriculum are the adults who support pupils' learning in a subject. In addition to the class teacher, there may be a special needs teacher, language support teacher, a nursery nurse, a student, a learning support assistant, a parent helper or other volunteer. Teachers and other adults in the classroom can help to

• foster a sense of security
• reinforce pupils' learning
• act as a role model for children
• model behaviour in science
• provide support for the children
• act as experts in their field

A high adult:child ratio helps to make the most effective use of materials and equipment and can assist in children's learning, primarily through the interaction between the adult and the children. Whilst firsthand experience, using physical resources, plays an important part in pupils' learning so too does high quality and supportive intervention on the part of adults. Bruner's research (Wood, 1998) suggested that children were capable of intellectual achievements at an earlier stage if supported by adult intervention and the use of carefully structured environments. This research built on the ideas of Piaget regarding children's stages of development. Piaget suggested the notion of *readiness*, that if a child found an experience too difficult to comprehend then this indicated that the child was not yet ready to learn (see Chapter 4). Both these ideas indicate the need for teachers to be sensitive to a child's abilities and development, and to be prepared to intervene to facilitate learning. Such intervention may take the form of questioning, guiding and instructing children, in an effort to extend and challenge their thinking. Bruner's model proposes facilitating pupils' progress through the use of appropriate support materials and intervention, providing children with *scaffolding* upon which they can construct increasingly advanced ways of thinking and understanding the world.

cS Case study

In a nursery setting the children were investigating magnets and magnetic materials. Miss P, the nursery nurse, was observing 3 children playing a magnetic fishing game. Amy asked Tom what colour 'fish' he had caught, Tom replied 'Blue'. Amy said she'd caught blue ones too and suggested only blue fish could be caught. Miss P identified this as a critical time in the children's learning, as the children may conclude that either *only* blue objects are attracted to magnets or that *all* blue objects are attracted to magnets, both incorrect. Miss P therefore intervened by asking Adam what colour 'fish' he had caught. Adam said 'red ones and blue ones'. Miss P suggested Amy and Tom try to catch one red 'fish' each. Amy caught a red one but Tom caught a yellow one. Miss P asked the children what colours they had caught so far. Adam correctly identified red, blue and yellow. Amy said she had thought only blue ones could be caught but now she had caught other colours. Through this Amy demonstrated that she was able to question her own thinking, in response to her explorations with scientific objects. Miss P asked the children if they knew how the game worked. Adam said 'The fish stick to the end of the fishing rod'. Tom added 'They stick to the metal bit'. Miss P asked if any of them could remember the name of the metal part, and reminded them it was called a magnet. She asked if they thought they could catch anything else other than 'fish'. The children decided to try to catch other objects in the Nursery with their fishing rods. Miss P was thus employing a series of focused questions to help the children to develop their thinking and to investigate their modified ideas. The children returned to Miss P with a range of small objects that they had 'caught'. Again Miss P used skilful questions to focus their attention on the similarities between the objects, i.e., they were all small, they were made of metal, etc.

The use of the teacher, or other adult, as a source of information for the child cannot be underestimated. It is essential that they are able to present information and ideas to children in ways that gain their attention and focus them on questioning and exploring, the quality of teacher talk therefore plays an important part in motivating and enthusing pupils towards science. Teacher talk is used for

- questioning – to explore children's ideas;
- directing – encouraging children to extend their explorations;
- explaining – painting a verbal picture of models and analogies in science;
- presenting more abstract ideas in science to children;

- eliciting – teacher talk is an important feature of the plenary to a teaching session, the conclusion to the lesson where the lesson objective may be recapped and children's learning explored.

Teachers therefore need to be able to think the content of a lesson through clearly in their own minds, and then be able to initiate and maintain a dialogue with the children throughout the lesson. This style of teaching uses guided discovery to ensure the children's learning is advanced through their own investigation and exploration; the teacher's role is therefore to be the guide, steering children through their development. The teacher needs to be mindful of how they convey information to the children, so that it supports the children's learning rather than information-giving being the focus of a teaching session.

Managing adults in science

Nurseries and schools involve other adults in the classroom, in addition to the class teacher. Most teachers are therefore involved in working with other adults at some stage. Organizing and managing possibly older and more experienced adults can be a daunting task for a student or beginning teacher. This is particularly true for those working within teams, e.g., in the Foundation Stage where the tradition of teamwork in a teaching situation is well developed. When working with children it is usual for Nursery nurses to have very similar roles and responsibilities to those of qualified teachers and yet they do not attract the same level of pay or status. It is therefore important that good, professional relationships are developed and the role of each member of staff within the team is established and clearly defined. Where an adult in the classroom is a voluntary helper, most schools have policies or policy statements that cover issues such as the volunteers' suitability for work with children and the need to maintain confidentiality.

Volunteers in the classroom – statement in a school's handbook

We extend a warm welcome to parents, visitors and friends who wish to support the learning of our children in the classroom. If you would like to assist in school in any way please contact your child's class teacher or the Head. We would like to assure all parents that voluntary helpers will assist the class teacher and work within the policies of the school. We therefore request that all helpers respect our children, assist them as directed by the class teacher and remember that we ask for confidentiality in matters concerning individual children in school.

If you feel you have a particular skill to offer the school please contact the Head. The staff and children look forward to working with you.

Visitors

The introduction of people who can talk about their experiences of science can be very stimulating for children. However, for children to acquire the maximum educational benefit from using human sources of information in this way, both the children and the visitor to the class need to be briefed. They both should have knowledge about the topic and have prepared questions to ask. The visitor may also wish to bring in sources of information with which to support their account.

CS *Case study*

Miss J's Year 5 pupils were studying The Victorians, a history topic with a science focus on materials. Miss J had contacted the local museum curator who agreed to visit the school and be questioned by the children. Miss J informed the curator that the children would be asking questions about the clothes worn by the Victorians and how clothes were washed before washing powders were invented. The curator was therefore able to prepare answers to possible questions by the children and to collect together items of Victorian clothing and washing equipment.

   The children were informed that the visit was going to take place and, working in small groups, they drafted a series of questions to ask in order to find out about the clothes worn and their care.

   The children worked through their questions and the curator was able to provide informed answers. He also demonstrated the Victorian way of washing clothes. This led to a discussion of whether the Victorian method was as good (or better) than the modern way.

   By preparing both the children and the curator, the teacher was able to ensure that the visit was a successful one that led to further learning. The next stage in the topic was to carry out investigations to compare the action of soap with washing powder, the visit led on to the children suggesting this as an investigation without prompting from the teacher.

Making the most of adult support in the nursery/classroom

In order to make the most of adult support in the nursery/classroom it is essential that the class teacher:

- ensures that the classroom is a welcoming place for all;
- uses the school policy on the role of support staff and procedures for briefing them;
- discovers the interests and abilities of potential helpers;
- asks volunteers if they can help on a regular basis, to provide continuity for the children and more satisfaction for the helper;
- avoids stereotyping, e.g., women cooking while men assist children in using the computer;
- involves non-teaching colleagues in planning activities – they need to be clear about what you want the children to learn and how you want them to go about this;
- makes sure that roles and responsibilities are clear – to the children as well as to the adults involved – e.g., classroom discipline, work areas to be supervised.

Partnerships between home and school

A child's education begins at home in the child's early years, and continues throughout the 3–11 phases of education and beyond. Teachers are therefore building on learning that has been begun by a child's parents, and parents are encouraged to carry on as active partners in their child's ongoing learning. The potential benefits of such a partnership are numerous:

- parents can support schools and nurseries by exhibiting positive attitudes towards education in general and science in particular;
- parents are able to become much more knowledgeable about their child's learning and the curriculum, e.g., the role of investigations;
- parents are able to undertake activities with their children that will help to support their learning;
- there may be increased motivation for the child;
- there may be an improvement in behaviour;
- there may be the development of more positive relationships, i.e., the partnership may help to avoid conflict between the home and the nursery/school;
- parents may possess particular scientific knowledge, understanding and skills.

Particularly with respect to science, an effective partnership and liaison between teachers and parents can have much more specific benefits for children's learning than indicated above. The development of positive attitudes towards science (Chapters 2 and 3) is crucial to a child's attainment in the subject area. Where teachers communicate with parents about the nature of the science curriculum, the parents will be in a better position to support their child's achievements in this area. Parents' own ideas about science may be quite negative and relate only to their own secondary school experiences. They may think science is about getting the *right* answer rather that it being a process as well as a body of knowledge. Their own scientific knowledge may be limited or patchy; this may result in the parent feeling unable or unwilling to support their child's learning in this area. It may also be that the parent knows much more than the teacher and thus may be able to offer help and support to the teacher. A partnership may therefore be used for schools and teachers to aid the parent and/or the teacher, to offer strategies and ideas for how parents can support their child's learning in science, and to emphasize the importance of observation, enquiry and analysis in science.

Keeping parents up to date about science in the primary school can be achieved in various ways. Displaying children's work in and around the classroom is an effective way of informing parents of the science being studied. Planning may also be displayed or available; to show the parent what science will be taking place within the ensuing few weeks. Parental involvement can be sought through inviting them into school to share in their children's work or to work with a small group. Parents and carers may also have a specific part to play in supporting science learning at home. This may be initiated by the child or carer, e.g., the child may be studying the conditions for plant growth in the classroom and may request to grow seeds at home, or the parent may suggest visiting the library to research facts about plant growth. A booklet may be prepared for parents on how they can help their children in science. The setting of formal homework tasks is now becoming more commonplace. It is a particularly useful way of both demonstrating the importance of science in the primary curriculum and of actively involving parents in their child's learning. It may be used to extend attainment in school through the provision of additional learning opportunities, although teachers do need to be mindful of both parental concerns and the age and maturity of the children involved. Homework tasks are not constrained by the requirements of the National Curriculum or the Early Learning Goals and so may be used to support a child's learning against the National Curriculum Programmes of Study and/or go beyond these to open children's minds up to a much wider scientific area. Please do remember that requests for parental support, with homework, should show consideration and awareness of the constraints on many parents in terms of both time and money: not every parent, for example, can afford to fund trips and visits or provide access to the Internet. Homework that uses the home and/or home situation as a resource is more likely to both make sense to the child and be facilitated by the parent or carer.

Science homework examples

Foundation Stage:
Draw the person who brings you to school. Label their eyes, ears, mouth and nose.

Key Stage 1:
Write a list of instructions for 'How to brush your teeth'.

Key Stage 2:
Make a list of objects in your house that have a spring in them. What does the spring do? Why does the object need a spring to work?

Resources beyond the nursery or school

An important resource in science, and an additional learning environment, is the space beyond the nursery or classroom. Many teachers make good use of the immediate outdoor area, the local environment and visits further afield. Outside visits offer real opportunities to link nursery and school experiences with the wider world and provide a wonderful stimulus for teaching and learning in science. Using visits to sites outside the school can introduce children to experiences they could not have inside the classroom e.g., observing wild animals in their natural habitat. Such visits therefore can make a significant contribution to the development of pupils' scientific knowledge and understanding, and can offer an insight into the use of science outside the classroom. Outside visits can also offer opportunities for community interactions and for linking the children's nursery and school science work with the wider world.

Starting points for using the local environment to support teaching and learning in science could include:

*A walk to identify different habitats, use of different building materials, etc.
*A visit to a local play area to observe forces in action;
*A visit to the local park to observe the changes in autumn;
*A visit to a health centre to collect information on the body and healthy living;
*A visit to a leisure centre to take part in physical activities;
*Watching a play in the theatre to experience the management of sound, colour and light;
*An exhibition, e.g., space travel at the local museum.

Taking pupils beyond the confines of the nursery or school environment involves careful planning. The teacher needs to consider the nature and purpose of the visit and the health and safety implications. A well-organized and executed visit can inspire and enthuse children about science, with the momentum lasting for a long time, whilst a poorly organized visit with a lack of control (which carries with it potential risks to the health and safety of the children) endangers the children and is unlikely to result in much planned learning, either during the visit or following the visit. Preparation is therefore needed to greatly increase the chances of a successful and safe visit.

Teachers begin by determining the appropriateness of the visit for their children. Younger children may benefit more from planned visits close to the nursery/school, where they are starting from the familiar, whilst older pupils are better able to cope with a longer journey. Local walks may be used to train young children in crossing roads safely before visiting further afield. Local visits also provide the opportunity to establish expectations about *public behaviour*, e.g., staying with designated adults, listening for dangers and instructions, how to deal with other adults. It is important to explain to the children that the standards of behaviour expected outside the school are even more rigorous than those inside the school or nursery, and that this is not just a matter of pleasing the teacher but is necessary for both safety issues and to ensure learning takes place. It must be recognized that once outside the school gates, the children are beyond their normal *closed* environment and consequently they are not so easily observed, held accountable or disciplined. They are also subjected to wider influences and so it may be less easy for teachers to exercise control over the children. In recognition of this there are LEA guidelines on adult:pupil ratios when taking children out of school. The student or newly-qualified teacher has a responsibility for finding out, and working within, the relevant LEA guidelines for the school/Nursery in which he/she is working.

Teachers often pre-visit a site, in order to find out what it has to offer. Things to note on a pre-visit are:

- ease of travel arrangements
- facilities for school visits, e.g., toilets, a classroom area, cloakroom
- availability and readability of labels
- height of displays
- ease of access of displays
- health and safety considerations

Teachers should always conduct a risk assessment prior to an outside visit, setting out any potential dangers facing the children and the measures to be taken to avoid the dangers and thus protect the children. A pre-visit will feed into the writing of the risk assessment, which must be made available to all adult helpers at the site and a copy is to remain on file in the school. When carrying out a risk assessment consideration is given first to *likelihood* of risk and *severity* of risk, and then to the steps to minimize the risks to the children.

Risk assessment

Venue or Activity	Day visit to Mr Straw's house, Worksop.
Contact	The Custodian, 7 Blyth Grove, Worksop, S81 0JG
Date Assessed	17.10.01
Assessed by	Mr Roberts (Year 1 class teacher).
Further information	Staff at Mr Sraw's house are retired teachers.

Hazard	Control measures
Travel	Ensure all children are correctly seated in the minibus and wearing seatbelts. Adult to child ratio, 1:10.
Crossing the road	Adults to ensure road is clear and guide children across.
Children walking around interior of house	1 adult from school + 1 adult from the house to escort groups of 10 children around the house.
Children sketching exterior of house	Private road. Children to be supervised by adults. Children to stay on pathway close to wall of house.
First aid	First Aid kit + inhalers to be retained by Class Teacher. Bassetlaw Hospital nearby if needed.

A pre-visit will provide valuable information for drafting letters to parents dealing with issues such as pocket money, clothing and footwear. The pre-visit will also assist in planning the visit and clarifying the educational purposes for the visit itself. It may be that it is neither possible nor desirable to try to do or see everything at the site, and so the use of children's time may be taken into account during the pre-visit. In addition to considering what learning will take place during the actual visit, where the learning fits in to the science topic being studied as a whole needs to be identified, together with any input to be given by an education officer or guide. Teachers must therefore give some thought to:

- What the children need to know or experience prior to the visit, and to plan for this in both the medium term and short term planning (see Chapter 3);
- The learning experiences to be delivered during the visit and who will deliver them, e.g., the teacher, an expert at the site, a knowledgeable volunteer attending the visit;
- How the children will record their ideas and information gained during the visit;
- The use of worksheets produced either by the class teacher or provided by the site visited. They can be useful in helping to focus attention and structure the collection of information, and can result in a visual as well as a written record;
- The opportunities afforded by the visit for handling objects and/or investigating;
- The opportunities provided at the site for reflection by the children, on what they have experienced.

 *Case Study*

Year group: 4
Visit: Elsecar Science Museum (South Yorkshire)
Purpose of visit: To access exhibits related to weight and gravity

Organization:
Four groups of children
Four activities
Groups to rotate around activities.

Activity	Details of activity	Adult responsible for activity
Activity 1	Investigation of gravity exhibit. Written observations.	Class teacher to supervise each group in turn.
Activity 2	Literacy focused activity. Record/represent given information about scientists/inventors in field of forces.	Learning Support Assistant to supervise each group in turn.
Activity 3	Free time to look more widely at the site and exhibits.	Volunteer parents to supervise groups.
Activity 4	Evaluate and categorize gifts in gift shop.	Volunteer parents to supervise groups.

A further consideration for the teacher is that of preparatory work with other adults accompanying the children. If the adults are expected to support the children's learning, as in the case study above, they do need to be briefed on the purpose, skills, concepts, attitudes associated with the visit, and on their roles on the visit.

 **Case study**

Year group: 4
Visit: Elsecar Science Museum (South Yorkshire).
Purpose of visit: To access exhibits related to weight and gravity.

Information for parents
*The children will leave school at 9.30 a.m. and return at 3.00 p.m.
*No special clothing is required.
*Please bring a packed lunch.
*All belongings may be locked in the museum's schoolroom during the visit.
*The children will work in four groups before lunch and will take part in a workshop after lunch.

You will be working with the different groups, in turn, in the gift shop. Each group is limited to 30 minutes in the shop, looking at gifts that are related to science study (I will point these out to you on the day: they include toy rocket sets, magnetic games, etc.). The children will identify the gifts, draw them, indicate why they are related to science study and categorize them using their own criteria.

Please ensure that the children are well behaved and polite; refer them to me if they do not behave appropriately.

Question the children about the gifts, to help them identify the science focus. You may wish to ask the children:

*the name of the gift
*the purpose of the gift
*how the gift works
*who is the gift aimed at, e.g., a young child, an adult, etc.

Reflective questions

Resources

In managing resources for science do you:

- Plan ahead to ensure that resources for science are available at the right time?
- Select and use a range of up to date, appropriate resources that support active, investigative learning?
- Monitor the use of potentially dangerous resources?
- Restrict pupil access to potentially dangerous resources?
- Ensure the resources are clearly labelled and easily accessible, so that the children know where to find them and where to return them?
- Organize resources for science to encourage children to take responsibility for obtaining them, using them appropriately and looking after them?

- Identify resources needed on medium term plans?
- Ensure that there are sufficient resources for the task in hand?
- Check regularly that resources are well maintained?

Learning environment

In establishing and maintaining an effective learning environment, do you consider:

- The use of the available space when teaching science?
- How the layout of the classroom fosters independence and responsibility in the children?
- The organization of resources ensure accessibility?
- The use and positioning of display?
- The use of quality display material?
- The use of captions, questions and arrowed boxes in display?
- The quality of presentation, e.g., are the display mounts cut straight and even, with square corners?
- The nursery/school guidelines about handwriting, to ensure that any handwriting displayed conforms to the guidelines?
- The use of labels? Are they clear? Are the spellings correct?
- Ensure the children's names are on their displayed work?
- If the display looks too crowded?
- The spaces between work when putting up a display? Remember that the spaces are as important as those occupied by the work.
- The height and level of the display?
- If the display conforms to the school/nursery conventions, e.g., style of mounting, use of colour, use of backing paper?
- The overall impression of the display; is it one of neatness and tidiness or one of sloppiness?

ICT

When planning to use ICT do you:

- Consider how to group the children? Ability groupings, mixed ability or friendship groups?
- Judge ability by ICT capability, reading ability or science ability?
- Consider how many children are able to work with a computer at any one time?
- Timetable the use of the computer?
- Ensure equal time for all on the computer? Is this measured by time or task?
- Ensure that all the children are involved when using the computer? Do they know what their role is?
- Monitor the use of the computer and the children's involvement in the task?
- Monitor the group dynamics from time to time, in the interests of equality of opportunity and personal and social development?
- Monitor and deal with groupings that clearly do not appear to work?
- Ensure the children are able to use the software?
- Use the children as peer tutors to demonstrate the use of software to their peers?
- Ensure equality in sharing successes, talking about their work on the computer and their expertise on the computer?

Using the wider environment

In addition to the statutory risk assessment to be carried out prior to visits into the community, do you consider:

- Is transport needed to the site?
- What route is to be taken?
- What are the safest crossing points, and are there any toilets en route just in case?
- The bus times, stopping places and alternative routes in the event of a non-arrival? Have I told the bus company that we are making the visit?
- What adult support is needed? Desired?
- If the accompanying adults are clear about the arrangements for the visit and their role?
- If the accompanying adults are responsible for a named group of children? Do the children know which adult to report to?
- The resources or equipment needed at the site?
- How the children will record their experiences?
- The information the children need? Do they know where they are going, why and what's expected of them?
- Whether any of the children have special needs?
- Has written permission been sought from the parents or guardians? (No child can be taken out of nursery/school without the parents' permission.)
- Have parents been informed in writing of the details of the visit, e.g., dates, times, lunchtime arrangements, clothing needs?
- Your familiarity with the site? Have you visited the site before or contacted the site by telephone or letter?
- What the domestic arrangements are – where will the children eat, sit, keep dry, and go to the toilet?
- Any particular hazards identified in the risk assessment?
- What the procedures are at the site in the event of an emergency or accident, for example a fire alarm?
- Access to an emergency kit, e.g., first aid, sick bags, 'wet wipes', spare clothing?

143

REFERENCES

Borrows, P. (ed.) (2001) *Be Safe: Some Aspects of Safety in School Science and Technology for Key Stages 1 and 2*, (3rd edn), Hatfield: ASE.

Carle, E. (1986) *The Very Hungry Caterpillar*, London: Hamish Hamilton.

Edwards, A. & Knight, P. (1994) *Effective Early years Education: Teaching Young Children*, Buckingham: Open University Press.

Farndon, J. (2000) *1000 Things You Should Know About Science*, Essex: Miles Kelly Publishing.

Feasey, R. (1998) *Primary Science Equipment*, Hatfield: ASE.

Green, P. (Undated) *Archimedes*, Hart-Davis.

Grey, D. (1999) *The Internet in School*, London and New York: Cassell Education.

Health and Safety at Work Act 1974 (1974), London: HMSO.

Qualifications and Curriculum Authority (1999b), *Early Learning Goals*, London: DfEE/QCA.

TTA (1999) *Using Information and Communications Technology to Meet Teaching Objectives in Primary Science*, London: Teacher Training Agency.

Wood, D. (1998) *How Children Think and Learn*, (2nd edn), Oxford: Blackwell.

SECTION 3

Accountability, special educational needs, equal opportunities and whole school issues

6 Monitoring, Assessment, Record Keeping, Reporting and Accountability

The terms monitoring, assessment, record keeping and reporting are all aspects of accountability and are becoming increasingly important for the primary science teacher. The student or newly qualified teacher must therefore know and understand each term and be able to apply them to their teaching. Monitoring is the term used to describe reviewing what is taught and learned within a classroom and across a whole Key Stage and/or a whole school. It is a crucial part of teaching, as what is learned may be very different to what has been planned! The assessment of children's learning provides valuable information regarding what has been taught and learned, which is used to plan subsequent teaching. Record keeping is essential to monitor what has been delivered, and is used to ensure progression and greater continuity for pupils across a Key Stage or across the age range in school. Reporting the results of assessment ensures that all involved in the teaching process, i.e., the children, the parents, the governors, the LEA, outside agencies, are fully informed of the achievements of the science curriculum being taught.

The chapter begins by expanding on the definition of the term *monitoring* and establishes that assessment, record keeping reporting and accountability are some of the facets involved. It then continues with a consideration of specific issues regarding assessment in science. It addresses what to assess and how to assess it and covers the meaning and use of various assessment strategies – formal, informal, diagnostic, formative, summative, evaluative, criterion-referenced and norm-referenced assessments are all explored. It outlines the practical forms of these assessment strategies, including classroom observations and marking pupil's work. Throughout, examples from the science curriculum are used to illustrate the various strategies for assessment. Included are case studies of whole school assessments and the moderation of assessments. Record keeping provides an important evidence base for teachers to support their assessments; the chapter contains a review of different types of record, again with examples specific to science.

The final section of the chapter focuses on reporting and the issues surrounding accountability. It includes a review of the statutory requirement to record and report children's attainment and offers suggestions on feeding back to children, reporting on pupil progress and reporting on the nature of the science curriculum. This section also provides an overview of target setting, which is now being used in primary science. Target setting takes the results of assessment, matches it to the known expectations of the children for their stage of learning, and is then used to plan future work that will develop the children's learning in science at an appropriate pace. The result of this process provides teachers with a valid base for evaluating their own practice, the science curriculum provided by the school and consequently aids in raising standards.

Monitoring Learning in Science

Monitoring what is taught, and learned, is the first stage in the accountability process. Accountability is becoming increasingly important within the primary sector. Teachers are accountable for the teaching and learning opportunities they provide in the classroom. They are accountable to the Head, the governors of the school, the parents, the LEA and the wider community. Monitoring thus provides evidence for the evaluation of the quality of teaching and learning within the science curriculum. Teaching may be monitored, formally and/or informally, by the class teacher and/or others, including other teachers, the Head, LEA advisers and Ofsted inspectors (see Chapter 9). The aspects of teaching to be monitored focus on the content of planned work and the teaching approaches used. The monitoring of learning has a number of related elements including assessment, record keeping and reporting. It is achieved through an evaluation of the science curriculum as received, in that it considers the intended outcome of a lesson or series of lessons alongside the actual outcome or outcomes. It is therefore achieved through the assessment, and thus the demonstration of, children's learning.

Monitoring learning in science involves

* observing children taking part in scientific activities
* observing children's recording of science
* assessing children's understanding in science
* observing individual science lessons
* self-evaluation of a science lesson
* reviewing class teacher's planning for science
* reviewing planning for science across the Foundation Stage or a Key Stage

Assessment

Assessment is the basic tool that is used to provide reliable information regarding learning in science; QCA (2001a) states that assessment informs '. . . teachers, parents and pupils about how a child is progressing at school'. The results of assessment can be helpful in a number of ways. It can be used to provide feedback on pupil progress, to plan subsequent steps in a teaching programme, and is now to be used to set targets with children, by diagnosing and responding to their difficulties (O'Hara, 2000). It is consequently important for teachers to be able to make sound assessments of pupils' progress, and then to be able to use these assessments to gauge the amount of scaffolding required to support further learning. Assessment can also be used to inform parents and future teachers about children's achievements, and this information on pupil attainment to date can be used to make the transition within and between schools more streamlined.

149

Assessment in science may focus on what a child has learned in a single teaching session, in a unit of planned science work, in a year or within the Foundation Stage or Key Stage. It is important to assess children's attainment in science as a whole; it is not just the pupils' abilities to demonstrate factual knowledge and understanding of scientific concepts, but also for evidence of attainment in relation to the process of scientific enquiry. Within the Foundation setting children are assessed with respect to the stepping stones and the Early Learning Goal of Knowledge and Understanding of the World. When assessing children's capabilities and knowledge and science, teachers may focus on the following areas:

- scientific skills, e.g., measurement, predicting
- scientific concepts, e.g., how sound travels; how electricity flows around a circuit
- scientific knowledge, e.g., the water cycle; the formation of day and night
- attitudes in science, e.g., curiosity, empathy

Assessment takes many forms, and the boundaries between the different forms are not always clearly delineated. It is possible for an assessment to involve a number of forms simultaneously, i.e., an assessment may be identified as criterion-referenced, formative and informal at the same time. A number of forms of assessment are briefly defined and explained below.

Formative and diagnostic assessments

Formative and diagnostic assessments both inform the next stage of the learning in science. Formative assessment is the term for ongoing, everyday assessment that is used to identify achievements made by a pupil, how these can be built upon and the next steps to be taken decided upon. Diagnostic assessments are made by the teacher to analyse and classify learning difficulties, so that appropriate assistance and interventions can take place. The ability to diagnose difficulties accurately is necessary in order to effectively match tasks and differentiation to the teaching activity. Formative assessment therefore establishes where a child has progressed to, whereas diagnostic assessment is concerned with why a child is not progressing. The assessments hence identify *what* the children should be learning and *how* they may learn it, i.e., how you should teach it. Scientific process and scientific content may be assessed using formative and diagnostic assessments, although it is often easier to make judgements about a child's knowledge or understanding of science content than it is to assess a child's ability to find out. However, for effective diagnosis and feedback in science, both these aspects of the curriculum must be assessed.

CS Case study

During a scientific investigation into the waterproofness of fabrics Mrs A was observing a group of four of her Year 3 children working together. Her focus was to assess the children's ability to take accurate measurements during the activity. The group had planned the investigation together and had decided to pour 15ml of water over each piece of fabric in turn and then measure the water that seeped through into the container below the fabric being tested. Each child was to test one fabric, assisted by the rest of the group. Mary, Susan and Peter measured the water accurately before pouring it over the fabric, but needed help to read the divisions of the beaker when the water had seeped through the fabric, as it required reading amounts that were not a whole number. The children were then able to calculate the amount of water absorbed by each piece of fabric. The children had thus met the objective of the lesson, to measure accurately, and now needed further practice on reading scales with intervals of less than 1. The fourth member of the group (Simon) found difficulty in measuring the 15ml of water needed to test the fabric. Mrs A correctly identified the problem as one of number recognition failure. Although Simon knows numbers to 50 he could not recognize the number 15 on the translucent beaker. Mrs A assisted Simon in measuring the water before and after the investigation; he calculated the difference unaided. The assessment thus diagnosed Simon's problems with reading the scale rather than problems with measuring accurately, and led to Mrs A providing more opportunities for Simon to read scales on translucent materials.

Summative assessment

Summative assessments are assessments made at the end of a period of teaching. This may be at the end of a unit of work, a term, a year or a Key Stage. The teacher may thus set activities purely for assessment purposes. These have the advantage of ensuring that the child is fully able to demonstrate their learning overtly, i.e., it is not dependent on the teacher *catching* the evidence of learning through observation or on the child recording the particular evidence needed to make sound assessments, as in the case of formative and diagnostic assessments. Summative assessment tasks may take many forms, from question and answer sessions, discussion, a practical activity or a formal set of questions. Summative assessments result in statements about achievement at a particular point in a child's education and are therefore a *round up* of what a child has achieved. The evidence is thus collected and recorded in a systematic way. The outcomes of summative assessment are used in various ways – by subsequent teachers of the child, by the whole school, by a child's subsequent school (in the case of transition) and as a basis for a formal report to the parents. Summative assessments are hence used as a measure of performance for children, their teachers and others. They are therefore of limited use to teachers in identifying and responding to the learning needs of their pupils on a day-to-day, week by week basis. The primary purpose of summative assessment is not to inform the next step in teaching and learning within a unit of work, this is the role of formative assessment. However, in some circumstances, the outcomes of a summative assessment may be used in a formative manner. This may occur when an end of summer term assessment is used as a starting point for science teaching in the autumn term, i.e., a Year 3 teacher may take the summative statements of the previous Year 2 teacher as a basis on which to plan the depth and range of ensuing science teaching.

CS *Case study*

Mr E's Year 6 class had spent half a term on the properties of materials. He wanted to assess the knowledge the children had gained through the topic and decided to present the assessment as a written, multiple-choice test. This would elicit the ideas the children held and provide practice for the children prior to the end of Key Stage statutory assessment. The results would not be used when planning the next half-term's work, which would focus on Forces.

Materials assessment

Q1. Which of these will heat up quickest if put in a cup of hot tea?

Plastic spoon	Wooden spoon	Metal spoon
☐	☐	☐

Q2. Which cup will feel hottest on the outside when filled with hot tea?

Plastic cup	China cup	Metal cup
☐	☐	☐

Q3. What is the temperature of water when it boils?

0 degrees centigrade   50 degrees centigrade   100 degrees centigrade

☐   ☐   ☐

Q4. Which of these will melt the slowest when heated?

25 grams of butter   25 grams of chocolate   25 grams of toffee

☐   ☐   ☐

Q5. What may happen when the ends of 2 magnets are put together?

They stick together   They push away   They get hot

☐   ☐   ☐

Q6. Which of these objects will be attracted to a magnet?

A glass marble   A steel paper clip   A wooden ruler

☐   ☐   ☐

Q.7 What gas is produced when a candle burns?

Oxygen   Nitrogen   Carbon dioxide

☐   ☐   ☐

Q.8 Which of these substances dissolves in water?

Sugar   Sand   Flour

☐   ☐   ☐

Q9. What method would you use to recover the sand from the water?

Sieving   Filtering   Evaporating

☐   ☐   ☐

Q10. Which of these liquids is an acid?

Vinegar   Soap   Milk

☐   ☐   ☐

Informal and formal assessment

All teachers carry out informal assessments continually. These may involve discussions with a child, classroom observations, spoken comments regarding the child's work or the amount of effort being made. It may also involve impromptu written comments on pieces of work as teachers move around the room. Because of its often unplanned nature, the children's comments and actions may throw up unexpected and unanticipated evidence of learning across a wide area of the curriculum. This type of assessment thereby provides a very wide-ranging evidence base, considered over an extended period of time. Informal assessments become almost second nature to the teacher. They provide information about pupil success and enable the teacher to diagnose learning needs as they occur. They are also used as the basis for a considerable amount of immediate, good quality feedback to pupils.

Formal assessment can only take place when teachers have planned beforehand for it to occur. It will therefore have an intended framework; will occur at a specified time, and the results will be formally recorded. Formal assessment consequently often results in a summative record, even though the data may subsequently be used formatively.

Formal assessment of a Unit of Work – Magnetism

The children, in a Year 5 class, had a series of 3 lessons on magnetism.
The teacher chose to assess the children's learning by giving the children a set of test questions, including the questions below.

What are the ends of a magnet called?
What is repulsion?
What is attraction?
Name two objects that are magnetic.
What is magnetic force?

The formal, summative test above was presented to the children as a quiz. It provided the class teacher with a useful source of information for determining the children's knowledge regarding magnetism. However, the teacher recognized the limitations of using only this approach to the assessment.

- The test could only elicit a small amount of the content covered during the two weeks.
- It was a test of memory rather than one that allowed the children to demonstrate their understanding.
- The test could not provide the teacher with any information regarding the development of the children's scientific skills or attitudes.
- The summative nature of the assessment meant that the teacher did not have the opportunity to respond to apparent misunderstandings and errors as they occurred.
- The teacher also did not have the opportunity to extend or consolidate the work, as the class were moving on to new areas of learning in the following week.

Consequently the teacher concerned had supplemented this formal and summative approach with informal, formative approaches to her assessments during this period. She had observed the children in their investigations and explorations using magnets. The teacher had also engaged in discussing the children's learning with them, by questioning them about their work.

Criterion-referenced assessment

Criterion-referenced assessment is that which seeks to assess pupils' achievement against a set of standards or competences, utilizing increasingly more demanding descriptions to judge and report on attainment. The Early Learning Goals and the National Curriculum level descriptions for science are the main standards used for criterion-referenced assessments for the 3–11 years range. The given criteria can be helpful for teachers to share the purpose of an activity with the children, thereby enabling the children to take more responsibility for their own learning and clarify what they need to do to be successful in the assessment. However, the criteria or statements made in the Early Learning Goals and the National Curriculum Level Descriptions for science do need a certain amount of interpretation by the teacher. To write a set of standards that are universally understood and are unambiguous in their interpretation is not an easy task and so teachers have to engage in *moderation.* Moderation is the term used to describe the process of developing shared understandings about what constitutes attainment against particular statements.

In the example opposite, an independent piece of recorded work by a Year 2 child about everyday appliances that use electricity, the criterion used to assess the work was drawn from the National Curriculum Attainment Targets (DfEE/QCA, 1999a, p. 23, Level 1). The work arose during a topic on *Our School*, the objectives for the lesson centred on recognizing appliances that use electricity to function (DfEE/QCA, 1999a, p. 81, PoS 1a). The recorded work provides some written and pictorial evidence that this child has recognized a range of everyday electrical appliances in this context.

Year 2 work recording *Things that use electricity in school*.

Norm-referenced assessment

Norm-referenced assessment involves making comparisons between the achievements of one child with the achievements of others. The *norms* are, for that reason, intended to describe the average or typical performance in that assessment only. Norm-referenced assessment differs from criterion-referenced, in that the standards to be attained are not necessarily the standards dictated by the National Curriculum or the Early Learning Goals. Norm-referenced assessments are used to make judgements about science teaching and learning by a particular group of children. It is useful where the children are particularly bright, and therefore functioning significantly above the expected level of attainment for their age, or are progressing in their learning but are achieving significantly below the expected level of attainment for their age. The children may be progressing in much smaller steps than are identified in the National Curriculum and norm-referencing may be needed to identify this learning. It may also be that the science work being assessed does not appear in the National Curriculum or the Early Learning Goals. The examples below and opposite are of two pieces of Year 2 science work. The children had been observing a pan of boiling water. The lesson built upon the children's observations of an ice cube melting. The comparison of the two pieces of work concluded that both pupils were able to demonstrate some factual knowledge about the change of state and were able to describe some key features of boiling. The comparison did however show that child A was better able to understand that the *bubbles* contained steam which subsequently left the pan.

Child A

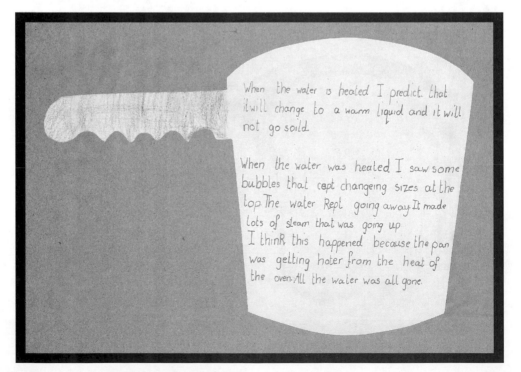

When the water is heated I predict that it will change to a warm liquid and it will not go soild.

When the water was heated I saw some bubbles that cept changeing sizes at the top. The water kept going away. It made lots of steam that was going up.
I think this happened because the pan was getting hoter from the heat of the oven. All the water was all gone.

156

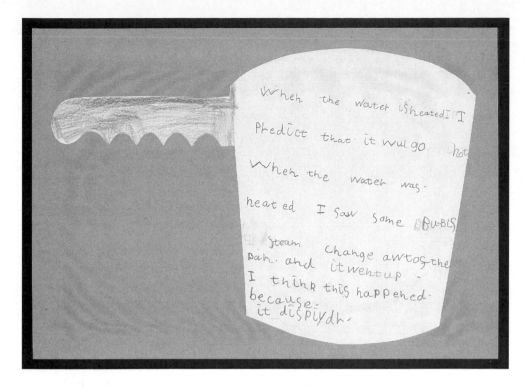

When the water isheatedI I
predict that it wul go hot
When the water was
heated I saw some Bubls
Steam change awtog the
pan. and it wehtup
I thihk this happened
because
it dispiydh

Baseline assessment

Baseline assessment is a unique assessment in the 3–11 age range. Currently it is carried out in the first few weeks of the Reception year, although following the introduction of the Foundation Stage the timing and structure of Baseline is to change. At the time of writing, Baseline is used to determine the children's attainment before any teaching in a formal setting. However, the Foundation Stage now covers teaching and learning for children aged 3–5 years and so the Baseline assessment may be considered to be inappropriate at this stage in a child's learning; it may be more appropriate for the assessment to be carried out at the end of Reception, prior to the child moving into Key Stage 1. The current arrangements are therefore to be replaced by a new national assessment for the Foundation Stage in the academic year 2002–2003. The new assessment will be known as the Foundation Stage Profile (QCA 2001b, p. 5) and will assess children's progress and achievements with respect to the Early Learning Goals at the end of the Foundation Stage. An end of Foundation Stage assessment would then be summative in nature and reflect the learning carried out under the umbrella of Knowledge and Understanding of the World. At the time of writing, therefore, Baseline assessment is used as a formative and diagnostic tool for Reception teachers, who use the results of the assessment to plan their teaching and the learning required by the children. The results are also used in the process of target setting, as explained later in the chapter.

The baseline assessments currently lean heavily towards personal and social development and literacy and numeracy, although they are also expected to consider the wider curriculum and so are relevant to the science aspect of the Foundation Stage curriculum, i.e., through Knowledge and Understanding of the World. The Early Learning Goals are the end of Foundation Stage expectations; the steps towards the expectations are categorized as Stepping Stones, as in the example below (DfEE/QCA, 2000a).

Stepping stones			Early Learning Goal for exploration and investigation.
Explore objects. Show an interest in why things happen and how things work.	Sort objects by one function. Talk about what is seen and what is happening.	Notice and comment on patterns. Show an awareness of change.	Look closely at similarities, differences, patterns and change. Ask questions about why things happen and how things work. (Adapted from DfEE/QCA 2000a, p. 88)

Baseline assessment is carried out mainly through observation. The table below shows how children's responses to ongoing activities in the Reception class may provide evidence for attainment against the stepping stones.

Child's response to activity	Stepping stone/Early Learning Goal
Children, with adult support, show some awareness of the world around them.	Explore objects. Show an interest in why things happen and how things work.
Children show an interest in features and changes in the world around them, in both the natural and the made world.	Sort objects by one function. Talk about what is seen and what is happening.
Children observe and explore the natural and the made world independently. Children show some awareness of similarity, pattern and change.	Notice and comment on patterns. Show an awareness of change.
Children explore and recognize features of living things in the natural and made world. Children look closely at similarities, differences, pattern and change.	Look closely at similarities, differences, patterns and change. Ask questions about why things happen and how things work.

Evaluative assessment

Evaluative assessment is used in order to appraise and influence school policies and planning on a wider scale than the subsequent planning by individual teachers. It is used to determine whether the overall aims of a unit of teaching in science, i.e., a series of related science lessons, are appropriate for the pupils, and whether the unit is effective in achieving those aims. *Evaluation* indicates making a judgement of some kind, for example, about the quality of resourcing for science, the appropriateness of particular teaching methods and/or learning strategies. Such judgements are based on information obtained through assessment, as assessment of actual outcomes provides a much more valid base for policy decisions than the use of impression or anecdote. Evaluative assessment therefore can be used to:

- determine the effectiveness of the school policy for science,
- determine the effectiveness of the school Scheme of Work for science,
- measure the extent of the breadth and balance of the science curriculum provided by the school or nursery,
- ensure progression and continuity in children's learning as they move through the school from the Foundation Stage, into Key Stage 1 and on to Key Stage 2.

Evaluative assessment

With the introduction of literacy and numeracy strategies into the school, a review of the time spent on science in Key Stage 2 was needed. Under the leadership of the subject coordinator, staff considered both pupil achievement and curriculum coverage. The evaluation resulted in the decision to timetable two sessions per week for the delivery of science. It was believed that this change would improve levels of attainment and ensure better curriculum coverage across the Key Stage. It would ensure time was spent on the teaching of scientific enquiry and the content aspect of the National Curriculum Order for science. This change in policy represented a move from the previous approach to science that relied on science-focused topics being taught at intervals across the key stage.

Assessment strategies

Having explored different forms of assessment (see above), the student or newly qualified teacher needs to consider how to use the various forms in practice. In order to do this there are three questions to answer:

- what is being assessed?
- what will be the criteria for success?
- what will be the mode or method of assessment?

What is being assessed?

When planning to make an assessment the teacher must be quite clear about what they are assessing. Many skills and/or understandings may be demonstrated in a learning session, including unanticipated outcomes, but not all will be assessed. It is the teacher's stated learning objective which determines what is being assessed, e.g., a certain skill, knowledge and/or understanding of a specific concept. For each learning objective the assessment opportunities provided need to be identified, as in the example below.

Year Group: **6**
Topic: Electricity

Learning objective	Learning activity	Assessment
To know that electrical components can be represented by specific symbols.	*Make an electrical circuit using the equipment provided. *Draw a sketch of the circuit. *Re-draw the circuit using the given component symbols.	Is the child able to draw a circuit diagram for a series circuit using component symbols?

What will be the criteria for success?

The assessment opportunity is most often posed as a question to which the answer is *yes* or *no*. Both the lesson objective and the assessment must therefore be clearly stated and easily measurable. The criterion for success is the benchmark for meeting the learning objective, i.e., it is the attainment necessary to demonstrate that the child being assessed has achieved the learning objective. The criteria may be set by the class teacher, the subject coordinator or be determined by the Early Learning Goals or the National Curriculum requirements, depending upon the nature of the assessment (as discussed above). For the example used in the previous section, the assessment opportunity is stated thus: Is the child able to draw a circuit diagram for a series circuit using component symbols? The criterion for success may be stated as:

❖ To draw a circuit diagram for a series circuit
   with at least three component symbols used correctly.

If children include three or more symbols correctly then they have met the learning objective; below three and they have not met the objective. The criterion for success may therefore be posed as a question for the teacher – How will you know if the children have achieved the learning objective? The table opposite gives further examples of how criteria for assessment are matched to learning objectives.

Learning objectives	Criteria for assessment
To ask questions about why things happen (ELG)	The children ask at least 2 questions about plants in the school garden.
To recognize that some materials are found naturally (KSI)	The children sort 8 materials into natural and man-made groups. At least 6 materials are correctly sorted.
To know the part played by evaporation and condensation in the water cycle (KS2)	The children correctly annotate a given picture with the terms evaporation and condensation.

What will be the mode or method of assessment?

The mode or method of assessment is also stated at the planning stage. It is important to use a range of strategies for assessment, to allow for all children to demonstrate their progress in science, irrespective of their abilities in other areas of the curriculum. A child may have an excellent understanding of a particular science concept but lack the writing skills to demonstrate it during a written assessment; it is therefore essential that the student and beginning teacher develop an understanding of a variety of modes of assessment. The main strategies used for assessment in science are classroom observations, marking pupils' outcomes (models, pieces of writing, drawings, paintings, tables, charts, ICT work, etc.) and set assessment tasks.

Summary of terms

Term	Definition	Example
Learning objective	The purpose of the teaching session.	To be able to draw conclusions from the results of an investigation.
Learning activity	What the children will be doing in the teaching session.	Carrying out an investigation into ice cubes melting in different areas of the classroom.
Assessment opportunity	An opportunity to assess a skill, attitude, knowledge or understanding held by a child. The opportunity is present in the activity.	Can the child draw conclusions from the results of his/her investigation?
Criterion for success	How the teacher knows if the child has met the objective.	At least one reference to previous science knowledge is included in the conclusion.
Mode of assessment	What outcome or piece of work you will assess.	Teacher participation in activity. Observe/listen to discussion by children of results.

Classroom observations

Teachers carry out classroom observations continuously throughout the day. These observations are frequently an informal and often unnoticed part of the ongoing interactions that occur in the nursery or classroom. Such observations are used to keep a check on children's progress and, as such, they are an integral part of a teacher's work with the children. They are essential for the continuous assessment of children's knowledge, skills and understandings. Not all science work carried out by children results in a piece of retainable evidence; the way in which children respond to an activity and are able to discuss their thoughts or interacts with a group may yield much more confirmation of their achievement than a written recording of their experiences. Classroom observation is therefore an essential assessment tool for children working individually or within a group; it is particularly useful for establishing the individual contributions made within a group task. It may be assumed that the strategy requires passivity on the part of the teacher; the reality is that it is a far more active process, and involves more than just sitting and watching. Classroom observation may also be used to support more formal assessments and be structured to assess learning against a particular aspect of the National Curriculum. In order to formalize the strategy, it needs to be both planned and focused, as noted in the introduction to this aspect of assessment.

Throughout the consideration of assessment of children's attainment it has been noted that assessments need to be reinforced with further information from other sources. It is more helpful if the children are made aware of the purposes for both the task and the assessment, as explaining what you are going to be observing gives the children the chance to demonstrate what they know or what they can do. However, the reaction of a child to a question, and the initial response, is not necessarily an accurate or reliable guide to knowledge and competence (SCAA, 1997). In the same way, observations of actions and behaviour can be misinterpreted. Consequently teachers need to reinforce their observations through careful questioning, discussion and/or further observations. Discussing activities with children is a crucial aspect of classroom observation, as it may lead to:

- evidence of a child's success;
- the identification and diagnosis of learning difficulties;
- a monitoring of progress over a period of time;
- the development of an insight into the ways in which a particular child learns and works.

The use of classroom observation is appropriate across the 3–11 age range. In the Foundation Stage the strategy provides the main source of attainment data. The observations involve the whole nursery and reception teams – teachers, nursery nurses, learning support assistants (LSAs), childcare assistants (CCAs), etc. Under the guidance of the teacher the team is able to focus on observing and talking with groups and individuals of pupils. Notes of such observations and conversations may be recorded during the teaching session, using a focus sheet, like the one opposite.

Foundation Stage practitioners, members of the nursery and/or reception team, may thus also use the focus sheet to identify future learning needs.

Focus sheet

Week:_____ Day: _____ Practitioner: _____

Activity: _____

Learning Objective: _____

Children's names	Comments	Future learning

In the primary school, where non-teaching support is either limited or non-existent, the strategy of observation requires the teacher to have particularly good classroom organization and management skills. The teacher needs not only to be able to concentrate on the small group or individuals being assessed, but also be aware of the rest of the class and their needs. A failure to cater effectively for their needs could lead to interruptions by the rest of the class, as they need to seek permission, mediation, instruction, advice and/or adjudication.

Summary of planning to assess science through classroom observation

- Identify assessments to be made.
- Do not try to assess children against large numbers of learning objectives, it is important to have a clear, focused and manageable objective or set of objectives.
- Do not try to collect assessment evidence for large numbers of children simultaneously through observation and discussion.
- Identify observations to be made/recorded, e.g., watching children's actions, listening to their conversation, listening to their presentations of work such as reading out their work or question and answer sessions.
- Make the maximum use of non-teaching support in the classroom, giving all information necessary to ensure assessments can be made, i.e., what is the role of the non-teaching support?
- Plan low-intervention tasks for children not being assessed.
- Assessment through formal classroom observation does not necessarily mean that the teacher is with the child/children being assessed at all times.

- Plan your intervention with the child/children. The assessment may take place through an independent activity, a teacher-supervised activity or a group discussion.
- When assessing a group of children, plan if you are to visit each child in the group in turn or the group as a whole, if you are to visit the group at regular intervals throughout the activity or at fixed points throughout the activity. Whichever option is chosen it is important to ensure that there will be sufficient time given to gather the necessary information required.
- It is important that the teacher considers the amount of their involvement with the task and how this will affect the assessments made.

 ## Key Stage 1 – Case study

Miss J's year 1 class were working on the role of drugs as medicines. Miss J wanted to assess if the children knew that all medicines were drugs of some sort. Within the classroom Miss J had set up a role-play area as a doctor's surgery. Miss J planned to assess the children's knowledge as they used the role-play area in groups of four. She set the criterion for success to be that the child must make a statement relating to medicines as drugs during the focused play. Miss J planned to observe the children at intervals during the teaching session and to involve herself with the play as a group member if needed. Other activities carried out during this time included observational drawings of medicine bottles and packaging, independent writing about a visit to the doctor and listening to stories on the headsets. All these activities required only minimal intervention by the teacher, thereby allowing Miss J to concentrate on the role-play area.

The children – Amy, Sam, Daniel and Faith – organized themselves in the role-play area. Amy took the role of the doctor, Faith the receptionist and Sam was Daniel's father. Miss J observed Sam and Daniel booking in and giving brief details about the reason for the visit, 'He's got a pain in his head.'

Faith filled out the necessary forms and took the boys to see the doctor. The doctor examined Daniel and pronounced that he had 'a bad case of 'flu'. Miss J observed that the boys were about to leave the doctor and heard Faith insist that they would all change places. Miss J asked Doctor Amy if there was anything she could do to help Daniel. Amy said she could give him some ointment and instructed Faith to go and get it. She returned with a package and gave it to Sam. 'Do you need to ask how to use it Sam?' asked Miss J. Sam asked the question. This led to all the children discussing how it should be applied. 'You need to put it on during the day,' offered Faith.

'You should say three times a day,' said Daniel, 'that's what doctor's say.'

'Why do they say that?' asked Miss J.

'Because it's medicine,' added Sam.

'You have to be careful 'cos its like a drug,' contributed Amy, 'and drugs are dangerous.'

'Are all drugs dangerous Amy?' asked Miss J.

'Yes,' replied Amy.

'No,' replied Sam, 'Not if the doctor says so.'

The children became distracted with the conversation and so Miss J suggested they carry on by changing roles.

When Miss J next visited the children their conversation had moved on and they were discussing what their mums gave them if they had a pain. Through listening to this conversation Miss J had evidence that all the children were aware of the dangers of medicines and clearly knew that medicines were drugs.

Assessing children's work

Following a science lesson where there are recorded outcomes, e.g., written work, a chart, a model or drawing, these outcomes may be used to assess the extent of a child's learning. As discussed earlier in the chapter, the work can first be assessed against the written learning objective on the short-term planning sheet, and then against the National Curriculum Level Descriptions or the Early Learning Goals. A collection of such pieces of work can illustrate a child's attainment over time and may be used as a benchmark for the assessment of others. Benchmarking requires the teacher or the school to collect exemplar material such as previous examples of children's work as a way of indicating the level of work expected from a particular group of children. Benchmarking is used in two ways:

- To aid the teacher in trying to determine the *levelness* of a particular piece of work.
- To assign a level of achievement to a particular child. In order to do this, more than one piece of work is usually required, to show the majority of points stated in a National Curriculum Level Description or the Early Learning Goal.

The examples below show a collection of three pieces of a Year 5 child's work on light and the eye (in Physical Processes). Together they can be used to provide evidence of attainment in science and to assign a National Curriculum Level to the child. The three short pieces each show that the child is able to '. . . use some abstract ideas in descriptions of familiar phenomena'. And is thus functioning at Level 5. (DfEE/QCA 1999a, p. 23)

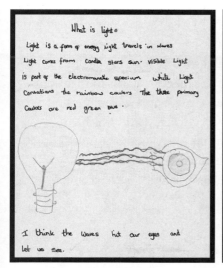

The work shows evidence of awareness that objects are seen when they enter the eye.

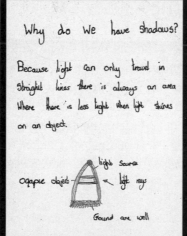

The work shows evidence of an understanding of how shadows are formed.

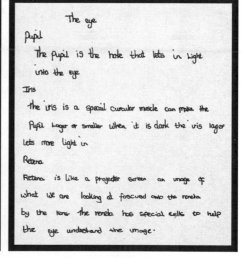

The work shows evidence of an understanding of how the eye works.

When assessing concrete outcomes the work may be assessed in conjunction with teacher: pupil discussions or classroom observations. It is important to recognize that concrete products alone may not provide sufficient and/or conclusive evidence of attainment. The recorded work may be incomplete in terms of the child's knowledge and understanding and a child's ability in science may be masked by difficulties with English, mathematics or art. It may be difficult to identify the features of a piece of work which indicate achievement and so it may be necessary to support judgements made on the basis of outcomes with reference to classroom observations of the process or discussions of the work with the child. Where assessments are supported by classroom observation the teacher's notes and comments made during the observation need to be attached, as these notes will form an important part of the evidence base for reporting pupil progress to parents (see later in the chapter). By sharing exemplar material with children it may provide the pupils with insights into the standards and expectations for their own work. In turn this may act as a spur to greater effort and higher achievement. Involving children actively in the process of assessment, through discussion of exemplar material and their own work in science, can be very helpful in enabling children to gain an insight into their own progress, strengths and weaknesses and can provide a useful starting point for setting targets for future learning, as discussed in more detail later in the chapter. This aspect of assessment can therefore provide immediate feedback on a child's progress, particularly for the older child, and inform future planning and teaching in science, by diagnosing and responding to difficulties.

Record Keeping

Record keeping – of what has been taught and learned – is used to ensure progression and greater continuity for pupils, across a Key Stage or across the age range in school. Recording pupils' coverage of the science curriculum, and of their attainment, provides an important evidence base for teachers with which to support their judgments, which are then reported, using the guidelines to be found later in the chapter. The recording of children's learning and experiences is therefore an essential part of the assessment and evaluation process. Such records are used for a variety of purposes, as in the table opposite.

Purpose	Example
To record past performance which is then used as the starting point for future teaching and learning.	Record of session evaluations.
To ensure that children are not repeating the same scientific content at the same level in subsequent classes.	Record of the exact content of a teaching session.
To monitor pupil progress over time, by illuminating patterns or problems.	Record of children's summative assessments.
To inform discussions with children on target setting.	Record of children's formative assessments.
To inform future teachers about a child's progress, needs, interests and capabilities.	Record of informal and formal assessments.
To facilitate transition within and between schools.	Record of children's summative assessments.
To provide an accurate and up-to-date profile of individual children's learning.	Record of informal and formal assessments.

Records of teaching

Records of teaching include all planning notes and records of the work carried out by the children. Planning notes (see Chapter 3) provide a record of the coverage of science in terms of the timing and content of the science work. All planning notes – long-term, medium-term and short-term lesson plans – form part of this record. Short-term lesson notes often include evaluations and show where they have been modified or adjusted in response to prior learning; this provides further evidence of how assessment has been used to inform future teaching. Records of work carried out by the children are another method of recording coverage of the science curriculum. This type of record enables teachers to record the activities and/or the objectives that their pupils have experienced or completed in science. The most popular form of this record is a tick list. Tick lists, like the example overleaf, are relatively quick and easy to use but do not necessarily indicate levels of achievement. They can be made more informative by using a colour-coded system, where red indicates below average performance, yellow average and green above average performance. It may be appropriate for the teacher to use the colour code or the children may use it to record effort within an activity.

Record of children's work

Name	Ask a question to be investigated	Plan how to find answer to a question	List sources of information needed to help with answering a question	List equipment needed for an investigation	Plan measurements/observations to be taken	Identify how the test will be made fair	Design own recording sheet for an investigation	Make a prediction

A = absent — = task not to be done (may be differentiated task or extension task)   / = task started
X = task completed   R = little understanding   O = partial ability/understanding   G = fully understands

Records of learning

It is a requirement that all schools and nurseries keep up-to-date records of children's progress and achievements; however, it is not feasible for the teacher to either remember all the observations they have made, or to record them all. The teacher therefore has to make judgements about what is appropriate to record. Written comments made during and after scientific activities may provide valuable evidence in terms of a child's learning, particularly for teachers working within the Foundation Stage. Younger children produce less in the form of concrete outcomes and so much of the evidence of the children's learning and development will be ephemeral in nature. Consequently, observation notes and teacher comments will form an important part of the record. These notes and comments may be formal or informal and may take many forms, e.g., recorded in a notebook, on a post-it note or in the form of a review on a planning sheet. The notes should indicate the level of achievement of the individual child, of a group, the success of an activity and may also record other incidents and observations that occur. As children get older and develop greater skills, they begin to produce larger quantities of concrete evidence that may be used to support teacher judgements; these are often retained in a portfolio of learning.

A portfolio is a collection of children's work that indicates attainment against given objectives. The work retained may be the original work, a photocopy or a photograph; it should arise from a broad range of activities in science and reflect the children's achievements across the science curriculum. It may be appropriate to involve the children in compiling their portfolios, by encouraging them to select their own examples and evidence for inclusion, in discussion with the teacher. The amount of work retained needs careful consideration; above all the portfolio must be manageable yet provide enough evidence for judgements to be made. Too narrow a range of work results in an impoverished evidence base; a wider range increases the chances of making accurate judgements concerning the children's capabilities. Portfolios also ought not to be full of out-of-date work. Reviewing the evidence base from time to time with children can be useful as a way of encouraging children to take a greater responsibility for their own learning, and to be involved in self-assessment, as pieces of work are superseded by subsequent and better examples.

A portfolio of evidence of children's learning in science may include

- teacher notes and comments
- drawings or sketches
- computer printouts
- written work
- graphs, charts and timelines

- photographs
- models
- diagrams
- paintings
- diaries
- plans
- posters

Whatever method or combination of methods is used in record keeping, recording coverage of the science curriculum and subsequent learning, it is important that teachers exercise a professional judgement about what to record and do not generate needless paperwork. The key to what to record is to consider its use in determining the relevance of the planned curriculum in science, a child's attainment in science and the needs of future learning. If it is not to be of use to these areas of teaching and learning, it is not worth recording. As indicated above, it must also be recognized that the level of recording – particularly short-term recording – may well vary depending upon the age of the pupils concerned.

Reporting and Accountability

There is a legal requirement for schools to inform parents and other interested parties of pupils' attainments, both individual attainment and the attainment of groups. (QCA 2000b, QCA 2001b). Reporting the results of assessment thus ensures that all involved in the teaching process, i.e., the children, the parents, the governors, the LEA and outside agencies, are fully informed of the achievements in the science curriculum.

Review of the statutory requirement to record and report children's attainment

The Head:

- Is to select a Baseline assessment scheme from the list of accredited schemes. The school's Governing Body makes the formal adoption of the scheme and informs the LEA.
- Ensures all children aged 4 or 5 must be assessed.
- Ensures all assessment data is given to the LEA, who will submit it to QCA.
- Identifies the children to be assessed at the end of Key Stages 1 and 2.
- Provides assessment results for the school's governing body.
- Provides assessment results for the LEA.
- Ensures that a summary of teacher assessment and test results in English and maths for all 7 year olds and in English, maths and science for 11 year olds is published in the school prospectus and governors' annual report, alongside comparative figures for the previous year.

- Ensures parents of all children (in all year groups) are provided with written reports on their child's progress.
- Ensures parents are provided with the opportunity to discuss their child's progress at least once a year.
- Ensures statutory requirements for the transfer of records between schools are carried out.

There are three strands to reporting and accountability:

- reporting to children
- reporting to parents
- reporting to other agencies

Reporting to children

Reporting to children involves the teacher in providing constructive feedback to the children on their efforts and attainment in science. This form of reporting may be informal or formal. It may be informal as much assessment in the classroom is informal, taking place every minute of every day in most nurseries and schools. It therefore takes place within the normal exchanges between children and adults; the teacher will give the child accurate, helpful and motivating feedback at the appropriate time. Such feedback needs to be given with regard to both verbal and non-verbal messages – oral and written feedback, body language, facial expressions and gestures – all of which can be used to reinforce and emphasize the messages given to children about their achievements and what they need to focus on in the future. Formal feedback to children is often in the form of marked work. Marking is an important (although sometimes time-consuming) aspect of teaching, which enables the teacher to provide written, practical feedback to pupils together with assessing where a child may need to go next to further their learning. It assists the teacher in monitoring what the children have done, what their learning needs are and any misconceptions the children may hold (see Chapter 4). Marking also sends a valuable message to the children about the importance of their work. If marking is carried out as the children are working, important issues may be dealt with as they arise, either where a child has explained a concept particularly well or where difficulties understanding a concept are arising. However, where there may be 30 or more pupils in a class, it is unreasonable to expect the teacher to be able to mark all children's work during a teaching session and be able to discuss the children's current work with them. This is especially true at the upper end of the age range where the children are more likely to produce increasing quantities of work.

- always be positive in written or verbal comments
- comment on at least one aspect of the work which shows progress from prior work or is particularly pleasing
- provide feedback which supports the children in improving and developing their knowledge, skills and/or understanding
- identify a target for the child to work on during future lessons
- refer back to the learning objective and comment on progress towards the objective
- praise children publicly within the class, specifying what you are praising – effort and/or achievement.

172

Reporting to parents

In nurseries and primary schools, where there is often a high level of day to day contact between teachers and parents, a great deal of informal and ongoing reporting takes place on a daily basis. Regular parent–teacher contact also provides insights into home circumstances, needs of the family and may contribute to parents' understanding of science in 3–11 settings. Such day-to-day meetings can thus be used as a two-way reporting system, offering both teachers and parents an opportunity to share information about the child's learning. Parents and carers have a particularly valuable part to play in pupil assessments of the youngest children, as they have a considerable amount of knowledge about their children that may enable the teacher to build up a more rounded picture of the child; whereas the teacher may report on the ongoing progress of the child within the Early Years setting. The Early Years teacher therefore needs to build up a supportive and sharing relationship with the child's parents or carers, in order to encourage them to share their knowledge and understand their role in the assessment process. Such a relationship is built up through the provision of opportunities for structured dialogue between parents/carers and teachers regarding the pupils and their progress. During the discourses between parents/carers and the teacher, the parents need to be reassured that the information they are supplying is for positive, helpful reasons and will not be used to discriminate against their child in any way. They also need to be made aware that in instances where special educational needs are identified (see Chapter 7), some of the information they give may have to be passed on to other professionals involved in the education and welfare of young children.

Teachers need to be professional in developing a home/school partnership by:

- ensuring parents feel welcome in the classroom
- explaining the ongoing work in the classroom
- taking advice from parents regarding their child
- working cooperatively with parents

Case study of informal reporting to parents

The Reception children sign into the classroom daily, by writing their names on a piece of paper that is folded and 'posted' in the class post box. Parents and carers are invited to help the children each morning. Ian's mum often talks to Miss R, the Reception teacher, about Ian's involvement in the class as she feels that Ian is shy and quite reticent in the classroom. Ian's mum asked Miss R about the autumn leaves 'game' he had played the day before. Miss R was delighted that Ian had talked to his mum about the game, as he had not discussed it with her. Miss R was able to tell his mum the game had involved ordering autumn leaves by their colour, from green to brown, and discussing why the colours were different. Ian had ordered the leaves well but did not contribute to a discussion about the colours. Miss R was therefore unclear about the extent of Ian's learning. Ian's mum informed Miss R that Ian had enjoyed the game and wanted to play it at home. He had said he needed lots of leaves, some old and some new, that had different colours on them. Ian's mum hadn't understood what he meant by old and new, however Miss R interpreted this as being leaves still living on the tree and ones which had fallen.

The case study illustrates how the home/school partnership enabled the teacher to report on Ian's work and progress in school, and use the information provided by the parent in assessing his learning.

Displaying medium-term and short-term planning in or immediately outside the classroom where it can be seen can be used to open dialogue between parents and carers about children's ongoing work and achievements and thus aid the development of appropriate home/school partnerships.

Formal reporting to parents takes place at parents' evenings and through an annual written report on their child's performance and achievement during the year. Schools have a statutory responsibility (QCA 2001b) to keep records on children that include the results of any national tests taken, and to provide an opportunity for parents to discuss their child's progress on at least one occasion within the academic year. There is no statutory format for parents' evenings and so they take different forms, e.g., an appointment time may be issued to individual parents or it may be organized as a 'drop-in' evening where parents attend at a time to suit themselves. There are many considerations to be made when arranging a parents' evening:

- The timing of the evening needs to be mindful of the constraints parents find themselves under, e.g., work patterns or care for other children;
- The amount of time given to each set of parents needs to guarantee the opportunity for meaningful dialogue, whilst ensuring all parents are able to speak with the teacher;
- The provision of an area where parents are able to look at examples of the children's work in science while they are waiting to see the teacher;
- The provision of an area where one set of parents is able to discuss their child quietly and without interruptions;
- The number of parents in or outside the classroom needs to allow for an atmosphere that is conducive to positive and productive communication between the teacher and parent.

In addition to the formal, verbal reporting at parents' evenings, every parent whose child is of statutory school age is entitled to an annual written report on their child's performance and achievement during the year. Reports are required to contain brief comments on the child's progress and achievements in each subject or area of learning studied as part of the school curriculum. The comments should be in the form of a series of short statements that outline a child's successes and his/her areas of weakness, as shown in the examples below. The report should contain information on a pupil's general progress that includes behaviour, attitude, academic attainment and attendance.

Examples of science comments made in annual reports to parents

Foundation Stage: Reception

Pupil name: _____ **School Year: 1999-00 (Reception)**
Knowledge and Understanding of the World: Peter displays an obvious interest in this area of the curriculum. He handles natural objects with care and asks appropriate questions. He is also able to extend his learning by suggesting further, related activities he could carry out. Peter now needs to work on sustaining his concentration within a given activity.

Key Stage 1: Year 2

Pupil name: _____ **School Year: 1998-99 (Year 2)**
Science: Amy is now able to make a prediction before carrying out an investigation. She is able to explain the reasons for her prediction. Amy is able to relate her results to her prediction, stating whether her prediction was 'right' or 'wrong'. Amy continues to be able to make a series of observations throughout an investigation and now needs to develop her ability to take a series of measurements, when appropriate, during an investigation.

Key Stage 2: Year 6

Pupil name: _____ **School Year: 1998-99 (Year 6)**
Science: John has worked hard this year to develop his skills in planning and carrying out scientific investigations. He is now able to consider the investigation needed to answer questions posed by the teacher. He can suggest the equipment needed to carry out his plan and works logically through his plan. John now needs to work on drawing conclusions from his results.

Reporting to other agencies

As noted on page 170, assessment data relating to science from Baseline and Year 6 statutory assessments is made available to the LEA, QCA, the school's governing body and parents. The data is provided alongside comparative data, thus comparing the school's performance to that of other schools and that of previous years. The data published is collective, i.e., individual children's achievements are not noted; reporting to other agencies therefore provides a means of accountability about the science curriculum delivered in school.

Target setting

Target setting is currently becoming more important in primary schools and thus in primary science. There is a statutory requirement (QCA, 2000b) for schools to set annual targets for the performance of children aged 11 years in the end of Key Stage 2 National Curriculum assessments. Governing bodies are responsible for setting and publishing the school's targets. In view of this, some schools are starting to use target setting to plan a child's progress through school. This form of target setting takes the results of assessments of a child's learning in science and matches it to the known expectations of the children for their stage of learning (using the Level Descriptions). The teacher is then able to plan future work that will develop the children's learning in science at an appropriate pace, in order for the child to attain the expected level for their age. This process is used to aid the raising of standards in science teaching and learning and thus provides teachers with a valid base for evaluating their own practice and the science curriculum provided by the school. It is also important that children are fully aware of, and involved in, the target setting process. This begins with the teacher sharing the teaching objective of the lesson (see Chapter 3) with the children and continues with the assessment of progress and target setting for further progress. The children may be encouraged to play an active part in this process by commenting on their own successes and achievements and carrying out joint target setting with the teacher. Parents may also be kept informed of their child's progress through sharing the targets set for their child in science. This information may be useful for the parent to track their child's progress through the year.

Reflective questions

Assessment

- Will your assessment allow pupils to demonstrate the appropriate skills, knowledge and/or attitudes?
- Will the assessment recognize the process of science as well as the content?
- Do you make use of open and closed questions during teaching to explore children's understanding?
- Do you make your assessment an integral part of teaching and learning?
- Do you match criteria for assessment to the learning objective?
- Do you plan to assess on a regular basis?
- When, where and how do you share the results of your assessments with pupils and parents?
- Do you ask children to reflect on their own progress and achievements so far?

- Are parents able to make a contribution to the assessment of their child in science?
- How do you assess children with special needs?
- How do you assess children, whose first language is not English, fairly?

Recording

- How do you ensure that your records are up to date and manageable, allowing information to be included and retrieved quickly and easily?
- Do your records show individual pupil progress and achievements, and indicate areas for improvement?
- Are your records accessible for all those that need them, including colleagues, parents and other adults with a right to the information and, in the case of Primary Records of Achievement and Experience (PRAE), the pupils themselves?
- Are your records ongoing and cumulative in nature, based on regular assessment in the form of classroom observations, discussions, directed tasks and tests?
- Do your records include evidence that supports the judgements recorded?
- Do you make use of the records that are passed on to you?

Reporting and accountability

- Do you make use of the Early Learning Goals or National Curriculum when reporting on pupil attainment?
- Do you suggest areas and ways in which children can improve on their attainment to date in science?
- Do you begin your comments by referring to positive factors and ensure any subsequent criticism is constructive in nature?
- Do you maintain a professional commitment to confidentiality when reporting to parents?

REFERENCES

O'Hara, M. (2000) *Teaching 3–8: Meeting the Standards for Initital Teacher Training and Induction*, London and New York: Continuum.

Qualifications and Curriculum Authority (1999a) *The National Curriculum: Handbook for Primary Teachers in England*, London: DfEE/QCA.

Qualifications and Curriculum Authority (2000a) *Curriculum Guidance for the Foundation Stage*, London: DfEE/QCA.

Qualifications and Curriculum Authority (2000b) *Key Stage 2: Assessment and Reporting Arrangements*, London: DfEE/QCA.

Qualifications and Curriculum Authority (2001a) www.qca.org.uk/ca/ 22.07.2001.

Qualifications and Curriculum Authority (2001b) *Foundation Stage and Key Stage 1: Assessment and Reporting Arrangements*, London: DfEE/QCA.

School Curriculum and Assessment Authority (1997) *Looking at Children's Learning*, London: SCAA.

Science and Children with Special Educational Needs

This chapter deals with the requirement on teachers in mainstream schools and maintained nurseries to provide an entitlement curriculum that includes children with special educational needs (SEN). Dealing effectively with SEN pupils in the classroom provides an exciting challenge for teachers, as these needs range widely and include physical disabilities, learning difficulties, emotional and behavioural difficulties and children who may be identified as very able, gifted or talented. It is important that children with SEN develop the same self-esteem as other pupils, and teachers have a part to play in facilitating this. This is not exclusive to the science curriculum yet science has an important role to play.

The chapter begins with an outline of some of the issues regarding special needs and considers the range and identification of needs that teachers may encounter in the 3–11 age range. The list of special needs given is intended merely to be a guide to the range of needs that the student and newly qualified teacher may encounter within their classroom, although in practice the range of SEN is both considerable and complex in nature and thus difficult to categorize. For the purposes of the chapter, therefore, different areas are considered individually, and yet in reality they may be inter-linked and the needs presented to the teacher may be much more complicated than this section of the chapter indicates. Also there is a need to view all pupils, including those with SEN, as individuals; consequently we need to be careful about taking one aspect of a child's life and using it to group together all children with a similar impairment into one indistinguishable whole. Even though two children may have dyslexia it would be a mistake to assume their educational needs are identical, as this may be the only connection between the two; in all other respects they may be very different individuals with very different needs. Furthermore, some children may experience special educational needs that are multiple. Therefore the chapter must be regarded as an introduction to the types of SEN possible in the classroom and used to consider effective teaching strategies and responses in science; readers wishing to look more closely into this area should visit some of the references and suggested further reading sources contained at the end of the chapter.

The revised National Curriculum outlines three principles through which to facilitate the inclusion of children with special educational needs:

- Firstly, teachers need to set suitable learning challenges.
- Secondly, they need to respond to pupils' diverse needs.
- Thirdly, they must overcome potential barriers to learning and assessment for individuals and groups of individuals (DfEE / QCA 1999a).

The chapter considers these three aims and offers suggestions on how the curriculum can be adapted and delivered to support the scientific learning of the expected 20 per cent of pupils with special educational needs in science, for there is much that teachers can do when planning and teaching science to make it both relevant and interesting to all children. Strategies to be used include establishing a clear structure in which pupils, including those with SEN, are encouraged to review previous work and learning, while new skills and concepts are presented in clear, unambiguous ways and are sometimes modelled by the teacher. Such practices should help to ensure higher success rates for all children, offering more opportunities for positive feedback to individual children. Teachers, therefore, need to find ways to foster independent pupil practice, whereby children with SEN have the chance to apply new knowledge and skills appropriately (Westwood, 1997). The chapter consequently focuses on how the student and newly qualified teacher can cater for special educational needs within their class, through the adaptation of planning and delivery of scientific activities, in order to support the scientific learning of all pupils in science. Effective teaching practices offer children 'the maximum opportunity to learn' (Westwood, 1997), and so liaison and discussion with other agencies, as listed in the chapter, is likely to be an important part of planning and delivering learning programmes that will best meet the specific needs of the children with SEN.

Special Educational Needs

Special educational needs is an umbrella term covering a range and severity of needs. The needs may involve social, emotional, sensory, physical, or intellectual factors, or may involve a combination of factors. Where the need is based on a learning difficulty or disability, rather than on a particular gift or talent, then this can range from mild to severe. Identifying children with SEN is not always an easy task. Children who experience a form of physical or sensory impairment may be fairly easy to identify, whereas a child who experiences hearing impairments, which are not immediately obvious or which are intermittent, may be much more difficult to identify. Furthermore, some learning difficulties are not instantly apparent; all that may be evident is the fact that children find it noticeably harder to achieve in certain areas of the curriculum than their peers. Some learning difficulties are quite specific, e.g., dyslexia and in some instances the difficulties may arise due to emotional and behavioural problems.

The suggestion that 20 per cent of children would experience some form of special educational need during their education that would merit additional provision of some kind appeared with the publication of the Warnock Report (DES) in 1978. This began a period of change within the area of Special Educational Needs provision. The Report, together with subsequent Education Acts (1981 and 1993), ensured the move towards greater integration of pupils with special educational needs into mainstream schooling. The Warnock Report not only influenced the move of some pupils with SEN out of special schools, but also suggested that many SEN pupils already existed in mainstream education (Stirton and Glover, 1998) but had not been identified as experiencing difficulties. It therefore recommended that these children would benefit from identification and support. Consequently, following its publication, the number of children in mainstream education identified as having SEN has increased both in terms of numbers and in terms of the range of needs. Underlying all the developments post-1978 was the belief that integration would greatly benefit all pupils, both those with SEN and those without, and that the benefits would impact on personal and social development and academic achievement.

The early identification of a special need is crucial. Failure to recognize a need, and therefore failure to modify the educational provision for the children involved, can result in low self-esteem, frustration, anger, cycles of under-achievement and alienation. It is therefore imperative that all partners in a child's education play a part in identifying and assessing children with special educational needs. The nursery and primary teacher may be the first professional to recognize signs indicating a special need, it is important they then go on to elicit knowledge of the child's conditions and needs from parents and carers of the child and other professions concerned with the education and welfare of children. Assessments of SEN consequently involve collaboration with external agencies and experts including medical practitioners, support teachers and/or educational psychologists.

Identifying Special Educational Needs

Special Educational Needs are deemed to exist when special provision has to be made for a child who:

- is affected by a disability which precludes or hampers efforts to access educational facilities on offer,
- is experiencing learning difficulties, i.e., is achieving significantly below the majority of his/her peers,
- is gifted or talented.

Code of Practice

The 1993 Education Act required the Secretary of State to issue a Code of Practice for special educational needs, giving practical guidance to LEAs and governing bodies of all maintained schools on their responsibilities towards all children with special educational needs (SEN). The Code of Practice requires all maintained schools to make appropriate provision for pupils with special educational needs and is designed to help schools make effective decisions. The list below shows the Code of Practice in operation at the time of writing. An updated Code is expected in school in 2002.

Code of Practice on the identification and assessment of Special Educational Needs

The fundamental principles of the Code are that:

☐ the needs of all pupils who may have special educational needs either throughout, or at any time during, their school careers must be addressed; the Code recognizes that there is a continuum of needs and a continuum of provision, which may be made in a wide variety of different forms

☐ children with special educational needs require the greatest possible access to a broad and balanced education, including the National Curriculum

☐ the needs of most pupils will be met in the mainstream, and without a statutory assessment or statement of special educational needs. Children with special educational needs, including children with statements of special educational needs, should, where appropriate and taking into account the wishes of their parents, be educated alongside their peers in mainstream schools

☐ even before he or she reaches compulsory school age a child may have special educational needs requiring the intervention of the LEA as well as the health services

☐ the knowledge, views and experience of parents are vital. Effective assessment and provision will be secured where there is the greatest possible degree of partnership between parents and their children and schools, LEAs and other agencies

The practices and procedures essential in pursuit of these principles are that:

☐ all children with special educational needs should be identified and assessed as early as possible and as quickly as is consistent with thoroughness

☐ provision for all children with special educational needs should be made by the most appropriate agency. In most cases this will be the child's mainstream school, working in partnership with the child's parents: no statutory assessment will be necessary

☐ where needed, LEAs must make assessments and statements in accordance with the prescribed time limits; must write clear and thorough statements, setting out the child's educational and non-educational needs, the objectives to be secured, the provision to be made and the arrangements for monitoring and review; and ensure the annual review of the special educational provision arranged for the child and the updating and monitoring of educational targets

☐ special educational provision will be most effective when those responsible take into account the ascertainable wishes of the child concerned, considered in the light of his or her age and understanding

☐ there must be close cooperation between all the agencies concerned and a multi-disciplinary approach to the resolution of issues

(DfEE, 1994)

The Code recommends that schools adopt a staged model of special educational needs, as shown below. The first three stages are school-based and school-driven; the subsequent two stages require the LEA to share the responsibility for the child with the school.

A staged model of Special Educational Needs

Stage 1: The class (or subject teacher) identifies and registers a child's special educational needs. The school's SEN coordinator is informed. The class teacher takes initial action, usually increased differentiation in the classroom.

Stage 2: The school's SEN coordinator takes lead responsibility for gathering further information on the child and for coordinating the child's special educational provision. An individual education plan is written and delivered by the child's teachers.

Stage 3: Specialists from outside the school support Class teachers and the SEN coordinator.

Stage 4: The LEA is consulted. They consider the need for a statutory assessment. A multi-disciplinary assessment may also be made at this stage.

Stage 5: The LEA consider the need for a statement of special educational needs. If a statement is made, the LEA monitor and review the provision.

(Adapted from DfEE, 1994)

Science and special educational needs

The National Curriculum Council (1992) identifies science as a subject with *characteristics* that enable pupils with SEN to achieve success. They give five reasons why science provides equal opportunities for all children, including those with SEN:

- science is primarily learning through first hand experience;
- knowledge and skills may be developed in small steps, concentration can therefore be maintained and developed;
- science captures the imagination and thus may help reduce behavioural problems;
- work in science often involves group work which promotes participation and communication;
- the variety of scientific activities allows pupils to share ideas and expertise and so pupils are able to help each other to succeed.

Effective teaching in science is that which ensures all children have access to a curriculum relevant to their needs. The key to achieving this is to match the delivery of the curriculum to the particular needs of a child. Consequently teachers need to know about the implications of a range of special needs and conditions, in order to provide for full involvement in the activities of the nursery/class, and to facilitate pupil learning. The teacher therefore needs to be able to identify the existence of a special need and to provide support to enable SEN children to have equal access to the curriculum, and its opportunities for appropriate learning experiences, including social experiences. It is advisable that the student or newly qualified teacher seek advice and guidance when they have suspicions that a child is experiencing learning difficulties. This can be sought initially from the school's SENCO (Special Educational Needs Coordinator) who has both expertise and experience in the area of Special Educational Needs. The SENCO is able to advise on early identification of needs and on teaching strategies that fit with the school's SEN policy and procedures. Further advice may then be sought from other relevant parties such as parents or support teachers.

Where a special educational need is confirmed, the teacher must then provide a relevant science curriculum that is mindful of the child's difficulties yet ensures access to the National Curriculum or Early Learning Goals requirements. The next section of the chapter will consider a range of needs and conditions and make suggestions how the teacher may support the scientific learning of children with such disabilities or needs. The chapter considers the range of needs and conditions under four main headings:

1. Physical disabilities
2. Learning difficulties
3. Emotional and behavioural difficulties
4. Gifted and talented pupils

Physical Disabilities

There are a great many physical disabilities that teachers may encounter in nursery and primary schools; only a brief overview of some of the more common conditions can therefore be given. In addition to physical disability some children may experience added problems arising from the impact of hospitalization, prolonged or numerous absences from nursery/school or even the reluctance to use available aids.

Key characteristics of some physical disabilities

Arthritis	Although this might be thought to be a disease of the elderly, some children do suffer from a form of rheumatoid arthritis. In such cases the children may be under medication or have to have physiotherapy. Although a reasonable and sensible amount of physical activity is desirable, excessive physical activity could result in the condition being exacerbated causing the child considerable discomfort and anxiety.
Asthma	Asthma appears to be becoming increasingly common in children and is caused by a narrowing of air passages in the lungs which make breathing difficult. While some children have only mild attacks, for others it can be far more serious and even life threatening. Triggers for attacks range from temperature changes and allergic reactions, to infections and excessive physical exertion. Serious cases may result in frequent or extended absences from nursery / school, interrupting a child's progress and could restrict their involvement in some activities such as PE or out of school work. Once again, where pupils feel self-conscious about their difference teachers may need to remind children about using their inhalers
Cerebral palsy	Cerebral palsy results from brain damage. Movement from 'a' to 'b' in the nursery / classroom may be awkward and jerky in nature, while at rest, the body may experience irregular and uncoordinated motion. This condition can also produce problems with balance and coordination. Depending on the seriousness of the condition some pupils may need wheelchairs, others may find fine-motor control impaired, or experience difficulties in speech and articulation. As with serious asthma, some children may find themselves absent from school resulting in their having to try to catch up with their peers. They may also experience a lower self-image as a result of their condition.
Cystic fibrosis	Cystic fibrosis is a genetic disorder that results in the appearance of thick mucus in the child's lungs. The consequences for the child include infections of the lungs and stomach and daily treatment including physiotherapy, medicines and special diets, all of which are necessary to ameliorate the effects of what is an incurable condition.
Diabetes	Diabetes results from difficulties with the body's production of insulin and a consequent inability to make use of sugar, causing it to build up in the body.

Diabetes cont.   Undiagnosed diabetes can result in:

- excessive thirst
- weight loss
- excessive urination
- fatigue

Children with diabetes often have to have insulin injections and they may also be placed on a diet that strictly controls their intake of carbohydrates. Meals have to be eaten at regular times in order to balance insulin with sugar. Where the balance breaks down children may find they have either too much or too little sugar in their bodies. Falls in blood sugar as a result of lack of food (hypo attack) can happen quite quickly and the results can include headaches, bad-temperedness, lack of colour, sweating, palpitations, or anxiety. Biscuits or sweets are sometimes used to rectify the situation. Excessive blood sugar levels can be far more serious, the onset is slower and if not dealt with can result in vomiting and diabetic coma. This is rare but hospitalization is essential where it occurs. Older children are often capable of recognizing when a problem is arising.

Epilepsy   Epilepsy is an unpredictable cerebral disorder caused by temporary changes in the brain's electrical activity. It can require control through drugs. Fits (sometimes referred to as seizures or convulsions) can be brought on as a result of illness, emotional and physical stresses, or a lack of medication. Minor fits (absence attacks) often appear as momentary lapses of attention. Major fits (tonic-clonic seizures) can result in facial or whole body spasms, loss of consciousness and loss of bowel or bladder control. Although frightening for the observer, teachers need to remain calm, reassure the rest of the class, loosen clothing around the child's neck, but must not put anything in the child's mouth. Place the child in the recovery position, check breathing and pallor, and monitor the length of the attack. If the situation persists for more than 5 minutes teachers are advised to seek medical help.

Hearing impairment   Some children experience hearing loss as a result of blockages that stop or impede vibrations in the air from reaching the inner ear, known as conductive hearing loss. Such blockages can be caused by a number of factors, even heavy colds, and they are often susceptible to medication and other treatments. Other hearing problems however may result from faulty nerve connections to the ear (sensori-neural hearing loss) and this can be both irreversible and profound in its effect. Hearing aids can be used to amplify sounds for children with sensori-neural problems but they will not cure the problem and can also distort the sounds a child hears. There can also be problems with children who feel self-conscious about having to wear a hearing aid and who consequently *lose it* or *forget* to bring it to school.

Signs of hearing loss can include:

- poor listening abilities (difficulties in comprehending spoken language)
- slow in learning to talk, limited vocabulary
- speech problems (articulation, discriminating and sequencing sounds)
- confused in class over instructions and tasks
- watching for cues from peers

Hearing impairment cont.	• hearing some sounds better than others (higher frequencies can be a problem)
	<div align="right">(Dean, 1996)</div>
Muscular dystrophy	Muscular dystrophy is an incurable wasting disease that affects motor skills rather than the brain. The condition is genetic and certain forms affect boys only. As the condition worsens the child may not be able to attend school. Working with families may be difficult and it needs to be done with sensitivity, as ultimately the condition is fatal.
Spina bifida	Spina bifida and other malfunctions of the spinal cord can range in their seriousness. For some children there may be only slight mobility problems. For some the condition can result in specific learning difficulties, for example, judging size, direction, shape, fine motor control, and personal organization.
Visual impairment	Visual impairment can have a range of causes and can result in moderate or severe problems with vision. It is also important for teachers to recognize that a child's eyesight may improve or deteriorate. As with hearing aids, children can be reluctant to wear glasses as a result of the stigma sometimes attached.

Signs of visual impairment can include:

- clumsiness
- pulling faces and squinting
- poor handwriting
- bringing text up close to the face
- poor coordination
- headaches and dizziness
- trouble seeing white / blackboard
- tiredness

(O'Hara, 2001 pp. 162–4)

Supporting the scientific learning of children with physical disabilities

It is clear that some scientific activities may present difficulties for some pupils with physical disabilities, e.g., working with equipment, manipulating equipment, taking measurements, going on visits and using audio-visual and documentary sources of information. Such difficulties therefore require some individual adaptation of the curriculum or specific consideration, as noted in the table below.

Specific considerations for the scientific learning of children with physical disabilities

Arthritis/ Spina bifida/ Cerebral palsy/ Cystic fibrosis/ Muscular dystrophy	The teacher needs to be aware of the mobility needs of children, both in and out of school. Cerebral palsy – Oral communication, e.g., through discussion may be difficult or the child may need extra time to contribute. Cystic fibrosis/ Muscular dystrophy – Absence for hospitalization may need to be allowed for.

Asthma	Consideration given to issues such as likely triggers for asthma attacks, e.g., use of fine powders when investigating solutions. The teacher must be aware of the signs of an asthmatic attack, the procedure to follow if an attack takes place, and know where a child's inhaler is stored.
Diabetes/ Epilepsy	Need to ensure pupils take the necessary precautions to keep their blood sugar levels stable. The teacher must be aware of the signs of epilepsy, possible triggers for attacks and the procedure to follow if an attack takes place.
Hearing impairment	Hearing-impaired pupils may find the of use visual clues, to back up verbal ones, helpful. Rephrasing and emphasizing key words or phrases is essential. New vocabulary or phrases to be introduced written down clearly. General noise levels should be kept down when giving instructions or initiating discussions. This involve cutting down on chatter, lifting furniture rather than dragging chairs, etc. Facing the child during discussions will aid attempts to lip-read. The teacher needs to be careful of moving around too much, as this can make it difficult for a hearing-impaired child to follow them and the cues that they are giving. Teachers must ensure they do not obscure their faces, e.g., with a book they are reading from or by moving around too much.
Visual impairment	Teachers supervising a visually impaired child may need to think of ways in which they can encourage them to use their other senses during visits and activities, i.e., touch, smell or hearing. Limit the visual demands made on children, e.g., looking from the white board to the teacher and back again quickly. Position the child to support vision, e.g., seated nearer to the white board in a well-lit area. When using written or visual resources avoid reflective papers and make use of larger print sizes, wider lines, and magnifiers. Where science activities require a degree of mobility, either around the classroom or during a visit, try to minimize potential obstructions.

In addition to the above specific considerations are some more general requirements:

• Some children may need additional time or alternative ways to complete scientific tasks and/or record their findings. The use of educational technology (video, ICT, concept keyboard) is one possible response to this.

• Resources may need careful consideration in order to ensure participation by all, including those pupils who may experience difficulties with gross or fine motor skills. This may involve providing specialist measuring and cutting equipment.

• Where a child is considered to be able to carry out a task unaided, the teacher may pair the child up with a peer who will assist the child to succeed in the given task.

- For educational visits out of school, a pre-visit it is advisable to identify access needs and to look for places where pupils could sit or rest if necessary.
- Prior to an educational visit all adult supervisors need to be properly briefed about supporting a child's health and education, for example an adult with an epileptic pupil who experiences an absence attack during a visit may need to repeat or check on information and instructions given.

 *Case study*

Mr J's Year 5 class were continuing their work on thermal insulators. After a discussion about how to keep an ice-lolly frozen without a freezer, the children were working in groups to carry out an investigation to identify which material would keep an ice cube frozen the longest time. Matthew has difficulties with his fine motor skills and is visually impaired, he therefore would not be able to wrap up the ice cubes or identify how much water had melted from the ice cube. Mr J put the children into groups to write their investigation plan prior to carrying out the investigation. He then worked with Matthew's group. The children decided to wrap each ice cube in a different material and at intervals in the day to measure the dimensions of the ice cube and how much water had melted from the ice cube. Mr J asked the children who would carry out the measuring and recording and how they would present their findings. The group decided that one child would wrap and unwrap the ice cubes, one child would do the measuring, a second child would check the measurements and Matthew would record the observations on the computer. They would work together as a team to record the investigation, using the computer and drawings. This ensured that all the group, including Matthew, were fully involved in the activity.

A physically disabled child may not be able to carry out an investigation, or be involved as part of a group in an investigation, but may add to the class work by carrying out a related activity. This may involve the child in researching the life and work of a scientist related to the concept being studied, e.g., Alexander Graham Bell when investigating sound, Thomas Edison when investigating electricity, Isaac Newton when investigating forces, using audiotapes and/or the Internet. During the plenary to the lesson the SEN child may deliver a biography of the scientist involved with the concept, and is thus achieving success through recording their work, and delivering it to their peers.

Learning Difficulties

Learning difficulties range from mild to severe, and from specific to complex. They may be rooted in problems located elsewhere such as in their social and emotional development; they may be cognitive and result in problems with the core elements of literacy and numeracy in the curriculum. Such difficulties have a profound influence across the curriculum; language acquisition is of particular importance, as it is both a precursor and co-requisite for learning in many areas of the curriculum including science. Without language there may be an inability on the part of the teacher to fully recognize a child's true potential and intelligence. Communication problems may therefore result in considerable frustration for the child and ultimately may lead on to withdrawal or aggressive behaviour. Special needs relating to literacy and numeracy therefore can have very severe consequences for pupils if not identified and addressed properly.

There are many indicators that may suggest a child is experiencing a learning difficulty of some kind. However, the presence of a single indicator does not necessarily mean that a child has a special educational need. A child who is frequently involved in off-task chatter or experiences difficulty in following instructions may merely be exhibiting typical child-like behaviour rather than indicating that they have a learning difficulty. The confirmation of a special educational need is more likely where a child displays a significant number of indicators, as listed below.

Possible indicators of learning difficulties

The child displays:

- little apparent awareness of, or interest in, the world around him/her
- little knowledge about the world around him/her
- limited evidence of previous experience in science lessons
- few interests, in or out of school
- difficulty in following instructions
- difficulty in relating learning in one area to work in another
- poor oracy skills
- limited vocabulary and/or speech
- reluctance to contribute to discussions
- a limited concentration span
- a tendency to be easily distracted
- a significant amount of off-task chatter
- hyperactive tendencies
- off-task behaviour, e.g., a prolonged involvement in activities in the classroom (planned or unplanned) other than the scientific one on offer
- a problem with literacy and numeracy
- attention-seeking behaviour
- work avoidance strategies, e.g., constantly sharpening their pencil
- an overt preference for practical activities
- a lack of interest in books and reading
- an over-reliance on adult help
- a disregard for adult help
- an inability to complete work effectively, by finishing slowly, never finishing anything, finishing quickly, carelessly or incompletely, or pretending to have finished
- a propensity for losing things
- poor personal organizational skills

The following table outlines some of the main, known learning difficulties.
This is only a brief overview and should not be regarded as a comprehensive list.

Key characteristics of some learning difficulties

Aphasia	Children with aphasia experience difficulties in understanding the meaning of words or difficulties in expressing themselves. Other pupils with aphasia know perfectly well what they want to say but have problems in producing and articulating the words, in some cases speech may be so garbled as to be almost unintelligible.

Autism

Autism is a lifelong disability, usually appearing by the age of three, in which a child will experience difficulties in communication and social skills, imagination and problem solving. Autism can occur by itself or it may be in association with other disabilities such as epilepsy. It is important to realize that some children with autism may combine their areas of difficulty with areas in which they are just as capable, and sometimes even more capable, than their peers, for example when it comes to drawing, musical ability, arithmetic, or memory tasks.

Communication difficulties may include:

- difficulties with non-verbal communication behaviour such as eye contact, expression and gestures;
- delays in or inability to develop spoken language;
- stereotyped and repetitive use of language.

Social skills difficulties may include:

- difficulties in developing relationships with peers;
- preferring solitary activities to ones involving reciprocal relationships with peers and others;
- treating people as inanimate;
- difficulties in sustaining conversations with others, can be stilted and halting;
- lack of spontaneous need to share experiences, interests pleasures;
- dislike of being touched.

Problem-solving, symbolic and imaginative play difficulties may include:

- lack of varied and spontaneous imaginative play, socio-dramatic role play;
- lack of interest in toys;
- inflexibility in the face of changes to routines and conventions;
- restricted and repetitive patterns of behaviour;
- all-consuming preoccupation with restricted area of interest (intensity and focus);
- extreme dislike of sounds, textures, tastes;
- repetitive mannerisms;

(Autism: Fact Sheets for Health Professionals)

Dyslexia

Dyslexia is a specific learning difficulty related to literacy that can inhibit children's ability to read, write and spell. Dyslexic children often confuse words and letters, but then so too do many children when they are learning to read and write. In dyslexic children, however, these difficulties persist in the face of

Dyslexia cont.   good teaching. Although primarily impairing children's written work and reading, dyslexia can also impact upon numeracy, coordination, behaviour and a child's ability to deal with time. Dyslexic pupils sometimes:• have difficulty learning to tell the time;

- show poor time keeping and general awareness;
- have poor personal organization skills;
- have difficulty remembering, for example days of the week, birthdays, years;
- have difficulty with concepts such as yesterday, today, and tomorrow.

(www.dfee.gov.uk/sen/hints.htm)

Dyspraxia   Dyspraxia is an impairment that affects motor coordination. Children with dyspraxia experience movement difficulties associated with correctly gauging their surroundings, working out what to do and executing particular movements. As this impairment affects muscle control it can impact upon speech resulting in poor articulation (Macintyre, 2000).

Supporting the scientific learning of children with learning difficulties

Once identified, the learning difficulties may be supported through an adaptation to the organization of teaching activities. There are many strategies to achieve this, some of which are listed below, together with case studies to demonstrate how the strategies have been used to facilitate the learning of children with special educational needs.

- delivering the lesson objective through a series of shorter activities rather than one extended activity
- establishing clearly understood routines
- allowing for the child to exercise some control over their work
- provide adult support during the activity, to read with or for a child, to act as scribe, to aid with practical work
- setting work at an appropriate level
- avoiding overlong strings of instructions during science lessons
- a reduced emphasis on teacher-centred approaches, i.e., *chalk and talk*, dictation
- a reduced emphasis on note-taking from books

CS Case study 1

Jonathon, a Year 6 child, has built up a good relationship with Miss P, a support assistant. Miss P often works with Jonathon, in a group, during Literacy. Mrs F, the class teacher, had planned a lesson to consolidate the children's knowledge of the movement of the earth and the moon. The introduction to the lesson involved a discussion and then the children were to record their work in written form. During the discussion Jonathon was distracted, Miss P focused his attention by quietly repeating questions to Jonathon andencouraging him to answer, thus **providing adult support** for Jonathon to access the activity. The children were then instructed to record their work. Miss P asked Jonathon how he would like to record his ideas, thereby giving Jonathon **control over his work**. He suggested a series of pictures. When the pictures were completed, Miss P helped Jonathon to annotate his work, using reference books for ideas but **not relying on copying the text**. Jonathon was pleased with his work and showed it to the class during the plenary session.

- a reduced emphasis on unstructured, free writing
- allowing for plenty of opportunity for reinforcement and repetition within the activity, and using and applying similar vocabulary and ideas in different contexts
- referral to previous science work, to help children make links and to understand their current work
- the use of scaffolding to develop skills and knowledge
- the use of thorough, careful questioning
- the use of investigative work to develop observational skills, attention to detail, descriptive skills, and to encourage children to ask their own questions for investigation
- supporting pupils' gradual progress in oracy and literacy

 *Case study 2*

Amy, a Year 2 child, was working within a group of six children to identify sources of light. The teacher, Miss D, **referred to the children's work** earlier in the week on identifying objects that used electricity to work. The group discussed which objects also provided light. Miss D then showed the children a series of pictures taken from a mail order catalogue and magazines, which they looked at, discussed and sorted into groups. The children then produced a collaborative list of light sources, with Miss D acting as scribe for the group. The teacher, by providing a series of short activities, had **provided the opportunity for children to reinforce their ideas** of light sources. Finally, the children completed a list of their own and illustrated their list with pictures, based on the pictures from the mail order catalogue and magazines. The writing task was therefore focused; the task **did not end with unstructured free writing**.

- careful choice of partners or groups for scientific tasks, as some children may find group tasks challenging
- use of story to introduce, explain or reinforce difficult concepts
- the use of computers to act as a stimulus to children who lack confidence in their literacy skills or who are autistic (Siddles, 1999)
- adapting and/or simplifying texts used in science – information texts, instruction texts etc.
- using taped texts and/or instructions
- providing more direct instruction, e.g., providing lists of key words, work cards worksheets and/or writing frames
- recording work pictorially
- recording work collaboratively
- recording work orally
- encouraging participation through praise for effort and achievement

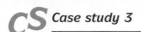

Alan, a Reception child, **finds group tasks challenging** as he does not relate well to his peers. Miss C, the Reception teacher, had planned for the children to work with autumn leaves. The activities included drawing a leaf, talking about the leaves and sorting them into groups. The children were to work on sorting the leaves with a partner and then choosing one to draw and discuss. Alan was asked to choose his own partner; he chose Miss S, the support assistant. Miss C suggested a third member of the group, Emma, and Alan reluctantly agreed. The children sorted their leaves, with Emma providing the commentary for sorting the leaves and Alan assisting her. Throughout the activity Miss S **encouraged** Alan's (and Emma's) **participation through praise for effort and achievement**. Both children then **recorded their work orally** on audiotape. Alan was encouraged to speak on the tape, which he did.

Emotional and Behavioural Difficulties

As with learning difficulties, the area of emotional and behavioural difficulties is a complex one. Listed below are some of the key characteristics shown by children with EBD (Emotional and Behavioural Difficulties) and AD(H)D (Attention-deficit (Hyperactivity) Disorder)

Key characteristics of some emotional and behavioural difficulties

Emotional and behavioural difficulties (EBD)	Children with EBD may exhibit a wide range of signs from extreme withdrawal to highly volatile, aggressive and disruptive behaviour. The causes of these patterns of behaviour are far from simple and may include multiple factors including:

- divorce/separation
- parental unemployment and poverty (free school meals, few holidays, outings, clothing)
- being placed in care, lack of contact with natural parents
- over-anxious parent (s)
- being compared negatively with sibling (s)
- affected by other sibling (s) previous school record and self-fulfilling prophecies
- frustration due to another impairment or learning difficulty
- physical or sexual abuse
- neglect

Dealing with EBD can be particularly 'intractable and frustrating for teachers' (DfE, 1994), as the learning difficulties are caused by emotional and behavioural factors that are beyond their control. Teachers need to exercise extreme care in identifying children as suffering from EBD as statistically there is a higher chance of some children being more prone to EBD than others, but EBD is not restricted to poor or working class children. Indicators that may suggest a child has emotional and behavioural difficulties can include:

192

EBD cont.

- loners / staying on the fringes or margins of activities
- seeking friendships with other age groups
- aggressive towards peers
- clingy / precocious
- disruptive
- spoiling other children's play
- immaturity
- poor self image, ('I can't do this', 'My drawing's rubbish!', 'Boring!')
- high anxiety
- attention seeking
- restless and easily distracted
- tearful / irritable / moody
- capable of tantrums
- distant, 'off with the fairies'

Attention-deficit (Hyperactivity) Disorder, AD(H)D

Attention-deficit (Hyperactivity) Disorder ought not to be confused with EBD. While AD(H)D may also present teachers with challenging behaviour, its origins are biological whereas environmental factors play a significant part in EBD. Not all children with Attention-deficit Disorder are necessarily hyperactive. The absence of attention and disruptive behaviour can be particularly challenging for teachers and it is important to remember that AD(H)D is a disability and that consequently care needs to be taken over punishing children for a disability. Teachers therefore are faced with trying to initiate strategies that will support the children in modifying their behaviour.

Indicators of an attention deficit:

- failure to give close attention, being careless and making regular mistakes
- forgetful of regular activities such as going to assembly, or PE.
- problems in sustaining enthusiasm, will avoid tasks requiring extended effort
- appears not to listen when addressed verbally
- appears unable to follow instructions, regularly fails to complete work / tasks
- difficulties in organizing self, often loses the tools necessary for the task (e.g., pencils, books, rubbers) thus avoiding work
- very easily distracted

Indicators of hyperactivity:

- constant fidgeting with hands and feet
- often unable to stay seated
- will move in an inappropriate fashion around the room, for example running, climbing over / under tables
- difficulties in playing without excessive noise
- will interrupt and intrude upon the activities of peers
- talks incessantly, blurting out answers to questions without observing classroom conventions and often without waiting for the questioner to finish the question
- difficulties in waiting for a turn

Supporting the scientific learning of children with emotional and behavioural difficulties

Children with emotional and behavioural difficulties often display disruptive behaviour in the classroom. They may also struggle to concentrate and focus on a task for the same length of time as their peers. It is interesting that it is often assumed that children with behavioural problems are merely attention seeking, and that by receiving attention they obtain satisfaction. However this is not always true. Children with EBD or AD(H)D may not understand or enjoy their behaviour or welcome the adult attention it brings. It may also be that they wish to change their behaviour and are willing partners in the management of their behaviour. It cannot be underestimated how challenging it is for the teacher to work with children who have these needs. The student or newly qualified teacher ought not to try to deal with them without the advice and support of their more experienced colleagues and outside agencies. When working with children with these needs it is important for the behaviour to be the focus for attention and not the child. The first step in addressing the need is to identify the context and the triggers for the behaviour; as it is the behaviour that is under scrutiny, the child may play an active part in this part of the process. The child's behaviour may manifest itself:

- during relatively unstructured activities
- at particular times of the day
- during certain methods of classroom organization
- when the teacher is doing certain things
- when the child is asked to do certain things

By recognizing these contexts, the teacher can begin to adapt his or her plans to avoid or reduce the incidences when disruptive behaviour is likely to occur. It is also advisable to give consideration to the teacher's response, and the response of other children, to such behaviour. When difficulties occur it is important that the teacher remains as calm as possible, however problematic this may be to achieve. Two strategies that may be employed involve either trying to keep the child productively engaged on the given task, e.g., by asking questions about the task, or by changing the task to defuse a potentially difficult situation, e.g., to a related science activity or a domestic chore. Use praise to demonstrate to the children that you are pleased they have continued their directed work.

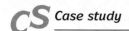 *Case study*

Colin, a bright Year 2 child, often displays attention-seeking behaviour during the introduction to lessons. Miss A, the class teacher, usually introduces lessons to the children when they are seated together on the carpet. She has observed that Colin demands the attention of his peers during these times by calling out, making noises and pushing other children. In order to manage this behaviour, Miss A ensures that Colin sits at the front of the carpet and then uses Colin to help her with the lesson introductions. This involves Colin passing pens for writing information on the whiteboard, holding equipment needed for introducing the task and holding examples of recording sheets needed for the task. By using Colin in this way Miss A is reducing the need for Colin to seek attention, as he is being given it as part of the lesson. (Miss A also ensures other children in the class have 'jobs', e.g., lunchbox monitors, book monitors, etc.) Miss A regularly praises the children for their behaviour on the carpet, including Colin. When requiring children to demonstrate she is able to reward all children for their behaviour, by asking them to assist her. Colin is also now included in this as his behaviour at the beginning of lessons is managed so well.

Further strategies can be effective in lowering the incidence of disruption, e.g.,

- using direct statements, instructions and directions rather than asking questions and demanding choices
- using adults to support in group settings
- appropriate pacing of lessons
- tightly structured lessons, using all the lesson time for directed activities
- known conventions and routines, used throughout the day. These reduce the need for teacher instruction at key points during the day, e.g., transition from one activity to another
- give specific targeted scientific tasks, e.g., a brief investigation, a short piece of writing, or a pictorial task
- clear expectations for both behaviour and completed work

CS *Case study 2*

Robert, a Year 3 pupil, is very enthusiastic about science but can be quite disruptive when working within a small group. He quickly becomes very frustrated at the pace his peers work at and will be quite physical in his response to his peers. Mrs J, the class teacher, chooses the group of children Robert works with to ensure the group will work **at an appropriate pace**. She also ensures that Robert's group has **adult support** throughout a task. The lesson on food chains was **tightly structured** with Mrs J providing 3 short tasks for the group to carry out – ordering a set of pictures to make a food chain; identifying their own lunchtime food chain, recording their understanding of food chains. A time limit for each task was given with **clear expectations for behaviour and completed work**. Both Mrs J and the adult support regularly praised the group for their efforts. Following the lesson Robert was allowed to read with a peer of his choice.

- build up the time spent on discussions, to aid children with low concentration spans
- be aware of triggers for misbehaving and work to avoid them, e.g., ensure the classroom layout allows you to monitor all children
- develop the insight to identify when disruptive behaviour is building up. intervene immediately. You are the teacher; demonstrate the impact that your presence as the teacher can have
- it may be possible to head off, divert or defuse an imminent outburst
- use your sense of humour, though not at the expense of the child, as an effective strategy for easing tensions in the classroom
- be patient with the children and expect to teach them strategies to deal with their behaviour, e.g., verbalizing anger, asking for equipment to be passed to them, expressing their feelings
- use non-teaching support staff to provide extra support for the children

CS Case study

Ellen is a 4-year-old child who attends Nursery full-time each day. Miss D, the Nursery teacher, has been informed by Ellen's mother that Ellen is very disruptive at home and suggested this was due to the influence of Ellen's 6-year-old brother. Miss D has observed Ellen in the Nursery setting and has **identified** that Ellen's **behaviour deteriorates during the day**, and is particularly problematic immediately after lunch. She is particularly aggressive with her peers when equipment needs to be shared. Miss D, in consultation with the SENCO, has identified the following strategies for managing Ellen's behaviour:
*The Nursery Nurse to work alongside Ellen every day, **supporting** her immediately after lunch, until it is clear Ellen will not disrupt the group.
*Ellen to be encouraged to spend time in the role-play area – a shop – where she will be required to work alongside her peers and **develop her turn-taking skills**.
*Miss D to **overtly teach** Ellen the **skills needed to work with others**, particularly asking for equipment to be passed, expressing their ideas to others, etc.

- use praise and reward for appropriate behaviour, be explicit about what is being praised and that it is the behaviour which is pleasing you
- reward a child with EBD or AD(H)D with an appropriate reward, discuss the form of the reward with the child
- reward determination and perseverance in addition to rewarding resulting work
- monitor pupil progress; provide positive feedback at regular intervals
- set small, achievable goals with the child. Review achievement with the child
- establish conventions associated with whole class speaking and listening

CS Case study

David, a very capable Year 6 child, had previously used a variety of strategies for attracting the teacher's attention – refusal to record work on paper, threatening other children sitting alongside him, climbing into cupboards, etc. In a one-to-one situation he was very amiable but became disruptive when other children were brought into a group. David's class teacher, Mr F, discussed David with the SENCO and David's mum.

It was clear that David enjoyed adult attention and did not want to share this with other children. During a science lesson on habitats David was able to contribute a great deal to the class discussion that preceded recording the features of two contrasting habitats. David was an avid reader of nature books and had a considerable amount of previous knowledge. Mr F **verbally rewarded** each contribution made by David and praised him for his **appropriate behaviour**, i.e., not calling out. He thanked children for putting up their hands and contributing so well. During the recording part of the activity Mr F ensured that David sat with children at his table and that all had sufficient books for reference. Mr F also asked David to help another child to structure his work. Mr F then **monitored** the children working and **provided positive feedback** by praising David for his own progress and that of the child he was helping. When Mr F visited the table he gave suggestions for what to record next and praised the outcome when he next returned to the table. During the plenary Mr F read out a selection of work, including David's and David's partner. He praised David for his own work and for helping his peer. In a later discussion with David Mr F **reviewed** David's **achievements** during the session, by discussing David's behaviour. David was pleased with his own work and that of the child he was helping. He asked if he could help the child again next week. Mr F agreed, but only if David could behave as well as this session. David asked if working with the child more often could be a reward for his own behaviour, Mr F agreed, thereby **discussing the form of the reward** with David.

Gifted and Talented Pupils

Where children are deemed to be gifted or talented there is a statutory requirement to deliver a relevant curriculum; this is their basic entitlement as stated in the National Curriculum (DfEE, 1999a). Exact definitions for the terms are difficult to produce although *giftedness* suggests ability in excess of their most able peers, i.e., the gifted child is not merely judged as *bright* but exceptionally bright, whereas *talented* suggests an advanced ability within a particular area, e.g., art or music. There is however a debate over the concept of *giftedness* and whether children should be singled out in this way. The National Association for Gifted Children (www.nagcbritain.org.uk/) sums up this debate through a series of questions. These are reproduced below.

Questions regarding the provision for gifted children

What is the most acceptable way to identify gifted children?
Do gifted children differ quantitatively or qualitatively from other children?
Is childhood giftedness the same as adult giftedness?
Does pre-school advancement signify later giftedness?

The checklist below was compiled by a Local Education Authority (Advisory Services Unit, Rotherham, 1995) for identifying gifted and talented pupils.

Checklist for the identification of gifted and talented pupils

The child:

- demonstrates thirst for knowledge
- learns easily
- original, imaginative, creative
- persistent, resourceful, self-directed, determined, single-minded
- informed in unusual areas, often beyond his/her years
- outstanding vocabulary, verbally fluent
- artistic/musical
- sceptical/logical
- numerical fluency
- independent worker, shows and takes initiative
- versatile, many interests
- shows unusual insight
- exhibits unusually extroverted or introverted behaviour in a group
- speed and agility of thought and preference for verbal rather than written expression
- shows leadership qualities

Supporting the scientific learning of gifted and talented children

The provision for gifted children is most likely to enable them to study the science curriculum in greater depth and at a faster pace than their peers. The scientific learning of the gifted and talented child can therefore be a challenge for the teacher; however, there are many sources of help for dealing effectively with these children. These include the science coordinator within school, the science coordinator for the next Key Stage, the designated teacher for gifted and talented pupils in school, and the National Association for Gifted Children. The children's needs are very specific and, if not addressed, may lead to a number of outcomes including:

- a child's potential being ignored
- boredom for the child, through the provision of work that is not suitably challenging
- they begin to dominate their more average peers
- they become intolerant of their peers
- overtly disruptive behaviour
- being hypersensitive to criticism and rejection
- denying their ability
- under-achievement
- showing concerns about their giftedness and question if they are able to keep pace with additional work

It is therefore essential to support children in maintaining their interest and motivation in the curriculum by planning an exciting, relevant and intellectually stimulating curriculum. This is much more than differentiating the curriculum; it is the provision of a more demanding curriculum. Within the National Curriculum (DfEE/QCA 1999a) there is the provision for children to study Programmes of Study outside their Key Stage; e.g., Key Stage 2 children may follow the Programmes of Study for Key Stage 3. This has obvious implications for the non-specialist teacher who plans the children's work, in that the teacher may be concerned at their own lack of scientific knowledge. The child's work rate together with his/her independence may also make great demands on the teacher, who still has to cater for the needs of the rest of the class. However, support given to the child will enable him/her to benefit from:

- the opportunity to have additional time for scientific study at a deeper level
- directed extension work
- the use of more challenging vocabulary and language
- the use of a wider variety in methods of *finding out*
- the opportunity to solve demanding problems
- project work
- independent investigations
- independent research
- teacher support, encouragement and praise
- teacher intervention – including inspiration, challenge and constructive criticism
- the opportunity to use and apply scientific ideas and skills in a range of different contexts
- sharing their work with a wider audience, e.g., via e-mail to other schools, working scientists
- contact outside school – with non-gifted peers, gifted peers and adults
- Opportunities for developing thinking skills

CS Case study

Her class teacher, Miss W, has identified Naomi (a Year 6 child) as gifted in science. Miss W has met with the school's SENCO, the science coordinator and Naomi's parents to discuss her needs in science. The science coordinator worked with Miss W's medium term plans to identify where Naomi could carry out **directed extension work**, where she could carry out **independent research** and where she could be introduced to the Key Stage 3 Programmes of Study, which would provide the opportunity **for scientific study at a deeper level.** An individual education plan was then drawn up by the school's SENCO that identified the extra provision being made for Naomi. It was also agreed to contact the local comprehensive school for support in delivering the Key Stage 3 Programmes of Study, possibly by offering Naomi the opportunity **to use and apply her scientific ideas and skills in a range of different contexts**. Through the secondary school Miss W was able to set up **contacts outside school** for Naomi with other children via e-mail and visits to other schools.

Reflective questions

- Do you take into consideration the range of special educational needs in your class when planning science?
- Do you set clear and appropriate learning objectives for all pupils?
- Do you adapt your teaching plans for the children with SEN?
- Do you plan the adult support you can offer the children with SEN?
- Do you plan carefully the introduction to your lesson so that all children understand the task?
- Have you allowed sufficient time for all pupils to complete their task in science?
- Has the lesson structure allowed for children to carry out smaller tasks if necessary?
- Do you modify your exposition or instruction in response to SEN children and their particular needs?
- Do you use scientific vocabulary and language at an appropriate level?
- Are you able to use verbal or physical models to explain concepts?
- Do you use a range of questions according to ability?
- Do you present tasks in science at appropriate levels of difficulty?
- Do you encourage children to set their own learning goals, with or without support?
- Do you ensure opportunities for success for all?
- Do you provide regular and immediate feedback for pupils?
- Do you monitor the attainment of all children, including those with special educational needs, and use the information to inform your decisions about progression?
- Do you make good use of available resources for SEN children?
- Do you make further resources for SEN children, e.g., games, glossaries, etc., to aid children in their work and to consolidate their learning?
- Do you consider the specific Health and Safety issues for SEN children (Chapter 10)?

REFERENCES

Advisory Services Unit (1995) *Report of the Very Able Working Party*, Rotherham: Department of Education.

Dean, J. (1996) *Managing Special Needs in the Primary School*, London and New York: Routledge.

Department For Education (1994) 'Circular Number 9/94: The Education of Children with Emotional and Behavioural Difficulties', London: DfE.

Department for Education and Employment (1994) *Code of Practice on the Identification and Assessment of Special Educational Needs*, London: DfEE.

Department for Education and Science (1978) *Special Educational Needs* (The Warnock Report), London: HMSO.

National Association for Gifted Children website, www.nagcbritain.org.uk.

O'Hara, M. (2001) *Teaching History 3–11: The Essential Guide*, London: Continuum.

Siddles, R. (1999) 'Teaching Children with Autistic Spectrum Disorders in Mainstream Primary Schools', in *The Autistic Spectrum: A Handbook*, London: National Autistic Society.

Stirton, J. & Glover, C. (1998) 'A Code in the Head: Special Educational Needs in the Mainstream Classroom', in Cashdan, A. & Overall, L. *Teaching in Primary Schools*, London and New York: Cassell.

National Curriculum Council (1992) *Curriculum Guidance 10: Teaching Science to Pupils with Special Educational Needs*, London: HMSO.

Qualifications and Curriculum Authority (1999a) *The National Curriculum: Handbook for Primary Teachers in England*, London: DfEE/QCA.

Westwood, P. (1997) *Commonsense Methods for Children with Special Needs*, (3rd edn) London and New York: Routledge.

SUGGESTED FURTHER READING

Autism: Fact Sheets for Health Professionals, http://hna.ffh.vic.gov.au/yafs/cis/facts/autism.

Autism-UK: Advice and Information, www.autism-uk.ed.ac.uk/advice.htm.

Babbage, R., Byers, R. & Redding, H. (1999) *Approaches to Teaching and Learning: Including Pupils with Learning Difficulties*, London: David Fulton.

DfEE (1997) *Excellence in Schools*, London: DfEE.

DfEE SEN website, www.dfee.gov.uk/sen.

Drifte, C. (2001) *Special Needs in Early Years Settings*, London: David Fulton.

Gerland, G. (1997) *Finding Out about Asperger's Syndrome, High Functioning Autism and PDD*, London: Jessica Kingsley Publishers.

Halliday, P. (1989) *Children with Physical Disabilities*, London: Cassell.

Jones, A. V. (undated) *Science for Special Pupils: Some Guidelines for Teachers*, Nottingham Trent University.

Macintyre, C. (2000) *Dyspraxia in the Early Years*, London: David Fulton Publishers.

McCall, C. (1983) *Classroom Grouping for Special Need*, Stratford-upon-Avon: National Council for Special Education.

Moss, G. (ed.) (1995) *The Basics of Special Needs: A Routledge/Special Children Survival Guide for the Classroom Teacher*, London: Routledge.

Moses, D. (2000) *Special Needs in the Primary School: One in Five?*, London: Cassell.

Office for Standards in Education (1994) *Exceptionally Able Children, October 1993: Report of Conferences*, London: DfE.

Qualifications and Curriculum Authority (1999) 'Circular 44/99 Shared World – Different Experiences: Designing the Curriculum for Pupils who are Deafblind', London: QCA Publications.

Vahid, B., Harwood, S. & Brown, S. (1998) *500 Tips for Working with Children with Special Needs*, Kogan Page.

Webster, A. & McConnell, C. (1987) *Children with Speech and Language Difficulties*, London: Cassell.

8

Science and Equal Opportunities

There is a wide social and cultural diversity in Britain today which is reflected in many school communities. Such diversity is to be acknowledged and viewed as an asset for teaching and learning, and therefore teachers need to be clear and explicit in their provision of a science curriculum that ensures equality of opportunity. The DfEE guidelines on equal opportunities (www.dfes.gov.uk) require schools to have an up-to-date policy on equal opportunities that is implemented through all documentation and actions. Teachers are expected to be aware of what constitutes discriminatory behaviour and to work to eliminate it from the classroom. The chapter thus begins with a consideration of the context within which nursery and primary teachers need to think about equal opportunities, by outlining the requirements of legislation such as the Race Relations Act (1976) and the Sex Discrimination Act (1975), and continues with an exploration of what constitutes discriminatory behaviour.

The chapter then goes on to identify the strands involved in equal opportunities teaching. (Special Educational Needs also raises issues of equality and entitlement; these have already been dealt with separately in Chapter 7.) Two inter-related strands will be considered – teaching *about* equal opportunities and teaching *through* equal opportunities. Teaching about equal opportunities means challenging the beliefs of some members of society about other members of society, whereas teaching through equal opportunities means ensuring the curriculum is relevant and accessible for all. The interpretation of equal opportunities in the classroom has therefore moved away from treating all children as the *same* towards treating all children *equally*. This has meant a move from providing all the children with the same experiences, to providing experiences that meet each child's needs.

The chapter hence establishes that equality of opportunity cannot, and ought not, to be avoided or ignored and that differences between people not only exist but also enhance the curriculum. The chapter therefore concludes with a consideration of the equal opportunities classroom and identifies approaches to teaching and learning in science, by addressing the classroom ethos, contexts and teaching methods used. Throughout the consideration, specific examples of teaching within the 3–11 age range are used to illustrate the points raised. This section of the chapter also considers the contribution of the equal opportunities classroom to the raising of children's awareness and understanding of values and attitudes such as fairness, respect and equity.

The Context of Equal Opportunities

Both the Race Relations Act (1976) and the Sex Discrimination Act (1975) place an onus upon schools to promote equal opportunities and positive relations between staff, pupils and parents. Both Acts also make direct or indirect discrimination, whether on the grounds of race, colour, ethnic and national origins or gender, illegal. Teachers therefore have a duty to actively work towards the elimination of all incidences of discrimination.

Race Relations Act (1976)

The Race Relations Act 1976 defines racial discrimination as discrimination on the grounds of colour, race, nationality or ethnic or national origins.

The Race Relations (Amendment) Act 2000 came into force in April 2001 and introduced the need for schools to promote race equality.

Sex Discrimination Act (1975)

The Sex Discrimination Act 1975 applies to both males and females and makes it unlawful to discriminate against a person on the grounds of his or her sex.

In order for teachers to be able to work towards eliminating incidences of discriminatory behaviour, they must first have an understanding of what constitutes discrimination. Discrimination is the translation of attitudes and beliefs into behaviour and action. It results in people being treated differently because of their colour, gender, religion, or class. The treatment they receive may be verbal abuse, harassment, and restricted access to services or even violence. Discriminatory behaviour may be direct, i.e., an individual is overtly treated unfavourably, or indirect, i.e., where an individual appears to be treated equally but where the outcome is discriminatory in nature.

Direct discrimination is where one person is treated less favourably than another would be in the same circumstances, on the ground of their sex or race.

Indirect discrimination is where a condition or requirement is applied equally to males and females, or to people of different races, but is such that it favours one group only.

Overt, direct discrimination is often easily recognized and condemned, whereas indirect discrimination is often much harder to recognize or accept. Indirect discrimination, which is not recognized by society, may become accepted as a normal practice (Lane, 1999). In due course the discriminatory behaviour may permeate the thought, speech patterns and actions of areas of society to such an extent that they are registered in institutional policies and practices. Institutional prejudices may then be transferred to personal prejudices, leading to a conduct and belief in superiority, and thus subordination of the different groups. The term prejudice is defined below.

Prejudice – a definition

Prejudice is defined as unfair behaviour towards individuals, e.g., unfavourable feelings, opinions or actions, carried out without reason. Prejudice may be supported by personal and cultural experiences and backgrounds, socio-economic factors, lack of information or lack of accurate information and 'different power relationships between people and groups' (Lane, 1999).
Prejudice often results in stereotyping of groups of individuals, i.e., alleged characteristics in one person begin to be attributed to all similar people. Prejudice is not restricted to any particular group of people, and is seen as an interpersonal matter between individuals or between individuals and groups.

It is the responsibility of teachers to address the issue of discriminatory behaviour through their teaching *about* equal opportunities, and to eliminate discriminatory behaviour in the classroom through their own practice in teaching. Discriminatory behaviour in the classroom may be direct or indirect and may be displayed by adults or by pupils. It creates barriers and obstacles to learning; this results in disadvantage or exclusion for some children. In order to address this behaviour teachers must examine their own practice and the actions of other adults and children in the classroom. Below is an outline of some of the incidences of discriminatory behaviour that may occur in the 3–11 years classroom.

Discriminatory behaviour in the classroom

Providing teaching for one group of pupils but not another, e.g., baking for girls and construction sets for boys in the Nursery.
Applying different standards of behaviour, dress and appearance to different groups, e.g., jogging trousers for outdoor P.E. for boys and gym skirts for girls.
Excluding pupils from activities, e.g., Muslim children not being allowed to attend Christmas parties in school.
Giving pupils an awareness of stereotyping in the world of work, e.g., all cleaners are female whereas all lorry drivers are male.

Allocating resources, e.g., boys using the computer on most occasions.
Access to other benefits favouring one group of pupils, e.g., the boys always asked to do jobs for the Head.

It is important that all staff, parents and pupils are aware of the need to promote equal opportunities in the classroom. Parents and pupils should therefore know that the school has an equal opportunities policy and is committed to equality of opportunity for all pupils. (www.dfes.gov.uk)

Equal Opportunities Teaching

Children come into the classroom with many ideas about themselves and those around them. Their ideas continue to be shaped by the numerous influences they encounter both in the classroom and beyond. Children's attitudes, behaviour and expectations of themselves and others are developed in the classroom using firsthand experiences and interactions with others, whilst the world around them provides other influences. A child's family will hold certain views which influence the child's own views, and society provides more cultural information and reinforcement on the role and place of different people in that society. Children are constantly exposed to images of black and ethnic minority peoples, to ideas of the roles of men and women in the home, in everyday life and in employment, through television, newspapers and other media. Equal opportunities teaching in the classroom involve teaching *about* equal opportunities and teaching *through* equal opportunities to be effective. Both aspects are needed to:

- address the issues around equal opportunities;
- equip pupils with critical thinking and reasoning skills;
- develop the children's attitudes towards others;
- address discriminatory behaviour, both in and out of the classroom.

Teaching about equal opportunities is direct teaching about the issues of discriminatory behaviour; it is therefore clearly discernible, i.e., is overt to the children. Teaching through equal opportunities is recognizing that discriminatory behaviour occurs but is not used in the classroom. It is consequently not clearly discernible to the child but is an ethos in which each child learns. Such teaching contributes to a child's acquisition of positive values and attitudes, to themselves, to each other and to science. This leads to an understanding of fairness, respect and equity. However, one lesson cannot achieve all this. Equal opportunities teaching is an ongoing commitment; teachers therefore need to commit themselves to establishing *and* maintaining an equal opportunities classroom.

Teaching about equal opportunities

Teaching about equal opportunities is much harder with the younger child than the older child. Younger children may not have been exposed to discriminatory behaviour or may not recognize it as such. Care must be taken, when introducing the issue, to ensure that children do not receive confused or conflicting messages from home and school. Within the classroom, science can be used to discuss, question and challenge discriminatory behaviour and prejudiced attitudes, particularly through the stories of scientists and their work. The stories of scientists, particularly from the past, show clearly examples of prejudice and discrimination of all kinds (see below). The issues they raise may be discussed at a level equal to the children's understanding and with regard to the time in which the scientist lived, to the present day or to both times. The stories of scientists can thus be used as starting points to explore children's own developing ideas. They may be used to deal with the children's:

feelings
emotions
sense of indignation and injustice
ideas of fairness, diversity and respect

Charles Drew

Charles Drew was a black scientist who lived in America. He was born on 3rd June 1904, the oldest of five children, and lived in Washington D.C. Although he wanted to be a doctor, his parents couldn't afford to send him to medical school and so he took a job coaching athletes, in order to save up enough money to train as a doctor.
In 1928 he attended McGill University Medical School and in 1933 he qualified, receiving Master of Surgery and Doctor of Medicine qualifications.
During his training Charles became interested in the problem of collecting, storing and keeping blood. He made many advances in this area and during World War II he became involved in setting up a military blood bank system. He became an expert in this area and was known world-wide. He was asked to set up a blood bank system in England; this was the foundation of the present Transfusion Service.
In 1950, at the age of 46, Charles Drew was involved in a serious car crash and needed treatment including a blood transfusion. At this time there were 'whites only' and 'black' hospitals, with blood from black and white donors also being segregated. Charles was first taken to a 'whites only' hospital and was refused treatment because of his colour. He was then taken to the nearest 'black' hospital but died on the way.

(Feasey, 1999)

Rosalind Franklin

Rosalind Franklin was born in England in 1920. At the age of fifteen she decided to become a scientist. In 1938 she passed the examination for admission into Cambridge University but her father disapproved of university education for women and refused to pay for her. Her aunt offered to pay but eventually her father backed down and allowed Rosalind to go.

At the age of 26, having been awarded her PhD, Rosalind began working on X-ray diffraction. In 1950 she joined a team of scientists at King's College in London studying living cells. Rosalind made great advances in X-ray diffraction techniques with DNA, and discovered crucial keys to the structure of DNA. However, unknown to Rosalind, a colleague of hers (Maurice Wilkins) shared her data with James Watson and Francis Crick who were also working on the structure of DNA. James Watson and Francis Crick published the proposed structure of DNA in March 1953.

Rosalind looked to carry out her work elsewhere. She was unhappy at aspects of her time spent at King's College, e.g., women scientists were not allowed to eat lunch in the common room where male scientists ate theirs. She was allowed to leave King's College on condition she would not work on DNA elsewhere.

(www.pbs.org/wgbh/aso/databank/entries/bofran.html)

Teaching through equal opportunities

The ethos and philosophy of equal opportunities teaching and learning in nursery and primary settings is grounded in the Education Reform Act 1988. The Act established that all children have a right to expect their teachers to provide them with every opportunity to achieve their full potential in the classroom, irrespective of their gender, race, ability or class. The National Curriculum Council (1990) states that all children are entitled to an education that will enable them to participate fully in society, an education that prepares them for the opportunities, responsibilities, choices and experiences of adult life. The challenge for teachers to deliver this entitlement is both complex and exciting. One reason for the complexity is that although teachers may wish to be fair-minded, their own background will inevitably influence their behaviour. The majority of serving nursery and primary teachers are drawn from a relatively narrow section of society, which tends to originate from white, middle-class backgrounds and so hold beliefs, attitudes and values based on their experiences (Marsh, 1998). However, many children in nursery and primary schools do not share this kind of background. Consequently, in order to address the issue of equality of opportunity in the classroom, newly qualified teachers may first need to question their own beliefs, views and behaviour, and reflect on their own ideas of equal opportunities. The model below shows the stages teachers may need to go through in their reflection on their teaching and the changes they may need to encounter before being ready to develop an equal opportunities perspective to their teaching.

Model of progression in teacher behaviour to promote equal opportunities (Nieto, 1992; in Lane 1999)

Tolerance

Enduring rather than embracing. The first step on the road to more equal treatment. To move beyond this, Nieto advocates trying to find out about the experience of groups and peoples different from your own in order to make connections and to develop compassion.

Acceptance and respect

Recognition that equality of opportunity is something to be striven for even if you don't know quite how to go about it. At this stage teachers are urged to start to reassess the curriculum and to look for multi-cultural, non-sexist approaches in teaching and learning.

Affirmation

For Nieto this represents the final stage in coming to terms with diversity. At this point teachers are more self-confident and knowledgeable and are thus willing to debate and disagree openly on the issues.

Teaching through equal opportunities is much more than treating all children equally; this may even result in indirect discrimination, as noted earlier in the chapter. The key to teaching through equal opportunities is to provide equality of opportunity in the classroom, i.e., to ensure that all needs are met equally. Therefore, although a teacher may believe that he/she provides equality of opportunity in the classroom, the reality may be very different. Upon reflection, the teacher may find that he/she does not consider individual needs but 'treats everyone the same', which may result in even greater inequality, as in the following case study.

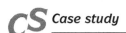 *Case study*

Mrs D teaches a year 3 class in a school that has a 20 per cent British Asian population and a gender mix of 2 girls to 3 boys. Mrs D's class reflects this trend, as within the class of 30 six children are British Asian and there are twelve girls and eighteen boys.
Mrs D planned to investigate sound travelling through different media, by investigating sounds in the air, listening to sounds along the floor and tabletop and making a string telephone. Mrs D was careful to ensure that all children were involved equally in the tasks. When recording their work Mrs D was mindful that the boys often used the computer and insisted that two girls presented their work using a graphics package. The follow up activity was to research information about sounds using a set of identical reference books which had been used earlier in the week with the more able Literacy group.
Mrs D was pleased that she had taught the lesson successfully, displaying overt equal opportunities teaching to the children. However she had discriminated against the lower ability children as they could not access the reference books, their reading ability was below that needed to decode the text. Two of the children would have benefited greatly from the provision of a bilingual text. Also, the boys appeared to use the computer more often because of their numbers in class and a much better use of the computer for the whole class was to have a CD Rom available for information to help the children with their investigations and research.

The delivery of the curriculum as in the case study above fails to meet each child's individual needs by not recognizing and taking into account their differences.

Adult conduct is hence central to the establishing of a learning environment in which the ethos is supportive of all the pupils, and so teacher expectations and teacher interactions with children need to be explored.

Teacher expectations, and behaviour, have a powerful impact upon pupil aspirations, achievement and self-esteem. Teacher expectations must therefore be relevant to children, to their ability and to their experiences and be shared with them. The children are thus aware not only of what is expected of them but also of the teacher's attitudes towards them and their belief in them. When working to identify and address the individual needs of children, teachers thus need to be mindful of their own ideas and behaviour and of the backgrounds of the children. The teacher must be careful not to fall into the trap of making stereotypical assumptions about their children concerning their intellectual, emotional, social and physical attributes (Adams, 1994). Consequently, their interactions with the child – both verbal and non-verbal – must convey their appreciation and understanding of the child's needs. This can primarily be achieved through recognizing the child's personal and cultural experiences and backgrounds, and building a curriculum that acknowledges these factors. The curriculum must also be determined with reference to the child's attitudes to equal opportunities. As acknowledged in the early part of this chapter, children do recognize that there are differences between themselves and others; even the youngest pupils discover these differences, particularly physical differences, and will begin to ask questions concerning them. To ignore these questions, and consequently the differences, is to ignore the issue of equal opportunities for the children. This is the context in which children's ideas of discrimination and prejudice are tested and developed. Children thus build up their ideas of both themselves and others in society. They also begin to make judgements about the worth of themselves and the worth of others. This leads to an understanding of their own expectations and their expectations of others. Promoting equality of opportunity therefore involves addressing the expectations and attitudes that children are acquiring, or have acquired.

A child's attitudes and expectations may be laudable, as they enable the child to meet his or her potential, or they may become barriers to their own learning, as they result in children having low expectations of themselves. If left unchallenged their attitudes and expectations may ultimately result in low job aspirations and life choices. Even quite young children may develop strong opinions about boys' and girls' attributes and about racial issues. If left unchallenged these opinions may have far-reaching affects. They may result in girls or ethnic minority pupils failing to fulfil their potential in science, due to a belief that the curriculum is inappropriate or irrelevant to them. It may also manifest itself in the same group of pupils under-performing, in order not to attract attention and so conform to stereotyping that undervalues their abilities. The teacher must therefore work

210

towards challenging these opinions, particularly children's opinion of themselves. This involves developing a child's self-confidence, as this is an important factor in overcoming under-achievement. The responsibility of the teacher is to provide a curriculum that is structured to develop self-confidence, by planning a curriculum that is relevant and accessible to all pupils. A child's self-confidence is needed to develop:

an enthusiasm for science,
an eagerness to investigate,
creativity in science,
curiosity about science,
an interest in explanations of concepts and phenomena.

Strategies for raising confidence and tackling discrimination in science

Strategy	Example
Consider the groupings of children in science lessons.	Decisions about grouping children in science must refer to children's abilities, children's developing attitudes, the gender mix of a group and the race mix of a group. Groups may be used to facilitate tolerance, empathy, fair-mindedness and equity.
Awareness of how black and white/boys and girls may react in science lessons.	The teacher must be mindful of stereotypical responses to science activities, e.g., boys are more able to work with electricity and girls enjoy working with plants, and provide activities which interest and motivate all children.
High expectations for all pupils – girls as well as boys, black as well as white – in science.	The teacher sets targets for children based purely on their attainment in science and not their attainment in Literacy or Numeracy or based on stereotypical ideas of race and gender.
Overtly teach the children that there are no gender or racially limited concepts in science. Use of black and female scientists as positive role models.	Refer to the work of scientists of both genders when introducing concepts new to the children.
Ensure learning materials appeal to all.	The teacher provides a range of learning materials, aimed at a range of abilities and interests.
Demonstrate value and respect for diversity and individual differences of pupils.	Ask a range of children to share their work, ideas and past experiences.
Use of knowledge about various cultures and backgrounds that might be present in the local community.	The teacher researches the scientific ideas of other cultures and presents them to the children for consideration.
Help children to recognize and challenge discriminatory practices and behaviour, in stories, in the classroom and beyond.	Discuss the events in stories. Ask various children their ideas about how the main characters behaved. Ask the children if they would like it if the same behaviour was displayed to themselves.

Challenge stereotypical responses – in yourself, in other adults and in children. Consider teacher/pupil interactions, to ensure all children are treated fairly.	As a teacher, reflect on events in the classroom with respect to equal opportunities issues.
Introduce children to ideas of fairness, justice and diversity.	Discuss with children the issues of fairness, justice and diversity in the classroom.
Insist on non-discriminatory language and procedures.	Older children should be expected to reflect on their behaviour in the classroom, with respect to equal opportunities
Praise for all children, boys and girls, black and white, for their achievements in science and their non-discriminatory language and behaviour.	Praise children for their achievements and their way of working, particularly in groups where all members have participated equally in a task.
Involve all parents in science teaching, to raise and broaden parental expectations of all pupils in science.	Invite parents in to school to help with science lessons and/or science events. Explain the science work being carried out and the expected achievements of the children.

The Equal Opportunities Classroom

The chapter so far has demonstrated that, in order to promote equal opportunities in the classroom, teachers need to plan to teach about equal opportunities issues, to address children's ideas and understanding of the issues, and to provide equality of opportunity for each child. As discussed previously in the chapter, to be effective in this teaching the teacher must first reflect on his or her own actions and beliefs, and may need to face up to some uncomfortable truths about his or her own ideas. Teachers may need also to consider their responses to the children's and society's prejudices and assumptions. Once these have been explored teachers must then begin to develop a science curriculum that contributes to the establishment of an equal opportunities classroom. Some issues to consider in this process are noted below.

Multicultural issues

In order to build a multicultural dimension into primary science teaching, the following must be taken into account:

cultural diversity in school and society;
that 'science' may mean different things in different cultures;

that the language of science may be complex, and so teachers need to provide help for children with these problems;

that pupils' own experiences, which should be the basis of science learning, may be very different due to cultural differences;

the need to avoid ethnic or cultural bias in tests and assessments.

(Adapted from 'Building a Multicultural Dimension into Primary Science', Peacock, 1990)

Gender issues

In order to promote science work which is relevant for girls and boys, the following may be taken into account:

illustrations, language, examples and models used in science should not have a purely masculine bias;

linking science investigations with other types of activity girls enjoy, e.g., discussion, creative writing;

emphasizing the application of science to everyday life;

starting with topics familiar and interesting to girls that lead to an understanding of all aspects of science.

(Adapted from 'GIST' final report, Manchester University Press, 1984)

The issues raised above begin to address the choices to be made by the teacher in developing an equal opportunities approach to teaching and learning in science. The classroom ethos, contexts and teaching methods must be explored further, in order to put theory into practice. The final part of the chapter therefore summarizes the considerations that teachers need to make in order to establish an equal opportunities classroom.

Planning

Planning which is sensitive to the children's backgrounds and beliefs is essential to the provision of equal opportunities. This may be achieved simply by building on children's current interests and being mindful of children's daily life, e.g., discussing the food choices made by different children in light of the BSE crisis. In this way, different cultural beliefs can be explored, understood and accepted.

Group work

Group work (see Chapter 4) offers most children a supportive and secure approach to developing their understanding and capability in science. The key to effective group work is the establishment of ground rules, e.g., following the conventions of conversation (listening to others, speaking in turn), dealing with bad behaviour, conflicts and disagreements through discussion and reasoned debate as part of the group. Group work therefore demands cooperation and respect for each member of the group and thus for the differences between people in the group.

Fairness

Children may be introduced to fundamental ideas about fairness through science activities, through the notions of fair testing and turn-taking when carrying out investigations.

Stories of scientists

The role of the stories of scientists in addressing equal opportunities has been discussed earlier in the chapter. Studying the stories enable pupils to find out about and discuss ways in which certain groups of people have influenced present scientific understanding, and how their work has affected the lives of others. Including the work and lives of scientists who are not the archetypal white man, helps to make diversity the norm.

Learning styles

It is reported (Marsh, J. in Cashdan and Overall, 1998) that socio-cultural factors may have an impact upon preferred learning styles. An awareness of the impact of such factors on pupil learning and behaviour may be a useful starting point for the consideration of curriculum delivery and teaching methods.

Learning experiences

Socio-cultural factors may also affect children's reactions to learning experiences in science. Children who have been brought up not to touch things until given permission may not readily involve themselves with interactive displays or hands-on activities and so may require extra encouragement or additional support. Children brought up not to question adults may experience difficulties during discussions or be reluctant to seek clarification about their work from their teachers. Other socio-cultural factors to consider involve children used to adult instructions being delivered as an order and therefore not responding with their own ideas about why and how things work, and the child not being allowed to make eye contact with an adult. This may lead the teacher to conclude that a child is either not listening or is not engaged in the task on offer.

Scientific enquiry

Scientific enquiry is based on the acquisition and use of skills, on open-mindedness and critical thinking, and on exploring the interpretations of scientific evidence. Discussing children's work, and more importantly their ideas, provides opportunities for reasoning, investigating and problem solving, and all children should be praised for questioning and sharing their ideas with the group/class. This approach values each child's contributions and so shows respect for differences of opinion and interpretation. Where children are able to bring to the discussion cultural ideas and explanations these too should be valued and discussed sensitively.

Scientific attitudes

Scientific attitudes are developed in the classroom (see Chapter 1) and may be relevant to both the science curriculum and the outside world. Development of positive attitudes towards science involves the willingness to modify views in the light of experience and additional information, and encourages the application of logic, developing an ability to engage in rational and reasoned discussion, based on evidence, in order to justify a point of view. Such attitudes and abilities constitute good preparation for the opportunities, responsibilities and experiences of adult life in a multi-cultural society.

Communication and recording

Using a variety of communication and recording techniques, and offering children the chance to describe and explain their ideas about science in a variety of ways, is an important way of promoting equality of opportunity in the science curriculum. Teachers must be mindful of the children who have English as an additional language, who are bilingual or multi-lingual or at the early stages of English acquisition. Teachers need to recognize that these children are no less intelligent than their English-speaking peers but merely lack the vocabulary needed to achieve in science. If possible, by providing a learning environment in which children are able to use their first language, children are able to express themselves clearly, and legitimacy for their first language is thereby provided in the classroom (Barratt-Pugh, 1994). Through being able to explain their ideas, they are then able to make a positive contribution to their learning of English and to their success in education generally (Marsh and Hallet, 1999). The use of bilingual teachers and support staff to facilitate the scientific work of pupils with English as an additional language is therefore invaluable in developing a multi-cultural learning environment. They may:

assist children in comprehending the English spoken word;
provide skilled assistance enabling the children to express themselves clearly and appropriately;
provide a model of how to use the English language appropriately, how to listen, and how to respond;
aid children in overcoming feelings of isolation and/or frustration;
ensure children do not avoid what goes on in the nursery or classroom;
ensure children are aware of what is happening in the classroom.

Displays

Careful use of display to value all children's work is essential in the equal opportunities classroom. Ensuring that displays and labels reflect the diversity and variety of children's backgrounds and traditions is also helpful in demonstrating equal opportunities in the classroom.

Marking work

Work must always be marked with respect to a child's socio-cultural background. Comments must be considerate and appropriate to the child's needs, but also reflect the objective of the lesson.

Communicating with parents

Communication with parents, both written and verbal, which reflects the diversity and variety of children's backgrounds and traditions, is helpful to the delivery of equality of opportunity. For some parents English is an additional language and this too must be considered. Again where possible communications may be made in the parents' first language, using bilingual assistants for support.

CS Case study

Mr N, the Year 5 teacher, was planning a Unit of science for his class that involved investigating contrasting habitats. He planned a visit to the local country park to observe the variety of nesting birds and the conditions provided by the country park, both natural and man-made. Two of his children had recently returned to school after visiting family in Pakistan. In order to use the two **children's current interests** Mr N decided to centre the work on the second, contrasting habitat in Pakistan. He could use the experiences and knowledge of the two children and supplement this with the use of secondary sources of information, i.e., books, CD Roms, TV programmes and the Internet. Through this study Mr N believed that **cultural beliefs could be explored, understood and accepted.**

Mr N planned for much of the work to be carried out in groups. Two groups would benefit from the knowledge of the children who had visited Pakistan and would promote the development of **cooperation and respect** within the group, **and thus for the differences between people in the group.** The whole class would benefit from their knowledge during plenary time, when the children would be **able to bring to the discussion cultural ideas and explanations.**

Mr N also planned a sharing assembly for the end of the Unit of work where parents would be invited to the presentation of the work to the school. This would provide **communication with parents**, and an opportunity for the parents to appreciate the school's response **to the delivery of equality of opportunity** in the classroom.

Reflective questions

How do you ensure that the principle of equality of opportunity permeates all planning and teaching in science?

Do you plan for equality of opportunity and the teaching about equal opportunities in your science activities?

Do you ensure that the curriculum is enriched and enhanced by positive reference to diversity?

Do you provide a variety of learning materials?

Do you ensure that all pupils have opportunities to develop their skills and confidence in science?

Do you provide a range of learning materials for hands-on experience?

Do you plan the breadth of curriculum content to appeal to all pupils?

Do you challenge stereotypical ideas and behaviours?

Do you use other resources that actively and positively promote the diversity of culture and gender roles in society?

Do you use attractively and professionally presented displays that incorporate objects, ideas, visual and written material from a range of cultures and geographical locations?

Do you introduce and discuss notions of right and wrong, fairness and inequality when teaching science?

REFERENCES

Adams, J. (1994) '"She'll have a go at anything": Towards an Equal Opportunities Policy', in Abbott, L. & Rodger, R. (eds) *Quality Education in the Early Years*, Buckingham: Open University Press.

Barratt-Pugh, C. (1994) 'We only speak English here don't we? Supporting Language Development in a Multilingual Context', in Abbott, L. & Rodger, R. (eds) *Quality Education in the Early Years*, Buckingham: Open University Press.

DfES (2001) 'Equal Opportunities', www.dfes.gov.uk.

Feasey, R. (1999) *Primary Science and Literacy*, Hatfield: ASE.

Kelly, A. (ed.) (1984) *GIST Final Report*, Manchester: Manchester University Press.

Lane, J. (1999) 'Action for Racial Equality in the Early Years', London: National Early Years Network.

Marsh, J. (1998) 'Schools, Pupils and Parents: Contexts for Learning', in Cashdan, A. & Overall, L. *Teaching in Primary Schools*, London and New York: Cassell.

Marsh, J. & Hallett, E. (eds) (1999) *Desirable Literacies: Approaches to Language and Literacy in the Early Years*, London: Chapman.

National Curriculum Council (1990) *Curriculum Guidance 3: The Whole Curriculum*, York: NCC.

Nieto, S. (1992) *Affirming Diversity: The Sociopolitical Context of Multicultural Education*, New York: Longman.

PBS On-line (2001) 'A Science Odyssey', www.pbs.org/wgbh/aso/databank/entries/bofran/html

Peacock, A. (1990) 'Building a Multicultural Dimension into Primary Science', *PSR* 12, Spring, ASE.

Race Relations Act 1976, HMSO.

Sex Discrimination Act 1975, HMSO.

Science and Whole School Issues

This chapter considers some of the whole school issues of which science is a part. The book has so far looked at numerous aspects of teaching and learning science in the curriculum, and now considers issues that involve science in the wider context. The chapter begins with a consideration of how parents, outside agencies and the community are informed of a school's ethos, interpretation and delivery of the subject area. Through this the chapter also explores how schools work effectively in partnership with governors and parents in the school curriculum. This section of the chapter concludes by discussing liaison between Key Stages, using specific examples of good practice. Through this, the notion of continuity and progression (see Chapter 3) as the children move through the 3–11 age range and beyond will be considered.

The final part of the section, and of the book, considers the role of the subject coordinator. The introduction of the National Curriculum in England and Wales in 1989 placed new pressures on primary school teachers in terms of their subject expertise. Teachers were faced with the task of developing their understanding and capabilities across a broad range of subjects, the recent developments in the Foundation Stage may, too, have a similar impact on teachers of the 3–5 age range. In many primary schools the response to the developments since 1989 has been to appoint curriculum coordinators for specific areas and subjects. However, the notion of curriculum coordinators was not new in 1989–90; it had previously been an underdeveloped idea (Bentley and Watts, 1994) and the developments in primary education since 1989 have done much to establish what the role involves. The current thinking has moved away from viewing coordination posts as rewards for general competence, resulting from long service and experience, towards a much more precise definition of the role. The definition now given to the role has enabled nurseries and schools to capitalize upon the collective subject strengths amongst their staff (Alexander, Rose and Woodhead, 1992, p. 21). Coordinators are now awarded the responsibility for curriculum planning in their subject areas, for the organization of resources, and for leading staff development. It is now recognized that all teachers, including teachers in the early part of their careers, are expected to shoulder some degree of curriculum responsibility. Titles may vary, and may include reference to curriculum coordinator, post holder and/or subject leader; this chapter will use the term *coordinator* to encompass all these titles.

In the past, training for the role of coordinator has often proved inadequate. Indeed many newly qualified teachers have to take on this increasingly complex and accountable role very early on in their careers, and preparation for it is now needed during ITT (Initial Teacher Training). In small schools, staff often have to take a lead in more than one subject area, and in other situations staff are asked to take on subject areas for which they have only a minimal subject background even though they may be very experienced as coordinators in other contexts. This section of the chapter is therefore intended to support teacher-training students with a subject specialism in science, and newly qualified teachers for whom science was studied as a core but non-specialist subject, to take a lead in the development of the subject across a school. The role of the subject coordinator, and some of the many skills needed by the effective subject coordinator, is explored through the scenario of the receipt of an Ofsted (Office for Standards in Education) inspection report. It begins with an analysis of the issues raised in the report, the formulation of an action plan in response to the report, and an overview of the resulting inservice work. The chapter therefore summarizes the role of the science coordinator in supporting teaching and learning across a school, and the challenge of maintaining and developing the impact of this core subject.

Whole School Issues

Maintained schools and Nurseries are accountable to parents, outside agencies and the community for their ethos, interpretation and delivery of a relevant curriculum, of which science is a part. The notion of accountability for the curriculum is not new; Docking (1990) writes that teacher accountability has been developing since the late 1970s. It was the Education Acts of 1980, 1981, 1986 and 1988 that made schools more publicly accountable. Schools continue to be accountable to the community, to parents, governors and the local education authority, and so must look for ways to inform the different partners in the education process. Accountability, in terms of children's attainment, has been explored in Chapter 6, accountability in terms of the delivery of an appropriate science curriculum must therefore be considered here. There are many ways in which the wider community may be informed of a school's interpretation and delivery of a subject area; this section of the chapter will explore four of them:

- school documentation
- school correspondence
- curriculum evenings
- dedicated curriculum days

School documentation

School documentation in the form of handbooks for parents, handbook for staff, policy statements, schemes of work and other written guidance may be made available to parents, governors and the LEA. It is through this documentation that the school's interpretation of national guidelines on the curriculum is conveyed to others. It is thus important that all documentation is appropriate to the school and is adhered to, for it is this that lays the foundations for good practice in science teaching in the primary school.

Guidelines for writing school documentation

Identify a need for documentation.
Is the documentation new or does it involve revising past documentation?
Access the Local Authority model.
Access other models.
Use models to provide headings for inclusion in school documentation.
Produce a first draft and circulate to colleagues.
Invite colleagues to comment on draft, add ideas, etc.
If necessary, delegate small groups to discuss and review the draft documentation.
Work with the groups then feedback to whole staff.
Use feedback from groups to redraft final version of documentation.
Present final draft to school governors for approval.

Handbook for parents

Schools often provide a handbook for the parents of children new to the school. The handbook will include a variety of information relating to the school's policies and procedures. They will include a statement regarding the description and outline of science teaching in the school. The handbook entry for each subject area should be fairly short and written in everyday language, in order to make it interesting to read and easy to understand. Where parents are known to have English as an additional language, the text should also be provided in alternative languages. The inclusion of children's work in the subject area enhances the comments made in writing and provides evidence of the policy in practice.

School handbook entry for science

From their early days in school our children are encouraged to observe and are introduced to details of texture, shape, pattern, etc. From these early explorations develops the ability to observe changes, a necessary skill in scientific development. Beyond this we encourage our children to adopt a scientific approach and attitude, as well as to acquire certain scientific facts. We expect our children to notice, to question, to hypothesize and investigate, to understand the notion of fair testing where appropriate, to record their work in a variety of ways and to relate their work to everyday life.

Handbook for staff

Staff new to a school, whether experienced or newly qualified, are often given general guidelines to school policies and practices in the form of a staff handbook. Information relating to science should include a statement regarding the delivery of the subject and a checklist for associated, in-school documentation for the teacher to refer to. The handbook should also contain a list of subject coordinators, including the science coordinator, for teachers to meet and discuss issues further.

Staff handbook entry for science

Science is to be taught for 2 sessions a week, approximately for $2\frac{1}{2}$ hours. We teach a balanced mix of investigational skills and content, through practical work wherever possible. Generally we provide differentiation at three levels for our children. We do not use a published scheme of work but have developed our own, which gives our planned coverage of the Early Learning Goals and the National Curriculum Order for science and suggested activities. The science coordinator keeps further sources of ideas and a range of books is stored in the staff room. Resources for science are mainly stored centrally, in the Maths and Science Store; electricity boxes and lenses are retained in each classroom.

Checklist of related documentation

National Curriculum Compendium
School Science Policy
School Science Scheme of Work
QCA Scheme of Work for Science (for reference only)
School Guidelines for Development of Sc1 Skills
School '10 minute science ideas'
Assessment, Record Keeping, Reporting and Target Setting Policy
School Planning Folder.

Science Policy

Each school or nursery will produce its own curriculum policies. The subject coordinator will lead the writing of the science policy, with all staff having input into the policy through comments or suggestions to be included in the policy. A subject policy is a succinct document which sets out the nursery's/school's overall rationale for teaching. It should be:

written in plain English
concise
a reference document for staff
relevant to the whole school
comprehensive

Draft science policy

A comprehensive policy will include:

A rationale – why teach science.
Aims – a description of the broad principles of science teaching.
Interpretation of the Early Learning Goals and the National Curriculum Order for science – what the school will teach in science.
Planning for science – details of long-term, medium-term and short-term planning issues.
Use of ICT in science.
Classroom organization and management – how science is taught in the school..
Cross-curricular links – where science fits into the whole curriculum.
Assessment, record keeping and reporting.
Meeting the needs of all pupils – differentiation of the science curriculum, SEN issues.
Equal opportunities and multicultural issues.
Continuity and progression in science – how this is ensured.
Links with the wider community – visits out of school, visitors into school, etc.
Safety in science.
Resources.
The role of the science coordinator
The role of the Head and Governors.

Scheme of Work

Schemes of Work (see Chapter 3) give details of how the requirements of national documentation are to be taught in the nursery and/or school. A Scheme of Work includes teaching objectives, suggested activities and pupil recording methods. Again the subject coordinator, in consultation with the rest of the staff, writes the scheme of work.

223

School correspondence

Many schools keep in contact with parents, governors and the community through letters, notices and termly or half termly newsletters. Information regarding events specific to science should be included, e.g., visits out to science centres, science projects and/or competitions, etc. School correspondence is a way of reaching all partners in education and informing them of current events in school, although when issuing the correspondence to children to take home teachers must be mindful that often the children need reminding to give letters, etc., to their parents. Addressing the papers, or putting names on the papers, helps to ensure delivery, and all correspondence should be followed up. The inclusion of reply slips to be completed by parents aids the process of following up correspondence.

Science entry in a school newsletter

Class 7 recently held a science poetry competition for the whole school. The winner of the under 7's poem was Dan Jones and winner of the over 7's poem was Emma Scott. Both children received a copy of Michael Rosen's book of science poems, 'Centrally Heated Knickers'.

The Head, Mrs Evans, presented the prizes in assembly this week. There is a display of some of the best entries to the competition in the school

Curriculum evenings

Curriculum evenings are an excellent vehicle for enhancing others' perceptions of how science is taught and what children learn about science. Parents, governors, LEA representatives and representatives from the community may be invited to attend. The events may be held immediately after school or later in the evening and last for around one hour. The language used should be everyday, out of courtesy for the non-professionals in the audience. The suggested format for a science curriculum evening is given below.

Suggested format for a science curriculum evening

3.30 p.m.	Coffee
3.45 p.m.	Introduction by the Head
	An overview of science in the school – national requirements, school interpretation, etc. – by the science coordinator
	Presentation of children's work, from Nursery to year 6, to demonstrate the range and depth of science work carried out in the school
4.15 p.m.	Question and answer session led by the coordinator and children, followed by thanks from the Head
4.30 p.m.	An exhibition of work, activities and investigations carried out in school
	Children to encourage, and help, adults to carry out the activities and investigations on display

Dedicated curriculum days

In order to share science work with the community, parents, etc., and to maintain interest in science in general, schools may organize dedicated curriculum days or weeks, to which all are invited. In March of each year a week of science, engineering and technology events is held nationally. Events range from local to national and include talks, exhibitions, radio and TV events. Some schools choose to organize an event of their own at this time. Suggestions include evening talks, a day devoted to science exploration, the organizing of an egg race (BAAS, 1983). The list below summarizes the events organized in one science (and technology) dedicated week.

Science and Technology week – Programme of Events

Visitors – each class to be visited by a visitor from the world of work. The visitor will set the class a challenge, which will require the use of science and technology to solve.

Displays – various hands-on displays to be put up around the school.

Weather-watch – weather recordings to be made daily.

Body-watch – P.E. time used for fitness work.

Science trail – provided by the science club.

IT – Year 6 to be 'roving reporters' for the week, recording the week's events.

Magazine – a school science magazine to be compiled after the week, using work from the week.

Visits – each class to have a relevant visit out of school.

Staff meeting – science-focused staff meeting during the week.

(Farmery, 1995)

Working with Parents and Governors in the Science Curriculum

Hornby (2000) writes about the increasing emphasis on parental rights within the Education Acts from 1980 to 1993 and that schools can now no longer afford not to work with parents. The establishment of a good relationship between parents and schools is now considered to be an essential requisite for providing the optimum education for children. Aspinall (1992) writes that keeping parents informed of the science curriculum is no longer a courtesy, that informed parents are better able to support their children which, in turn, helps teachers enormously, while Watkinson (1992) suggests that the parental (and home) role is vital for the development of scientific skills, concepts and understandings in young children. It is therefore vital that the student or newly qualified teacher has a good knowledge of strategies or techniques for working effectively with parents. The list below outlines some of these ideas.

To work effectively with parents teachers must

Have an understanding of parental perspectives (i.e., be able to see and understand parental points of view);

Be aware of family dynamics;

Be able to view children within their family units;

Know what they can do to help the parents of children experiencing difficulties, either with the curriculum or problems affecting them and their work in school;

Know how to work with parents who are experiencing difficulties themselves;

Have knowledge of the range of services and resources available to parents.

Be aware of the beliefs and customs of the ethnic groups with which they work.

Adapted from 'Improving Parental Involvement', Hornby, 2000

Parents are therefore now viewed as partners in their child's education. Many references have been made throughout the book to their involvement in the science curriculum, including the important role they play in assessing and monitoring learning in science (see Chapter 6). Parents are to be kept informed through the suggestions made at the beginning of this chapter and through ongoing, day-to-day interactions between the school, the class teacher and the parent. Students and newly qualified teachers therefore not only need to be aware of strategies for working effectively with parents but also need to develop the inter-personal skills needed to relate to parents in a non-threatening environment. Advice for working with parents of the children in the school should be sought from more senior members of the school staff. The skills needed also relate to a teacher's interactions with a school's governing body. The governing body will be made up of representatives from the community, the LEA, school staff and parents. The governing body is responsible for the establishment of school policies and plays an active role in ensuring the policies are put into practice. Members of the governing body are therefore encouraged to visit the school during the day, to sit in on lessons (as pre-arranged with the Head) and attend school events. The science coordinator and/or class teacher may therefore communicate directly with the governing body on matters related to the science curriculum.

Liaison between Key Stages

When children move through the Key Stages – from the Foundation Stage to Key Stage 1, from Key Stage 1 to Key Stage 2 and from Key Stage 2 to Key Stage 3 – the requirements of the curriculum, including the science curriculum, inevitably change. Teaching for each Key Stage is planned using the Early Learning Goals (DfEE/QCA, 1999b) for the age group 3–5 years, and the National Curriculum (DfEE/QCA, 1999a) for children in Key Stages 1 to 3. In each Key Stage the requirements build on previous teaching and learning, and so an understanding by teachers is needed of what children have experienced in science in previous years. Liaison is the term used to describe how teachers from each Key Stage receive information about the children. Liaison may involve meetings, joint projects and/or the transfer of written information. Copies of children's Records of Achievement now form part of a child's educational record (QCA, 2001) and schools are required to transfer this information when a child transfers to a new school. A common transfer form is to be sent to the receiving school that contains information about the child, including Key Stage test results and teacher assessments. The form therefore requires information about a child's achievements in science to be submitted to the receiving school. Where a child moves from one Key Stage to another, this information is also made available. However, there is much more schools can do to both aid the transition for the children and provide information for the receiving Key Stage. QCA (1998) reports that the majority of schools ensure pupils are well prepared for transfer between Key Stages, particularly in the areas of pastoral care and special educational needs, but there are concerns that children do not progress as they should, particularly when moving from Key Stage 2 to Key Stage 3. The report acknowledges that transferring assessment information is important in order for each Key Stage to build upon prior attainment, and also suggests three further strands to ensure progress is made:

more effective use of assessment data;
planning for curriculum continuity and progression;
monitoring pupil's work.

The suggestions made refer to Key Stage 2/Key Stage 3 transfer, but are equally applicable to other Key Stage transfers. Cheshire County Council (1997) published the results of a project based on developing materials for effective cross-phase liaison and suggested that meetings between staff were a very important part of the process. Their recommendations are summarized in the list below.

Requisites for effective cross-phase liaison

meetings between teachers – to build up a professional relationship;
agreed meeting dates and agendas – to ensure meetings are used for the purpose of liaison issues;
support from the Senior Management Team – to acknowledge the importance of cross-phase liaison;
good communication – to keep all involved in the process informed and to avoid misunderstandings;
equal contribution – all teachers involved need to be able to contribute to the planning and delivery of liaison;
common objectives – how and why the liaison is taking place;
moving forward – keeping the process going;
planning – to keep the process on track, using the time available .

Adapted from Cheshire County Council (1997)

Effective liaison, taking into consideration the three strands suggested above for ensuring pupil progress, may involve various strategies. The table overleaf sets out some of the strategies that may be used, together with examples of good practice.

Strategies for effective, cross-phase liaison

Strategy	Explanation
Exchange of Common Transfer Form	Statutory requirement to transfer copies of Records of Achievement, Key Stage assessment results and teacher assessments.
Exchange of examples of children's work	Children's workbooks and other recorded work (including assessed work) passed on to receiving teacher, to increase awareness of children's achievements.
Cross-phase meetings	Termly meetings between teachers in different phases of education, to share experiences, discuss current science work and related issues – see Case study 1 below.
Cross-phase assessment moderation	Work to be assessed against national standards (see Chapter 6) shared at meetings, to agree on achievements made and to develop a common understanding of national standards.
Cross-phase assessments	One assessment activity to be carried out in each Year group, e.g., a simple investigation, the results of which are discussed and moderated – see Case study 2 opposite.
Joint curriculum projects	A project that begins when the children are in one phase of education and completed in the subsequent phase of education – see Case study 3 opposite.
Shared teaching	Teachers moving between Key Stages, e.g., a Year 6 teacher (KS2) teaching a session in Reception (Foundation Stage) or a Year 7 teacher (KS3) teaching a Year 6 class. The teaching may be carried out solely by the teacher from another phase or may be team teaching. Both teachers, to ensure the work is pitched at the correct level, will plan the lesson together. Shared teaching provides valuable information for the teacher in the next phase of education regarding the children's attitudes and aptitudes.

 ## Case study 1 – Cross-phase liaison between Nursery and Reception

At Fenchurch Primary School children transfer from the LEA-maintained Nursery school on the same site, to Reception, in September and January. Planning for curriculum continuity and progression is achieved through termly meetings for the teachers, Nursery nurses and support staff. The respective Heads of the two schools provide cover for the classes to allow for the meetings during the school day. The two teachers take turns to draw up an agenda; Miss B (a Nursery nurse in Reception) minutes the meetings and provides all staff with a copy after a meeting has taken place. The meetings have a basic agenda, which is added to when needed. The basic agenda is:

Current planning, including details of topic ideas
Current assessments taking place
Ideas for future planning/topics/visits
Resource issues – resources needed/resources to be shared
AOB

At the meetings all the Foundation Stage practitioners have a voice and are involved in discussions about current issues, including current science work and related issues. The meetings ensure there is continuity and progression in the children's learning as past experiences and achievements are shared, and the practitioners in the different phases of Nursery and Reception education, share their expertise.

 ## Case study 2 – Cross-phase liaison between Key Stage 1 and Key Stage 2

In order to address the issue of collecting and using assessment data more effectively, Mrs E (the science coordinator) planned to use a series of staff meetings to work with her colleagues. At the first meeting Mrs E presented the staff with a question 'Will the flattened part of a plasticine ball get bigger or smaller if we drop it from different heights?' The staff were asked to discuss how this question could be presented to each teacher's class, and how the children could carry out the necessary investigation. The staff were then asked to carry out the investigation with their class and report back the following week.

At the next meeting the staff shared their children's work, giving explanations of how the task was carried out. The staff were clearly able to see the progression in the children's scientific enquiry skills.

At the next staff meeting the pieces of work were moderated and assigned a National Curriculum Level of Attainment. Staff from both Key Stages were able to work together to agree on the standards reached.

The next meeting involved the staff in identifying the scientific enquiry skills already held by the children and the skills they needed to be taught to move the children on.

(Adapted from Farmery, 1999)

 ## Case study 3 – Cross-phase liaison between Key Stage 2 and Key Stage 3

St Gerald's Secondary school identified the need to work much more closely with its feeder schools, as the Year 7 children were not attaining the levels expected in science, following their end of Key Stage 2 SATs results. Miss J, the Key Stage 3 coordinator for science, contacted the LEA for suggestions for developing cross-phase liaison between Key Stage 2 and Key Stage 3. The LEA recommended the Cheshire County Council's Bubbles project (1997), which had been used successfully in other schools in the area. The project involved a series of activities based on the theme of 'bubbles' and focusing on scientific enquiry skills. The activities were carefully planned, easy to resource and well explained. A list of activities to be carried out in Year 6 was followed by a list of activities to be carried out in Year 7. The benefits of the project were apparent to Miss J – the children's skills would be developed, there was continuity in the science being offered and the Year 7 teachers would get to know the children and their achievements. Miss J began the project by contacting the head of St Gerald's and the heads of the feeder schools. Permission was granted to carry out the project and meetings were arranged with all Year 6 and Year 7 teachers. Details regarding the delivery of the activities were agreed and the project ran in the summer term in Year 6, to be concluded in the autumn term in Year 7.

The Role of the Subject Coordinator

The coordinator may have a range of roles and responsibilities, the specific responsibilities of the subject coordinator may be provided by schools in different ways. They may be issued as part of the job description for a new appointment or as a written list of responsibilities, together with a curriculum plan for the subject, as in the following boxes.

_____ Nursery / Infant / Junior School

Job description

Class teacher / Science Coordinator, CPS (Common Pay Spine)

General duties

Class teacher for a Year 6 class. This responsibility includes:
the planning, preparation, delivery and assessment of a varied and relevant curriculum;
ensuring a stimulating, active learning environment for pupils through good classroom organization and display;
motivating children by personal influence and by awareness of needs.
To work as part of the staff team, adhering to the school's behaviour policy, showing consideration to colleagues, assisting in curriculum development, and involvement in extra curricular activities.

Specific responsibilities

To be responsible for the development of the science curriculum across the school to ensure breadth and balance, progression and continuity.
To develop and maintain the science policy, guidelines and schemes of work.
To keep up to date with local and national developments in the science curriculum.
To liaise where appropriate with other curriculum coordinators.
To lead staff development in science.
To support teaching and learning in science across the school.
To be responsible for monitoring and purchasing resources for science across the school.

_____ Nursery / Infant / Junior School

Curriculum Coordinator responsibilities:

To be responsible for the effective running of the subject at a Key Stage.
To be responsible for policy discussions.
To provide explanation and practical application of subject.
To liaise with the Head, Deputy Head, Key Stage and Year Group Coordinators.
To support colleagues in meeting the requirements of an effective class teacher.
To provide a good model of practice in line with school policy.
To monitor class practice of the subject by developing good working
relationships, being positive, anticipating and resolving problems.
To bring issues of concern to the attention of the Senior Management team.
To evaluate the implementation of policy and practice.
To know the aims of the School Development Plan with respect to the subject.
To play an active part in the performance management system of the school.
To be part of the School Management structure.
To promote a positive approach and keep abreast of modern education
practice.
To respect confidentiality at all times.

_____ Nursery / Infant / Junior School

Plan for a Curriculum Area:

Rationale for the subject in school.
Policy for delivery of subject.
Scheme of Work for coverage of subject.
Organization of subject.
Progression through school.
Differentiation.
Special needs provision.
Health and Safety issues.
Resources.
Assessment, Recording and Record-Keeping.
Portfolio of Moderated work.

The Subject Coordinator will have a clear overview of the subject in school.
He/she will also have a clear plan for how the subject is to move forward.

One of the keys to being a good science coordinator is the development of subject expertise. The work of Alexander et al. (1992, pp. 20–21) had emphasized the importance of 'curricular expertise' as a precursor to quality in teaching and stressed the need for coordinators to possess such expertise. This necessitates knowledge and an understanding of science, an understanding of the factors that promote effective learning in science and the skills needed to teach science successfully. Developing subject expertise can be achieved in a variety of ways – through keeping up to date with current thinking and current trends in the world of primary science teaching, through local school networks, through the LEA, by accessing relevant websites on the Internet (e.g., the DfEE standards site, the virtual teachers centre, etc.) and by involvement with the professional body, the ASE (The Association for Science Education). Subject expertise therefore needs to be considered in terms of the subject within the school and also the development of the subject outside school. This is one of the central responsibilities of a subject coordinator, the ability to move a subject forward originates from this aspect of the coordinator's role. Hence, in addition to developing their own subject expertise, the coordinator must also be capable of disseminating such expertise to others within the school, in order to continue to develop quality teaching and learning across the school. One of the main challenges facing the science coordinator today is ensuring the subject retains its core area status in the school and that sufficient time is given over to its study. This is crucial for the maintenance and development of the subject. The introduction of the Literacy and Numeracy Strategies into schools has had a profound impact on the status of science – and on other subjects in the curriculum – and on the opportunities for teaching and learning in science. Similarly, parallel changes to the priorities for initial teacher training (DfEE, 1998) are also likely to impact upon the preparedness of some newly qualified teachers to deliver quality teaching in subjects other than Literacy and Numeracy, although science does fare better than the Foundation subjects. The introduction of the Desirable Outcomes for Children's Learning (SCAA, 1996) and the Early Learning Goals (DfEE/QCA, 1999b) have added a further dimension to the need to develop progression and continuity in science, and yet the existence of national documentation alone cannot ensure adequate and effective coverage of science. The science coordinator must consequently be able to promote the development of science through working alongside colleagues in their classrooms, demonstrating lessons or approaches to learning, and by conducting curriculum development meetings or Inset days. The responsibilities of the subject coordinator therefore encompass the roles of educator, advisor and facilitator.

As an **educator** you will have to help your colleagues to develop their own subject knowledge and understanding in history. Inspiring and motivating colleagues has to be underpinned by an ability to empower and enskill those colleagues. Insufficient attention to the latter can undermine attempts to inspire and motivate by reinforcing feelings of inadequacy, both real and imagined, amongst staff.

As an **advisor** you will need to have an eye to future developments in the teaching of history and be able to communicate not only with colleagues but also with parents and governors and the head teacher in the school.

232

As a **facilitator** you will need to create a climate of trust and openness in which change can occur. To be effective as a leader you have to become effective as a supporter.

(Bentley and Watts, 1994, pp. 159–160)

The Ofsted Report

One of the main vehicles for demonstrating the requirements of a science coordinator is the response to an Ofsted inspection and its report. The many skills deemed as being necessary for being an effective subject coordinator are used at this time. Ofsted Inspections are carried out in maintained schools at least once every six years, although the time difference between inspections varies from school to school. An Ofsted team will spend time in a school observing lessons, meeting staff and reading school documentation. The Inspection team also consults parents, governors and children. The inspection, and the subsequent report, will focus on the quality of education provided, the educational standards achieved, the management of finances and the spiritual, moral, social and cultural development of the pupils. The Inspections are intended to aid school in improving through identifying strengths to be built on and weaknesses to be addressed. The science coordinator can expect to be fully involved in the Inspection process and its follow-up, in consultation with the school's Senior Management Team. The next section of the chapter will hence focus on an Ofsted report for a primary school, the response to it and the skills needed to effect the response. The report used has been adapted from an actual school's Inspection report, to illustrate the demands made on a subject coordinator following the receipt of an Ofsted report.

Adapted Ofsted Inspection Report for Curriculum Areas and Subjects

Science

Standards of attainment in science at Key Stage 1 are not significantly different from the National Average. Pupils are not working to achieve at higher levels. Work on experimental and investigative science is below what could be expected at this stage whilst work on the remaining aspects of science shows a much better match to the standards expected. Pupils are able to resolve problems and develop their vocabulary successfully. Display work shows sound work on the senses, the body, plants and magnets.

Pupil results in the Key Stage 2 SATs were below the National Average. Attainment in experimental and investigative science is not consistently satisfactory. Evidence of previous work displayed indicated sound work on electricity, food chains, the body and the water cycle. Pupils' recall of recent knowledge was satisfactory but less secure when discussing earlier work.

Pupils make good progress in planned activities. They gain new knowledge and their scientific vocabulary is being extended successfully. The National Curriculum assessment indicates that progress is not reflected in the level of success gained in the tests.

Pupils show a good attitude to their work and carry out practical work sensibly. The range of available resources is good, well organized and readily accessible.

The coordination of science across both Key Stages is good. The role is well defined. Good progress is being made in implementing the school's scheme of work. Assessment procedures are clearly defined. A structure to raise pupils' level of attainment is now in place.

In order to respond to the report, the coordinator must be able to:

Interpret the report;
Accept the comments;
Summarize the comments;
Work out a plan of action which builds on the noted successes and addresses the identified weaknesses;
Lead the staff through change.

Interpret the report

The effective subject coordinator must be able to read the Ofsted report and, more importantly, be able to interpret what has been read. This is not only true for the Ofsted report but also other documentation. The curriculum in the 3–11 age range has been in a constant period of change for some years. Over the last ten years there have been numerous initiatives, strategies and curriculum updates, e.g., Desirable Learning Outcomes (SCAA, 1996); Early Learning Goals and the Foundation Stage (DfEE/QCA, 1999b); National Curriculum and Key Stages 1 and 2 (DES, 1989; DfE, 1995; DfEE/QCA, 1999a); National Literacy Strategy (1998); National Numeracy Strategy (1999). Each of these documents requires a response from schools at a local level and it is usual that the coordinator is involved in preparing a response.

Accept the comments

The Ofsted report may make statements that the coordinator, and the school, may not agree with. However, it must be accepted that the report details what has been observed during a short space of time and what is apparent through documentation provided by the school. The coordinator must therefore accept that the Report reflects what is discernible to a knowledgeable observer and must work to improve what has been observed. This may be through a change in practice, a change in policy and/or a change in school documentation, to ensure that the observer does see what is on offer in the school.

Summarize the comments

The coordinator must be able to summarize the comments made in the Ofsted report, to identify the key points of the report that need action. The key points of the report above can be summarized thus:

Key Stage 1
Standards of attainment are around the National Average.
Pupils not working to achieve at higher levels (than National Average).
Work on experimental and investigative science is below what could be expected.
Work on other aspects of science (Sc2/3/4) shows a much better match to the standards expected.
Pupils are able to solve problems.
Pupils develop their vocabulary successfully.
Display work shows variety of science work.
Evidence of work on the senses, the body, plants and magnets.

Key Stage 2
Results in Key Stage 2 SATs below the National Average.
Work in experimental and investigative science not consistent.
Display work shows variety of science work.
Evidence of work on electricity, food chains, the body and the water cycle.
Pupils able to recall recent knowledge.
Pupils less able to discuss earlier work.
Good progress made in planned activities.
Pupils gain new knowledge successfully.
Pupils' scientific vocabulary is being extended successfully.
SATs results indicate that progress made is not reflected in the tests.
Pupils show a good attitude to their work.
Pupils carry out practical work sensibly.

Coordination
Coordination of science across KS1 and KS2 is good.
The role of the coordinator is well defined.
The range of resources is good, well organized and readily accessible.
Good progress in implementing the school's scheme of work.
Assessment procedures clearly defined.
A structure to raise pupils' level of attainment in KS2 SATs is now in place.

Working out a plan of action

In response to the report an action plan must be devised. The coordinator will use the summarized points from the Inspection report to work out a plan of action that builds on the noted successes and addresses the identified weaknesses. In order to do this, the points are sorted into those which:

235

- Indicate success
- Indicate a weakness
- Are relevant to both key stages
- Are relevant to one key stage.

The sorting of the summarized points on the previous page is shown in the tables below.

Key Stage 1

Strengths	Weaknesses
Standards of attainment are around the National Average	Pupils not working to achieve at higher levels (than National Average)
Work on other aspects of science (Sc2/3/4) shows a much better match to the standards expected	Work on experimental and investigative science is below what could be expected
Pupils are able to solve problems	
Evidence of work on the senses, the body, plants and magnets	

Key Stage 2

Strengths	Weaknesses
Good progress made in planned activities	Results in Key Stage 2 SATs below the National Average
Pupils gain new knowledge successfully	SATs results indicate that progress made is not reflected in the tests
Evidence of work on electricity, food chains, the body and the water cycle.	Work in experimental and investigative science not consistent
Pupils able to recall recent knowledge	Pupils less able to discuss earlier work
Pupils show a good attitude to their work	
Pupils carry out practical work sensibly	

Both Key Stages

Strengths	Weaknesses
Display work shows variety of science work	Attainment against National Average and above
Pupils' scientific vocabulary is developed and extended successfully	Work on experimental and investigative science is inconsistent/below expected average

Coordinator role

Strengths	Weaknesses
Coordination of science across KS1 and KS2 is good	
The role of the coordinator is well defined	
The range of resources is good, well organized and readily accessible	
Good progress in implementing the school's scheme of work	
Assessment procedures clearly defined	
A structure to raise pupils' level of attainment in KS2 SATs is now in place	

By summarizing the report and sorting the report issues into grids the points for action can be clearly defined. Using the model Inspection report in this chapter, the points for action can clearly be defined as:

Work in experimental and investigative science needs developing across both key stages;
An understanding of the requirements of the different Level Descriptions;
An understanding of the requirements of children in the Key Stage 2 SATs;
Strategies to develop children's recall of previous science.

The coordinator is then able to work with the Senior Management Team and the governors to provide a written response to the Ofsted report. The school has at least one week from receipt of the draft report to comment on matters of factual accuracy, and forty school working days from the receipt of the full report to respond in writing. It is the responsibility of the governors to prepare a Governors' Statement and the responsibility of the coordinator to prepare a written action plan, to be submitted to the Ofsted team. (The boxes overleaf set out the responses to the Ofsted report being used in the chapter.) The vast majority of coordinators in nursery and primary settings receive little or no non-contact time in which to carry out their coordination responsibilities, and so the written response has to be completed in their own time. Effective personal organization and time management are therefore crucial to the success of both the written response to the Ofsted report, the action plan, and the general role of the science coordinator.

Governors' Statement

During the next term we intend to review our work in science, commencing with an audit and a review of planning, to lead to clearer objectives. The issues of experimental and investigative science and National Curriculum assessments will then be addressed.

Science Action Plan

The principal aim of the Science Action Plan is to raise attainment of children in science. The action plan will build on the positive aspects of the report and focus on staff training, monitoring the delivery of science and general support given by the co-ordinator.

Staff training will take place over one term, through weekly staff meetings and an Inset day. The scheme of work will be reviewed.

Monitoring of science will be based on the scheme of work.

The coordinator will continue to keep up to date with current ideas in the teaching of science and use this to support colleagues.

Target Setting and Monitoring the Action Plan

Staff responsible: Head, Senior Management Team, Science coordinator, assessment coordinator, Year group staff

Date to be reviewed: End of current school year

Targets	Criteria for success	Action
Improvements in SATs in Years 2 and 6.	A 20 per cent increase in number of children obtaining the National Average.	Review requirements of SATs tests. All staff to be aware of requirements. Develop programme of 'revision' work.
Improvements in higher levels of SATs in Years 2 and 6.	Children to achieve at a higher level than National Average.	Support by coordinator.
Development in children's use of Sc1 skills.	Children to demonstrate expected ability in Sc 1 assessments.	Staff training on teaching Sc1 skills. Staff understanding of whole investigations to be developed.
Children to become more independent in whole investigations.	Children able to carry out whole investigations.	Implementation of an end of Year Sc1 assessment.
Children, and parents, to be informed of targets set in response to learning objectives for year.	Children know own targets for science.	Teachers to set achievable targets for class. Targets to be reported to parents.
To collect work for a school portfolio on assessed science work.	A portfolio set up and retained by coordinator.	Put into place fully requirements of school assessment policy. Carry out Year Group standardization meetings.

Lead the staff through change

The Ofsted report, and its response by the school, may necessitate *change* on behalf of the coordinator and/or the staff. The change may be required in personal understanding, in curriculum practices and/or personal thinking. It must be accepted however that there are practitioners who embrace and support change and those who oppose it. The role of the coordinator is hence to:

understand that there are changes needed;
clearly identify the changes to be made;
set a programme for change;
understand the implications of the proposed changes for their institution.

The coordinator must be able to recognize, accept and work with the feelings that such change may inspire in some of their colleagues. These feelings may be intensified if there are changes to be made to their practice on a number of fronts simultaneously. In order to support their colleagues through these feelings, the science coordinator must be able to reflect upon their own views regarding change in general. They must then consider their responses to the immediate changes being considered. Finally, coordinators must be mindful that they are the subject *expert* and so their reaction may be very different to that of other, non-specialist staff and so it may be helpful to consider their own feelings when changes have been introduced in other subjects. However, the reactions of the coordinator and the staff cannot always be anticipated, as everyone can find himself or herself supporting or opposing change at different times. Their reaction will be dependent on both the immediate circumstances and the change proposed. Being a supporter or opposer of change may also be dependent upon personality, as indicated below.

Supporters of change

May be characterized as progressive, positive and forward looking
May invoke change for the sake of change
May not allow time for change to be effective
Are open to new ideas
Seek to improve curriculum through change

Opposers of change

May be characterized as reactionary, negative, backward looking
May oppose change without giving it due consideration
May not allow time for change to be effective, and be negative in their responses to it
Oppose all ideas that differ from what they consider to be the norm
Prefer to maintain *status quo*
Do not accept that the curriculum will improve through change

The coordinator must therefore be able to recognize whether there is to be change for the individuals and/or for the curriculum, whether the changes proposed are quite insignificant or quite major, and if they will be welcomed by individuals or may be actively resisted. Being aware of the probable responses will aid the coordinator in planning the implementation of changes. The change may be perceived as an exciting opportunity that offers teachers an opening to experiment with their teaching and to be creative in their interpretation of the curriculum. Alternatively, it may be perceived as threatening to the teacher's interpretation of the curriculum and critical of his or her present practice. There are many factors that may influence the response to change to practice, including:

The origin of the change, e.g., those that originate nationally, and are thus backed by the force of national legislation and have potentially considerably more impetus than locally originated change;
Little input into externally imposed changes by teachers;
Changes that are internally inspired, albeit possibly more relevant to the development needs of the nursery/school, may be viewed as less effective than national developments;
External pressures on teachers and on teacher time being cited as reasons for not taking up internal changes;
Priority in the curriculum for Literacy and Numeracy;
Everyday pressures on teachers – planning, paperwork, assessment, etc.;
The perceived threat of the change to the stability of the curriculum;
Anxiety about the new skills and knowledge needed;
Concerns based on a professional assessment of the proposals;
Concerns, worries and consequent resistance based on emotional responses.

Specific personal and professional changes required by the Ofsted report may include:

a disruption to established routines and practices,
a change to documentation for the subject,
a possible redundancy of old resources,
perceived threats to teacher status through loss of confidence and self-esteem,
a revision, renewal or learning of scientific knowledge and skills,
loss of, or change to, previously held beliefs and ideas,
anxiety for staff whose own experiences at school were less than satisfactory and so
   question the proposed changes.

The science coordinator must therefore be aware of potential staff feelings, threats to the implementation of the change and the possible effects of the change. To be successful in bringing about curriculum change in science, the coordinator will need a range of skills – as shown on the opposite page. The skills will ensure that the coordinator is able to empathize with their colleagues, reassure them, discuss their fears, put together a training package if needed and ultimately persuade them of the potential benefits of any change.

Skills needed to implement change:

empathy

communication – the ability to listen as well as speak

subject knowledge

organizational skills

planning skills

ability to set, and meet, short-term goals

understanding of how change improves teaching, pupil attainment and learning

the ability to see changes through to a conclusion

leadership style – lead by example. Be well prepared, enthusiastic, caring, and aware of group dynamics

motivational skills

facilitation of teamwork

interpersonal skills

understanding of what is to change and why

pre-empting problems to be overcome

Delivering the Action Plan

Once the Action Plan has been written and approved by the school's governing body and subsequently by the Ofsted Inspection team, the coordinator must then present the Plan to the staff. This thus begins the process of developing teaching and learning across the school, through initiating and leading staff development. This may involve a series of staff meetings and/or Inset days. A suggested programme of Inset in response to the Ofsted report being considered here is given below.

Inservice plan to deliver Action Plan

Week 1	Audit present delivery of science
	Feedback from Ofsted
	Expectations from Inset
Week 2	Evaluation of SAT results
Week 3	Using Level Descriptions
Week 4	Recapping – how to use children's' previous knowledge
Week 5	Scheme of Work – where are we now?
Week 6	Review of Scheme of Work
Week 7	Planning for science
	Learning objectives
Week 8	Experimental and Investigative science
	Feedback from previous Inset
	Year group priorities

Week 9	Whole investigations
Week 10	Whole investigations – progression from Reception to Year 6
Inset Day	Assessment issues
	End of Year Sc1 assessment

The Action Plan may also be addressed through informal workshops and demonstration lessons, in addition to formal, whole school Inservice. The purpose of the Action Plan is to ensure all staff have sufficient knowledge to deliver quality teaching and learning, by building on identified strengths and addressing identified weaknesses across the school. The coordinator must therefore be able to use many skills to lead staff through the staff development. The skills needed here include:

communication skills;
chairing meetings;
working with others;
evaluative and reflective skills.

Communication skills

It is imperative that the coordinator is able to communicate effectively with staff collectively and on a one-to-one basis. It may be assumed that all teachers are natural communicators, as much of the teacher's role involves communicating with others. However, communication may take many forms and may vary in its effectiveness. There are therefore many considerations involved with communication. Some of these are stated below.

Considerations involved with communication

Has communication actually taken place?
Does the person being communicated with understand what has been said?
Was the place for communication well chosen?
Did the communication take place in a quiet area or in a corridor?
What time was allowed for the communication?
Did the communication take place during a quiet time or was it during a break or lesson time?
Was the person being communicated with focused on the task in hand?
Was the person being communicated with too busy to take things in properly or to respond?
Is there an acceptance or general mistrust of messages in school?
Was enough notice given for the communication?
Was the communication one-sided?
Were staff included and/or asked for their views and opinions?
Was the language used in the communication clear?
Did the communication involve excessive use of jargon or unfamiliar acronyms? (Both can intimidate the listener and allow ambiguity to creep in.)
Was too much information given at one time?

A further consideration is that there may be many subject coordinators in the school trying to develop their area in school and so there is much competition for staff meetings and for communication to staff. What is needed in school is a coordinated approach to communicating between subject coordinators and the staff. There is a danger that if individual coordinators do not work together there will be an information overload for the staff, resulting in communications being ineffective. A coordinated approach would ensure that all subjects are represented at regular intervals in staff meetings, in staff information documents and notice boards. The relative advantages and disadvantages of some of these communication methods are presented below.

Communication method	Advantages	Disadvantages
Staff meetings	Same message given to all staff Effective use of coordinator and staff time Allows for two-way communication	Requires pre-planning Coordinator must have chairing skills May be intimidating for some staff Can reduce input from less confident colleagues
Staff information documents	Same message given to all staff Effective use of coordinator and staff time Information can be accessed at a time suitable to the staff Available for future reference	May not be read May not be followed Provides for one-way communication only No opportunity for immediate feedback
Noticeboards	Good for communicating simple information such as dates and times Not wasteful of resources – time, paper, etc. Consistent message to all staff	Need to be maintained and kept up to date May not be referred to Information may not be retained No opportunity for immediate feedback
Informal conversation	Non-threatening Free-ranging Two-way Scope for further discussion	Inconsistent Unreliable Inefficient use of coordinator time Needs a professional approach Information easily forgotten Not all staff have same access to information

The coordinator will use verbal communication in formal and informal settings. It must be considered how the two forms necessitate the same skills, and ways in which they differ. Both forms must involve the coordinator in listening as well as speaking, to ensure both participants feel involved and are able to check that each understands the other and share an agreed view of what has been communicated. Verbal communication is a valuable strategy for coordinators as it can be used for many purposes – praise, recognition, information, messages, etc. It is also valuable in that coordinators will receive instant feedback – either verbal or non-verbal – on their own performance and effectiveness. Both participants in the communication will be mindful of the non-verbal elements of the communication – the body language – and the tone in which the communication was delivered. These are equally as important as the content of the communication.

Listening skills

Face the speaker
Make eye contact
Take up (and maintain) a relaxed and open posture
Avoid negative, non-verbal communication, e.g., folded arms, distracted air, etc.
Use positive, non-verbal communication, e.g., nodding agreement, smiling, etc.
Use encouraging verbal devices, e.g., hmmm, yes, etc.
Analyse what your colleague is saying
Consider what is being said and what is not being said
Avoid interrupting the speaker
Be aware of the tone of the speaker and non-verbal signs being given
Clarify points made by asking questions
Use focused questions to ascertain specific details
Use exploratory questions to encourage the speaker to provide general information, their views, positions, ideas and opinions
Use clarification questions to demonstrate interest, to elicit further information about what has been said, and to investigate the attitudes and ideas of the speaker in more detail
Use emotional questions to ascertain feelings of speaker
Use behavioural questions to determine how the speaker has acted/will act in response to the communication

A major disadvantage of verbal communication is that it may easily be forgotten or remembered inaccurately. The communication, therefore, may need to be repeated or reinforced. It must be consistent and continuous and the coordinator will need to check that there is a shared understanding about what has been said. The timing of verbal communications is crucial to its effectiveness. The information needs to be disseminated in good time and in an appropriate setting, when both participants are able to listen, ask questions and focus on the communication without being distracted by what is happening around them.

Formal verbal communication	Informal verbal communication
Coordinator has an *audience*.	Coordinator available for informal, one-to-one meetings.
Style and delivery of communication will be considered beforehand.	Style and delivery of communication may not be considered beforehand.
Staff able to discuss together what is happening in science in school as a whole and provide a collectively agreed opinion.	Collect information/ideas from various staff. Use to form a picture of what is happening in science in school.
May be used in parents' meetings, governors' briefings.	May involve individual discussions with parents, outside agencies.

Written communication skills are essential for the coordinator, as it is not always possible to engage in verbal communication with all members of staff. This may be due to time constraints or because written communication is a preferred method of information transfer. There are many factors to consider when utilizing written communication.

Written communication does not allow for two-way conversation. There is therefore no opportunity for verbal questioning or clarification of the information.

Precision is essential to ensure there is no ambiguity in the information communicated.

The communication must be checked for misspelled or misused vocabulary.

All written communication must be checked for meaning and redrafted to reduce the possibility of misinterpretation by the reader.

Care must be given to the presentation to interest the reader, e.g., use of bullet points, note form or short sentences.

Do not be tempted to over-complicate what is being communicated, be direct and to the point.

Consider the audience – do not use terms and acronyms that are specific to teaching when communicating with parents.

Care should be taken when considering the use of humour. The coordinator must be assured that the audience will not be offended or consider the use to be unprofessional.

The communication must be relevant to the audience.

The use of written communication to inform of changes to practice must be considered carefully; it may not be the most effective method of communicating this change.

Chairing meetings

An essential part of the role of the coordinator is to organize and lead meetings, including staff meetings, parents' evenings, and governors' meetings. It is the skill of the coordinator that ensures that a meeting is deemed a success by all involved.

Mr F, the science coordinator, was asked by the Head to chair a governors' curriculum meeting following the receipt of the Ofsted Inspection Report. Mr F drew up an agenda and circulated copies to all members of the sub-committee in advance of the meeting. The agenda items were:

> Welcome and introductions
> Summary of the Ofsted findings
> The school's Action Plan
> AOB.

The Head had asked that the meeting be an informal meeting that would last no longer than 45 minutes. Mr F opened the meeting by introducing himself and thanking the governors (five in all) for attending the meeting and showing such interest in the science response to Ofsted. He then asked the governors to introduce themselves. Mr F stressed that the meeting was to be informal but informative and asked that the governors interrupt him at any time to ask questions or make comments and suggestions. He then continued by reading out the summary of findings. Miss P, a parent governor, enquired if Mr F believed the findings to be accurate, Mr F agreed that they were. Mr N, an LEA governor, stated that the findings were not indicative of what he had seen in school, Mr G (another parent governor) agreed with Mr N. Mr F, the coordinator, **listened to everyone**'s point of view and **encouraged all the meeting's participants to be involved** in the discussion. However, the discussion did begin to move towards discussing individual children and so Mr F **moved the meeting forward** by summarizing the different points of view but acknowledging that the school needed to respond to the actual report received, and thus **returned the discussion to the point of the meeting**. Mr F then presented the governors with the science Action Plan and how it was to be delivered. The governors made many comments about this and, at times, Mr F needed to **seek clarification of comments made** in order to respond to them. Seeking clarification also aided the governors in understanding each other's points of view. The meeting moved on to AOB (any other business). This was a crucial point of the meeting as Mr F wished to fully inform the governors yet **keep the meeting to time** and **keep the meeting on track**. The governors used this time to seek further clarification and to establish a role they could play in the science Action Plan. Although at times Mr F did feel he was **refereeing the discussion** rather than chairing it the outcome of the meeting was very positive. He felt that the sub-committee had a good understanding of the strengths and weaknesses in the school and were committed to helping the staff to work towards further improvements. The meeting was thus deemed a success for all the participants. He closed the meeting by once again thanking the governors for attending and taking such an active part.

The case study above demonstrates how the different facets of the meeting were ensured. Each meeting must therefore:

allow for an exchange of ideas,
ensure the information is communicated accurately,
generate a general agreement and consensus of opinion,
result in a commitment to a particular course of action or decision,
inspire the attendees,

result in the attendees being enthusiastic about the recommendations of the meeting,
be of relevance to the attendees,
balance the needs of the task in hand, the individual attendees and the group of attendees as a whole,
ensure that the group is able to function as a team where the individuals in the group feel valued,
lead to success for all concerned,
result in the meeting being considered a good use of the attendees' time.

Organizing and chairing a meeting consequently needs careful preparation, from considering whether a meeting is the most effective method of communication to whether the meeting will involve dialogue only or will require more active participation by the meeting members. As a new coordinator, you must seek advice from more experienced members of staff to ensure relevance of the meeting to the intended audience. It is also helpful to think back to a successful meeting you have attended and a less successful meeting you have attended. Consider what made the meeting successful/ unsuccessful and how you can structure your meeting to suit your style of delivery and result in the meeting being deemed a success. The lists below indicate some of the features of a successful meeting and of an unsuccessful meeting.

Features of a successful meeting:

The meeting is necessary. It is considered to be the most efficient method of communication.
There is a clear purpose for the meeting, which is shared with the attendees.
The meeting is relevant to all staff attending the meeting.
An agenda is used, given out to participants before the meeting starts, and adhered to.
Colleagues are expected to be active participants in the meeting, rather than passive recipients.
Participants are provided with copies of all documentation needed or under discussion.
The meeting is chaired effectively (see notes on chairing meetings on the next page).
The discussion is summarized.
Decisions are reached.
Decisions are clarified – through repeating the decision to all present as a check on understanding and agreement.
Minutes are taken, to ensure that an accurate record of the meeting is kept.

Features of an unsuccessful meeting:

The meeting is not needed at this time; an alternative method of communication could be used, which may be faster and more efficient.
The meeting is not relevant to all the participants.
An agenda is not used or adhered to.
The venue is too small or not appropriate to the meeting.

Participants in the meeting are not encouraged to contribute to the discussion.
Ideas and contributions from others are ignored.
The meeting does not move along at a good pace, resulting in participants having paired
    conversations not relevant to the purpose of the meeting.
Minutes of the meeting are not kept.
Decisions are not made.
The discussion is not summarized, participants do not share the same opinion of the
    meeting outcome.
The outcome of the meeting is not evaluated.

To chair a meeting effectively you must be able to:

encourage all participants to be involved,
listen to everyone,
seek clarification of comments made,
keep the meeting to time,
keep the meeting on track,
keep the discussion to the point,
move the process forward,
use non-verbal gestures and/or statements to draw people back to the original agenda,
referee the discussion – argument and disagreement is productive within a meeting, but it
    must not be allowed to descend to aggression or bullying.

Working with others

As stated earlier in this section, in delivering the Inservice plan, the coordinator begins the process of developing teaching and learning across the school through leading staff development during staff meetings and/or Inset days. This requires the coordinator to work with a range of staff, from very experienced staff to relatively inexperienced staff, from staff who actively welcome change to staff who are frightened of or negative towards change. The coordinator must therefore develop the skills to work effectively with all staff. Working with others includes providing support for colleagues. This is achieved through the delivery of the inservice work and through being available for staff to confide in, to consult with and to offer advice to. In order to support their colleagues effectively, the coordinator must have the skills to be able to empathize with individual members of staff, to assist them to identify their successes in science and then to build on these. Where it occurs, the coordinator must be able to work with staff to reduce the amount of resistance to proposed change and move colleagues towards commitment to the changes deemed necessary. To do this the coordinator will need to provide:

Empowerment and enskilling, i.e., increasing teachers' knowledge and skills, reinforcing their current thinking, encouraging their colleagues to view the issues from different perspectives.
Offer training through workshops, working with colleagues, sharing experiences.
Relevance: offer focused support that is specific to the age range(s) concerned.

Establish what are the direct curriculum development benefits and application for classroom practice.
Realism: what can be achieved in the time available?

The coordinator's role therefore differs markedly from that of a primary classroom teacher alone with the class. The coordinator must work with others in order to be effective. It calls for adequate subject knowledge, an understanding of interpersonal relationships and the ability to work effectively as part of a team or group. The skills needed include an understanding of National Curriculum and/or Early Learning Goals documentation and their interpretation, SATs data, Local Management of Schools, inspection arrangements, appraisal or performance related pay, and how these may impact on curriculum change. The coordinator, also as noted previously, may need to overcome resistance to change. They may need to lead by example and demonstrate that the change needed may be best achieved through working together collaboratively. The list below illustrates the main considerations needed to develop collaborative work.

Developing collaborative work

mediate the relationships within a group
ensure there is an agreed purpose
encourage contributions from all staff – experienced and inexperienced
promote the different and complementary strengths that staff bring to collaborative work
show enthusiasm
offer praise, recognition and practical support to the group
ensure credit is given for the efforts of others
information is shared
constructive criticism is accepted
seek advice
demonstrate confidence

Working with others, implementing change, sharing expertise, etc., does not automatically ensure that colleagues change their practice sufficiently or result in people working harder. Motivation to do this is crucial to the implementation of change; teachers may be motivated by intrinsic or extrinsic factors. Intrinsic factors are: feelings, actions and comments of others; extrinsic factors are physical rewards, e.g., pay or allowances. Examples of both factors are shown in the table overleaf, although it must be noted that motivation factors may be a combination of these or other factors.

Intrinsic factors	Extrinsic factors
A sense of achievement and success	Pay
Professional recognition from colleagues, parents or pupils	Paid allowances
	Positive relationships with colleagues
Awarded responsibilities	High quality leadership in the school
The opportunity to be creative	High quality working environment
Variety and interest in their role	Membership of a supportive team
Career advancement	
A sense of vocation and dedication	
A commitment to the children, their learning and welfare	

The science coordinator may be unable to change or improve the extrinsic factors that motivate staff; the focus is therefore around the intrinsic factors. There are many ways in which the coordinator can influence staff motivation through intrinsic factors:

Model motivated behaviour – show that you are motivated about developments in the science curriculum.
Be direct in praising the achievements of others.
Give credit for the efforts of others.
Involve others in developments in the teaching and learning of science.
Keep colleagues informed about developments in science.
Ensure the staff are clear about their roles and responsibilities in science.
Set attainable and realistic targets for colleagues.
Provide good leadership in the subject.
Communicate with others in clear, concise ways.

Coordinators also need to be able to detect a lack of motivation or deterioration in motivation for science, e.g., absence from meetings, avoidance, lack of punctuality, or poor performance in science teaching and meetings, and may need to work individually with such staff, to raise their motivation. This again may be through leading by example and providing individualized help. The coordinator must also be able to lead staff in curriculum planning for science. Curriculum planning, organization and delivery may form part of the coordinator's ongoing role or may arise from an Ofsted inspection. The coordinator must have an overview of all curriculum issues in school relating to science. This overview may result through observation, monitoring, discussion and planning meetings and involve the coordinator in establishing effective teaching approaches, techniques and methods in science teaching. The main vehicle for this is in writing and maintaining the school's Scheme of Work for science, which sets out these effective teaching models (see Chapter 3). The coordinator may be called upon to lead curriculum medium-term and short-term planning, to aid groups of teachers and/or individuals. The coordinator thus motivates the staff and provides concrete assistance through providing ideas and establishing how quality teaching and learning in science may be achieved.

Evaluative and reflective skills

Following the delivery of the inservice plan, the plan must be evaluated in terms of its effectiveness in meeting the objectives of the Action Plan. The coordinator must also be able to reflect on his or her own performance in the delivery of the plan. The skills needed to evaluate this have been discussed in detail in Chapter 4, in the section on evaluating own performance in the classroom. The coordinator must be able to be objective at this time, recognizing his or her own and the Action Plan's strengths and weaknesses to be addressed. The advice of colleagues is also to be sought, as they have received the Action Plan and will be able to supply information needed regarding the coordinator's performance and the advances made towards meeting the objectives set out in the Action Plan. This will start a cycle of development, followed by evaluation and reflection, followed by action planning, followed by delivery of the development. The skills needed are therefore necessary to the ongoing improvement of teaching and learning in science.

Summary

The role of the science coordinator can appear very daunting, and so in the early stages of your career as a coordinator you do need to try to work out your immediate priorities for the role and work purposefully towards them. Enlist the help of colleagues who are supportive and constructively critical. This will help you to develop your presence as the subject coordinator and build up your confidence for working with less supportive or less confident members of staff. As your skills as a coordinator develop, you will begin to work with staff who are willing to work with you, by offering your support and knowledge of the science curriculum. At all times ensure you involve the key people on the staff (including the Head teacher) in your activities as the science coordinator. This will make certain that you work within the school's policies and practices and will provide the support you need to be most effective.

Strategies for improving your organization and efficiency as a coordinator

Draw up a plan for what you want to achieve as coordinator
Break down the plan into daily, weekly and termly plans
Commit the plans to paper
Distinguish between what is essential and what is desirable, and between what you must
  do and what others can do

Try to work to time-scales and deadlines
Identify the amount of time you can give to the role
Review how your time is spent
Consider using the time available in different ways
Look for ways in which more time can be made available for your role
Always keep your objectives in mind

Reflective questions

Change

Do you know what your attitude to change is?
How would you respond to colleagues whose attitude is the same as yours?
How would you respond to colleagues whose attitude is not the same as yours?
How would you deal with colleagues who oppose change?
How would you deal with colleagues who are apprehensive of change?
How would you deal with colleagues who cannot implement change?

Leading staff development

How will you ensure colleagues:

Build on their successes?
Experience achievement?
Understand the developments and their impact?
Participate in decision-making?
Share in the responsibilities for developing the science curriculum?
Share in the ownership of the curriculum?
Develop confidence in science?
Plan and organize their work in science?

Communication

What forms of communication are you familiar with?
Are you able to share your views with others?
Are you a good listener?
Are you able to empathize with others?
Can you accept contributions from others and value them equally?

REFERENCES

Alexander, R., Rose, J. & Woodhead, C. (1992) 'Curriculum Organisation and Classroom Practice in Primary Schools: A Discussion Paper', London: DES.

Aspinall (1992) *Keeping Parents in the Picture in Primary Science: A Shared Experience*, Hatfield: ASE.

British Association for the Advancement of Science (1983) 'Ideas for Egg Races', London: British Association.

Bentley, D. & Watts, M. (1994) *Teaching and Learning in Primary Science and Technology*, Buckingham: Open University Press.

Cheshire County Council (1997) *Bubbles: Bridging the Gap KS2/3 Liaison*, Cheshire: Zeneca.

Department for Education (1995) *Key Stages 1 and 2 of the National Curriculum*, London: DFE.

Department for Education and Employment (1998) *The National Literacy Strategy*, Cambridge: Cambridge University Press.

Department for Education and Employment (1999) *The National Numeracy Strategy*, London: DfEE.

Department for Education and Science and the Welsh Office (1989) *Science in the National Curriculum*, London: HMSO.

Docking, J. (1990) *Primary Schools and Parents: Rights, Responsibilities and Relationships*, London: Hodder and Stoughton.

Farmery, C. (1995) 'Science and Technology Week', *PSR* 38, pp. 20–21, Hatfield: ASE.

Farmery, C. (1999) 'Progression in Experimental and Investigative Science', *PSR* 58, pp. 12–14, Hatfield: ASE.

Hornby, G. (2000) *Improving Parental Involvement*, London and New York: Cassell.

Qualifications and Curriculum Authority (1998) *Building Bridges: Guidance and Training Materials for Teachers of Year 6 and Year 7 Pupils*, London: QCA.

Qualifications and Curriculum Authority (1999a) *The National Curriculum: Handbook for Primary Teachers in England*, London: DfEE/QCA.

Qualifications and Curriculum Authority (1999b) *Early Learning Goals*, London: DfEE/QCA.

Qualifications and Curriculum Authority (2001) *Assessment and Reporting Arrangements*, London: QCA.

Rosen, M. (2000) *Centrally Heated Knickers*, London: Puffin.

School Curriculum and Assessment Authority (1996) *Nursery Education: Desireable Outcomes for Children's Learning on Entering Compulsory Education*, London: DfEE/SCAA.

Watkinson, (1992) (ed.) *Primary Science: A Shared Experience*, Hatfield: ASE.

Index

256